THE RIFLE AND THE HOUND IN CEYLON

THE RIFLE AND THE HOUND IN CEYLON

BY

SIR SAMUEL W. BAKER, M.A. F.R.S. F.R.G.S.

PACHA AND MAJOR-GENERAL OF THE OTTOMAN EMPIRE: GOLD MEDALLIST OF THE ROYAL GEOGRAPHICAL SOCIETY, AND GRANDE MEDAILLE D'OR DE LA SOCIETE DE GEOGRAPHIE DE PARIS: AUTHOR OF 'EIGHT YEARS IN CEYLON' 'ALBERT N'YANZA, GREAT BASIN OF THE NILE' 'NILE TRIBUTARIES OF ABYSSINIA' 'ISMAILIA'

NEW EDITION

WITH ILLUSTRATIONS

GYAN

Published by

Gyan Publishing House
5, Ansari Road
Daryaganj, New Delhi-110002
Phone: 011-47034999, 9811692060
E-mail: books@gyanbooks.com

Distribution Network
gyanbooks.com
India, USA, Canada, UK, Australia, France

ISBN : 978-81-212-3959-2 (PB)
First Published, 1874

2nd Impression 2020

Printed at: Gyan Press, Delhi.

The
Rifle and the Hound in Ceylon
Author: Sir Samuel W. Baker

INTRODUCTION.

THE love of sport is a feeling inherent in most Englishmen, and whether in the chase, or with the rod or gun, they far excel all other nations. In fact, the definition of this feeling cannot be understood by many foreigners. We are frequently ridiculed for fox-hunting. "What for all dis people, dis horses, dis many dog? dis leetle (how you call him?) dis 'fox' for to catch? ha! you eat dis creature; he vary fat and fine?"

This is a foreigner's notion of the chase; he hunts for the pot; and by Englishmen alone is the glorious feeling shared of true, fair, and manly sport. The character of the nation is beautifully displayed in all our rules for hunting, shooting, fishing, fighting, &c.; a feeling of fair play pervades every amusement. Who would shoot a hare in form? who would net a trout stream? who would hit a man when down? A Frenchman would do all these things, and might be no bad fellow after all. It would be *his way* of doing it. His notion would be to make use of an advantage when an opportunity offered. He would think it folly to give the hare a chance of running when he could shoot her sitting; he would make an excellent dish of all the trout he could snare; and as to hitting his man when down, he would think it madness to allow him to get up again until he had put him *hors de combat* by jumping on him. Their notions of sporting and ours, then, widely differ; they take every advantage, while we give every advantage; they delight in the certainty of killing, while our pleasure consists in the chance of the animal escaping.

I would always encourage the love of sport in a lad; guided by its true spirit of fair play, it is a feeling that will make him above doing a mean thing in every station of life, and will give him real feelings of humanity. I have had great experience in the characters of *thorough* sportsmen, and I can safely say that I never saw *one* that was not a straightforward honourable man, who would scorn to take a dirty advantage of man or animal. In fact, all *real* sportsmen that I have met have been really tender-hearted men; men who shun cruelty to an animal and who are easily moved by a tale of distress.

With these feelings sport is an amusement worthy of a man, and this noble taste has been extensively developed since the opportunities of travelling have of late years been so wonderfully improved. The facility with which the most remote regions are now reached renders a tour over some portion of the globe a necessary adjunct to a man's education, and a sportsman naturally directs his path to some land where civilisation has not yet banished the wild beast from the soil.

Ceylon is a delightful country for the sporting tourist. In the high road to India and China, any length of time may be spent *en passant*, and the voyage by the Overland route is nothing but a trip of a few weeks of pleasure.

This island has been always celebrated for its elephants, but the other branches of sport are comparatively unknown to strangers. No account has ever been written which embraces *all* Ceylon sports: anecdotes of elephant shooting fill the pages of nearly every work on Ceylon; but the real character of the wild sports of this island has never been described, because the writers have never been acquainted with each separate branch of the Ceylon chase.

A residence of many years in this lovely country,

where the wild sports of the island have formed a never-failing and constant amusement, alone confers sufficient experience to enable a person to give a faithful picture of both shooting and hunting in Ceylon jungles.

In describing these sports I shall give no anecdotes of others, but I shall simply recall scenes in which I myself have shared, preferring even a character for egotism rather than relate the statements of hearsay, for the truth of which I could not vouch. This must be accepted as an excuse for the unpleasant use of the first person.

There are many first-rate sportsmen in Ceylon who could furnish anecdotes of individual risks and hairbreadth escapes (the certain accompaniments to elephant shooting) that would fill volumes; but enough will be found in the few scenes which I have selected from whole hecatombs of slaughter to satisfy and perhaps fatigue the most patient reader.

One fact I wish to impress upon all.—That the colouring of every description is diminished and not exaggerated, the real scene being in all cases a picture, of which the narration is but a feeble copy.

CONTENTS.

CHAPTER I.

CHAP. II.

CHAP. III.

CHAP. IV.

CHAP. V.

CHAP. VI.

CHAP. VII.

CHAP. VIII.

CHAP. IX.

CHAP. X.

CHAP. XI.

THE

RIFLE AND HOUND

IN

CEYLON.

CHAPTER I.

WILD COUNTRY. — DEALINGS IN THE MARVELLOUS. — ENCHANTING MOMENTS. — THE WILD ELEPHANT OF CEYLON. — "ROGUES." — ELEPHANT SLAUGHTER. — THICK JUNGLES. — CHARACTER OF THE COUNTRY. — VARIETIES OF GAME IN CEYLON. — "BATTERY FOR CEYLON SPORT." — THE ELK, OR "SAMBER DEER." — DEER COURSING.

It is a difficult task to describe a wild country so exactly that a stranger's eye shall at once be made acquainted with its scenery and character by the description. And yet this is absolutely necessary if the narration of sports in foreign countries is supposed to interest those who have never had the opportunity of enjoying them. The want of graphic description of localities in which the events have occurred, is the principal cause of that tediousness which generally accompanies the steady perusal of a sporting work. You can read twenty pages with interest, but a monotony soon pervades it, and sport then assumes an appearance of mere slaughter.

Now, the actual killing of an animal, the death itself, is not sport, unless the circumstances connected with it are such as to create that peculiar feeling which can only be expressed by the word "sport." This feeling cannot exist in the heart of a butcher ; he would as soon slaughter a fine buck, by tying him to a post and knocking him down, as he would shoot him in his wild native haunts—the actual moment of death, the fact of killing, is his enjoyment. To a true sportsman the enjoyment of a sport increases in proportion to the wildness of the country. Catch a six-pound trout in a quiet mill-pond in a populous manufacturing neighbourhood, with well cultivated meadows on either side the stream, fat cattle grazing on the rich pasturage, and, perhaps, actually watching you as you land your fish : it may be sport. But catch a similar fish far from the haunts of men, in a boiling rocky torrent surrounded by heathery mountains, where the shadow of a rod has seldom been reflected in the stream, and you cease to think the former fish worth catching;—still he is the same size, showed the same courage, had the same perfection of condition, and yet you cannot allow that it was sport compared with this wild stream. If you see no difference in the excitement, you are not a sportsman; you would as soon catch him in a washing tub, and you should buy your fish when you require him; but never use a rod, or you would disgrace the hickory.

This feeling of a combination of wild country with the presence of the game itself to form a real sport is most keenly manifested when we turn our attention to the rifle. This noble weapon is thrown away in an enclosed country. The smooth bore may and does afford delightful sport upon our cultivated fields; but even that pleasure is doubled when those enclosures no longer intervene, and the wide-spreading moors and morasses of Scotland give an idea of freedom and undisturbed nature. Who can compare grouse with partridge shooting? Still the difference exists not so much in the character of the bird as in the features of the country. It is the wild aspect of the heathery moor without a bound, except the rugged outline of the mountains upon the sky, that gives such a charm to the grouse-shooting in Scotland, and renders the deer-stalking such a favourite sport among the happy few who can enjoy it.

All this proves that the simple act of killing is not sport; if it were, the Zoological Gardens would form as fine a field to an elephant shot as the wildest Indian jungle.

Man is a blood-thirsty animal, a beast of prey, instinctively; but let us hope that a true sportsman is not a savage, delighting in nothing but death, but that his pursuits are qualified by a love of nature, of noble scenery, of all the wonderful productions which the earth gives forth in different latitudes. He should thoroughly understand the nature and habits of every beast or bird that he looks upon as game. This last attribute is indispensable; without it he may kill, but he is not a sportsman.

We have, therefore, come to the conclusion, that the character of a country influences the character of the sport. The first question, therefore, that an experienced man would ask at the recital of a sporting anecdote would be, "What kind of country is it?" That being clearly described to him, he follows you through every word of your tale with a true interest, and, in fact, joins in imagination in the chase.

There is one great drawback to the publication of sporting adventures — they always appear to deal not a little in the marvellous; and this effect is generally heightened by the use of the first person in writing, which at all events may give an egotistical character to a work. This, however, cannot easily be avoided if a person is describing his own adventures, and he labours under the disadvantage of being criticised by readers who do not know him personally, and may, therefore, give him credit for gross exaggeration.

It is this feeling that deters many men who have passed through years of wild sports from publishing an account of them. The fact of being able to laugh in your sleeve at the ignorance of a reader who does not credit you, is but a poor compensation for being considered a better shot with a long bow than with a rifle. Often have I pitied Gordon Cumming, when I have heard him talked of as a palpable Munchausen, by men who never fired a rifle, or saw a wild beast, except in a cage; and still these men form the greater proportion of the "readers" of these works.

Men who have not seen cannot understand the grandeur of wild sports in a wild country. There is an indescribable feeling of supremacy in a man who understands his game thoroughly, when he stands upon some elevated point and gazes over the wild territory of savage beasts. He feels himself an invader upon the solitudes of nature. The very stillness of the scene is his delight. There is a mournful silence in the calmness of the evening, when the tropical sun sinks upon the horizon, a conviction that man has left this region undisturbed to its wild tenants. No hum of distant voices, no rumbling of busy wheels, no cries of domestic animals meet the ear. He stands upon a wilderness, pathless and untrodden by the foot of civilisation, where no sound is ever heard but that of the elements, when the thunder rolls among the towering forests, or the wind howls along the plains. He gazes far, far into the distance, where the blue mountains melt into an indefinite haze; he looks above him to the rocky pinnacles which spring from the level plain, their swarthy cliffs glistening from the recent shower, and patches of rich verdure clinging to precipices a thousand feet above him. His eye stretches along the grassy plains, taking at one full glance a survey of woods, and rocks, and streams; and imperceptibly his mind wanders to thoughts of home, and in one moment scenes long left behind are conjured up by memory, and incidents are recalled which banish for a time the scene before him. Lost for a moment in the enchanting power of solitude, where fancy and reality combine in their most bewitching forms, he is suddenly roused by a distant sound made doubly loud by the surrounding silence — the shrill trumpet of an elephant. He wakes from his reverie; the reality of the present scene is at once manifested. He stands within a wilderness where the monster of the forest holds dominion; he knows not what a day, not even what a moment may bring forth; he trusts in a protecting power and in the heavy rifle, and he is shortly upon the track of the king of beasts.

The king of beasts is generally acknowledged to be the "Lion;" but no one who has seen a wild elephant can doubt for a moment that the title belongs to him in his own right. Lord of all created animals in might and sagacity, the elephant roams through his native forests. He browses upon the lofty branches, upturns young trees from sheer malice, and from plain to forest he stalks majestically at break of day, "monarch of all he surveys."

A person who has never seen a wild elephant can form no idea of his real character, either mentally or physically. The unwieldy and sleepy looking beast, who, penned up in his cage at a menagerie, receives a sixpence in his trunk, and turns round with difficulty to deposit it in a box; whose mental powers seem to be concentrated in the idea of receiving buns tossed into a gaping mouth by children's hands; this very beast may have come from a warlike stock. His sire may have been the terror of a district, a pitiless highwayman, whose soul thirsted for blood; who, lying in wait in some thick bush, would rush upon the unwary passer-by, and know no pleasure greater than the act of crushing his victim to a shapeless mass beneath his feet. How little does his tame sleepy son resemble him! Instead of browsing on the rank vegetation of wild pasturage, he devours plum-buns; instead of bathing his giant form in the deep rivers and lakes of his native land, he steps into a stone-lined basin to bathe before the eyes of a pleased multitude, the whole of whom form their opinion of elephants in general from the broken-spirited monster that they see before them.

I have even heard people exclaim, upon hearing anecdotes of elephant-hunting, "poor things!"

Poor things, indeed! I should like to see the very person who thus expresses his pity going at his best pace with a savage elephant after him: give him a lawn to run upon if he likes, and see the elephant gaining a foot in every yard of the chase, fire in his eye, fury in his headlong charge; and would not the flying gentleman who lately exclaimed "poor thing!" be thankful to the lucky bullet that would save him from destruction?

There are no animals more misunderstood than elephants; they are naturally savage, wary, and revengeful, displaying as great courage when in their wild state as any animal known. The fact of their great natural sagacity renders them the more dangerous as foes. Even when tamed there are many that are not safe for a stranger to approach, and they are then only kept in awe by the sharp driving hook of the mohout.

In their domesticated state I have seen them perform wonders of sagacity and strength; but I have nothing to do with tame elephants; there are whole books written upon the subject, although the habits of an elephant can be described in a few words.

All wild animals in a tropical country avoid the sun. They wander forth to feed upon the plains in the evening and during the night, and they return to the jungle shortly after sunrise.

Elephants have the same habits. In those parts of the country where such pasturage abounds as bamboo, lemon grass, sedges on the banks of rivers, lakes, and swamps, elephants are sure to be found at such seasons as are most propitious for the growth of these plants. When the dry weather destroys this supply of food in one district, they migrate to another part of the country.

They come forth to feed at about 4 P. M., and they invariably retire to the thickest and most thorny jungle in the neighbourhood of their feeding place by 7 A. M. In these impenetrable haunts they consider themselves secure from aggression.

The period of gestation with an elephant is supposed to be two years, and the time occupied in attaining full growth is about sixteen years. The whole period of life is supposed to be a hundred years, but my own opinion would increase that period by fifty.

The height of elephants varies to a great degree, and in all cases is very deceiving. In Ceylon an elephant is measured at the shoulder, and nine feet at this point is a very large animal. There is no doubt that many elephants far exceed this, as I have shot them so large that two tall men could lie at full length from the point of the forefoot to the shoulder; but this is not a common size; the average height at the shoulder would be about seven feet.

Not more than one in three hundred has tusks; they are merely provided with short grubbers, projecting generally about three inches from the upper jaw, and about two inches in diameter; these are called "tushes" in Ceylon, and are of so little value that they are not worth extracting from the head. They are useful to the elephants in hooking on to a branch and tearing it down.

Elephants are gregarious, and the average number in a herd is about eight, although they frequently form bodies of fifty and even eighty in one troop. Each herd consists of a very large proportion of females, and they are constantly met without a single bull in their number. I up her man until either he or she is killed. If any young elephants are in the herd, the mothers frequently prove awkward customers.

Elephant-shooting is doubtless the most dangerous of all sports, if the game is invariably followed up; but there is a great difference between elephant killing and elephant *hunting;* the latter is sport, the former is slaughter.

Many persons who have killed many elephants know literally nothing about the sport, and they may even leave Ceylon with the idea that an elephant is not a dangerous animal. Their elephants are killed in this way, viz.—

The party of sportsmen, say two or three, arrive at a certain district. The headman is sent for from the village; he arrives. The inquiry respecting the vicinity of elephants is made; a herd is reported to be in the neighbourhood, and trackers and watchers are sent out to find them.

In the meantime the tent is pitched, our friends are employed in unpacking the guns, and, after some hours have elapsed, the trackers return: they have found the herd, and the watchers are left to observe them.

The guns are loaded, and the party starts. The trackers run quickly on the track until they meet one of the watchers who has been sent back upon the track by the other watchers to give the requisite information of the movements of the herd since the trackers left. One tracker now leads the way, and they cautiously proceed. The boughs are heard slightly rustling as the unconscious elephants are fanning the flies from their bodies within a hundred yards of the guns.

The jungle is open and good, interspersed with plots of rank grass; and quietly following the head tracker into whose hands our friends have committed themselves, they follow like hounds under the control of a huntsman. The tracker is a famous fellow, and he brings up his employers in a masterly manner within ten paces of the still unconscious elephants. He now retreats quietly behind the guns, and the sport begins. A cloud of smoke from a regular volley, a crash through the splintering branches as the panic-stricken herd rush from the scene of conflict, and it is all over. X. has killed two, Y. has killed one, and Z. knocked down one, but he got up again and got away; total, three bagged. Our friends now return to the tent, and, after perhaps a month of this kind of shooting, they arrive at their original head quarters, having greater portion of the herd may at other times be perhaps easily killed. There is no certainty in a shot. An elephant may be discerned by the eye looming in an apparent mist formed by the countless intervening twigs and branches which veil him like a screen of net-work. To reach the fatal spot the ball must pass through perhaps fifty little twigs, one of which, if struck obliquely, turns the bullet, and there is no answering for the consequence. There are no rules, however, without exceptions, and in some instances the following of the game through the thickest jungle can hardly be avoided.

The character of the country in Ceylon is generally very unfavourable to sport of all kinds. The length of the island is about two hundred and eighty miles, by one hundred and fifty in width; the greater portion of this surface is covered with impenetrable jungles, which form secure coverts for countless animals.

The centre of the island is mountainous, torrents from which form the sources of the numerous rivers by which Ceylon is so well watered. The low country is flat. The soil throughout the island is generally poor and sandy.

This being the character of the country, and

vast forests rendered impenetrable by tangled underwood forming the principal features of the landscape, a person arriving at Ceylon for the purpose of enjoying its wild sports would feel an inexpressible disappointment.

Instead of mounting a good horse, as he might have fondly anticipated, and at once speeding over trackless plains till so far from human habitations that the territories of beasts commence, — he finds himself walled in by jungle on either side of the highway. In vain he asks for information. He finds the neighbourhood of Galle, his first landing place, densely populated: he gets into the coach for Colombo. Seventy miles of close population and groves of cocoa-nut trees are passed, and he reaches the capital. This is worse and worse — he has seen no signs of wild country during his long journey, and Colombo appears to be the height of civilisation. He books his place for Kandy; he knows that is in the very centre of Ceylon — there surely must be sport there he thinks.

The morning gun fires from the Colombo fort at 5 A.M., and the coach starts. Miles are passed, and still the country is thickly populated—paddy cultivation in all the flats and hollows, and even the sides of the hills are carefully terraced out in a laborious system of agriculture. There can be no shooting here!

Sixty miles are passed; the top of the Kaduganava Pass is reached 1800 feet above the sea level, the road walled with jungle on either side. From the summit of this pass our newly arrived sportsman gazes with despair. Far as the eye can reach over a vast extent of country, mountain and valley, hill and dale, without one open spot, are clothed alike in one dark screen of impervious forest.

He reaches Kandy, a civilised town surrounded by hills of jungle — that interminable jungle! — and at Kandy he may remain, or, better still, return again to England, unless he can get some well known Ceylon sportsman to pilot him through the apparently pathless forests, and in fact to "show him sport." This is not easily effected. Men who understand the sport are not over fond of acting "chaperon" to a young hand, as a novice must always detract from the sport in some degree. In addition to this, many persons do not exactly know themselves; and, although the idea of shooting elephants appears very attractive at a distance, the pleasure somewhat abates when the and of course their weight is proportionate, that of a buck in condition being about 400 pounds when gralloched. I have killed them much heavier than this on the mountains, but I have given about the average weight.

The habits of this animal are purely nocturnal. He commences his wanderings at sunset, and retires to the forest at break of day. He is seldom found in greater numbers than two or three together, and is generally alone. When brought to bay he fights to the last, and charges man and hound indiscriminately, a choice hound killed being often the price of victory.

The country in which he is hunted is in the mountainous districts of Ceylon. Situated at an elevation of 6300 feet above the sea is Newera Ellia, the sanatorium of the island. Here I have kept a pack and hunted elk for some years, the delightful coolness of the temperature (seldom above 66° Fahr.) rendering the sport doubly enjoyable. The principal features of this country being a series of wild marshy plains, forests, torrents, mountains, and precipices, a peculiar hound is required for the sport.

A pack of thorough-bred fox hounds would never answer. They would pick up a cold scent and open upon it before they were within a mile of their game. Roused from his morning nap, the buck would snuff the breeze, and to the distant music give an attentive ear, then shake the dew from his rough hide, and away over rocks and torrents, down the steep mountain sides, through pathless forests; and woe then to the pack of thorough-breds whose persevering notes would soon be echoed by the rocky steeps, far, far away from any chance of return, lost in the trackless jungles and ravines many miles from kennel, a prey to leopards and starvation! I have proved this by experience, having brought a pack of splendid hounds from England, only one of which survived a few months' hunting.

The hound required for elk-hunting is a cross between the fox-hound and blood-hound, of great size and courage, with as powerful a voice as possible. He should be trained to this sport from a puppy, and his natural sagacity soon teaches him not to open unless upon a hot scent, or about two hundred yards from his game; thus the elk is not disturbed until the hound is at full speed upon his scent, and he seldom gets a long start. Fifteen couple of such hounds in full cry put him at his best pace, which is always tried to the uttermost by a couple or two of fast and pitiless lurchers who run ahead of the pack, the object being to press him at first starting, so as to blow him at the very commencement: this is easily effected, as he is full of food, and it is his nature always to take off straight *up* the hill when first disturbed. When blown, he strikes down hill, and makes at great speed for the largest and deepest stream; in this he turns to bay, and tries the mettle of the finest hounds.

The great enemy to a pack is the leopard. He pounces from the branch of a tree upon a stray hound, and soon finishes him, unless of great size and courage, in which case the cowardly brute is soon beaten off. This forms another reason for the choice of large hounds.

The next sport is the "Deer Coursing." This is one of the most delightful kinds of sport in Ceylon. The game is the Axis or spotted deer, and the open plains in many parts of the low country afford splendid ground for both greyhound and horse.

The buck is about 250 lbs. live weight, of wonderful speed and great courage, armed with long and graceful antlers as sharp as needles.

He will suddenly turn to bay upon the hard ground, and charge his pursuers, and is more dangerous to the greyhounds than the elk, from his wonderful activity, and from the fact that he is coursed by only a pair of greyhounds, instead of being hunted by a pack.

Pure greyhounds of great size and courage are best adapted for this sport. They cannot afford to lose speed by a cross with slower hounds.

CHAP. II.

NEWERA ELLIA. — THE TURN-OUT FOR ELK-HUNTING. — ELK-HUNTING. — ELK TURNED TO BAY. — THE BOAR.

Where shall I begin? This is a momentous question, when, upon glancing back upon past years, a thousand incidents jostle each other for precedence. How shall I describe them? This, again, is easier asked than answered. A journal is a dry method of description, mingling the uninteresting with the brightest moments of sport. No, I will not write a journal, it would be endless and boring. I shall begin with the present as it is, and call up the past as I think proper.

Here, then, I am in my private sanctum, my rifles all arranged in their respective stands above the chimney-piece, the stag's horns round walls hung with horn-cases, powder-flasks, and the various weapons of the chase. Even as I write, the hounds are yelling in the kennel.

The thermometer is at 62° Fahr., and it is mid-day. It never exceeds 72° in the hottest weather, and sometimes falls below freezing point at night. The sky is spotless, and the air calm. The fragrance of mignonettes, and a hundred flowers that recal Old England, fill the air. Green fields of grass and clover neatly fenced surround a comfortable house and grounds. Well fed cattle of the choicest breeds and English sheep are grazing in the paddocks. Well made roads and gravel walks run through the estate. But a few years past, and this was all wilderness.

Dense forest reigned where now not even the stump of a tree is standing; the wind howled over hill and valley, the dank moss hung from the scathed branches, the deep morass filled the hollows; but all is changed by the hand of civilisation and industry. The dense forests and rough plains, which still form the boundaries of the cultivated land, only add to the beauty. The monkeys and parrots are even now chattering among the branches, and occasionally the elephant in his nightly wanderings trespasses upon the fields, unconscious of the oasis within his territory of savage nature.

The still, starlight night is awakened by the harsh bark of the elk; the lofty mountains, grey with the silvery moonlight, echo back the sound; and the wakeful hounds answer the well known cry by a prolonged and savage yell.

This is "Newera Ellia," the sanatorium of Ceylon, the most perfect climate of the world. It now boasts of a handsome church, a public reading room, a large hotel, the barracks, and about twenty private residences.

The adjacent country, of comparatively table land, occupies an extent of some thirty miles in length, varying in altitude from 6200 to 7000 feet, forming a base for the highest peaks in Ceylon, which rise to nearly 9000 feet.

Alternate large plains, separated by belts of forest, rapid rivers, waterfalls, precipices, and panoramic views of boundless extent, form the features of this country, which, combined with the sports of the place, render a residence at Newera Ellia a life of health, luxury, and independence.

The high road from Colombo passes over the mountains through Newera Ellia to Badulla, from which latter place there is a bridle-road, through the best shooting districts in Ceylon, to the seaport town of Batticaloa, and from thence to Trincomalee. The relative distances of Newera Ellia are, from Galle, 185 miles; from Colombo, 115 miles; from Kandy, 47 miles; from Badulla, 36 miles; from Batticaloa, 148 miles. Were it not for the poverty of the soil, Newera Ellia would long ago have become a place of great importance, as the climate is favourable to the cultivation of all English produce; but an absence of lime in the soil, and the cost of applying it artificially, prohibit the cultivation of all grain, and restrict the produce of the land to potatoes and other vegetables. Nevertheless, many small settlers earn a good subsistence, although this has latterly been rendered precarious by the appearance of the well known potato disease.

Newera Ellia has always been a favourite place of resort during the fashionable months, from the commencement of January to the middle of May. At that time, the rainy season commences, and visitors rapidly disappear.

All strangers remark the scanty accommodation afforded to the numerous visitors. To see the number of people riding and walking round the Newera Ellia plain, it appears a marvel how they can be housed in the few dwellings that exist. There is an endless supply of fine timber in the forests, and powerful saw-mills are already erected;

but the island is, like its soil, "poor." Its main staple, "coffee," does not pay sufficiently to enable proprietors of estates to indulge in the luxury of a house at Newera Ellia. Like many watering places in England, it is overcrowded at one season, and deserted at another, the only permanent residents being comprised in the commandant, the officer in command of the detachment of troops, the government agent, the doctor, the clergyman, and our own family.

Dull enough! some persons may exclaim; and so it would be to any but a sportsman; but the jungles teem with large game, and Newera Ellia is in a central position, as the best sporting country is only three days' journey, or one hundred miles, distant. Thus, at any time, the guns may be packed up, and, with tents and baggage sent on some days in advance, a fortnight's or a month's war may be carried on against the elephants without much trouble.

The turn-out for elk-hunting during the fashionable season at Newera Ellia is sometimes peculiarly exciting. The air is keen and frosty, the plains snow-white with the crisp hoar frost, and even at the early hour of 6 A.M. parties of ladies may be seen urging their horses round the plain on their way to the appointed meet. Here we are waiting with the anxious pack, perhaps blessing some of our more sleepy friends for not turning out a little earlier. Party after party arrives, including many of the fair sex, and the rosy tips to all countenances attest the quality of the cold even in Ceylon.

There is something peculiarly inspiriting in the early hour of sunrise upon these mountains — an indescribable lightness in the atmosphere, owing to the great elevation, which takes a wonderful effect upon the spirits. The horses and the hounds feel its influence in an equal degree; the former, who are perhaps of sober character in the hot climate, now champ the bit and paw the ground: their owners hardly know them by the change.

We have frequently mustered as many as thirty horses at a meet; but on these occasions a picked spot is chosen where the sport may be easily witnessed by those who are unaccustomed to it. The horses may, in these instances, be available, but as a rule they are perfectly useless in elk-hunting, as the plains are so boggy that they would be hock-deep every quarter of a mile. Thus no person can thoroughly enjoy elk-hunting who is not well accustomed to it, as it is a sport conducted entirely on foot, and the thinness of the air in this elevated region is very trying to the lungs in hard exercise. Thoroughly sound in wind and limb, with no superfluous flesh, must be the man who would follow the hounds in this wild country, — through jungles, rivers, plains, and deep ravines, sometimes from sunrise to sunset without tasting food since the previous evening, with the exception of a cup of coffee and piece of toast before starting. It is trying work, but it is a noble sport: no weapon but the hunting knife; no certainty as to the character of the game that may be found; it may be either an elk, or a boar, or a leopard, and yet the knife and the good hounds are all that can be trusted in.

It is a glorious sport certainly to a man who thoroughly understands it; the voice of every hound familiar to his ear, the particular kind of game that is found is at once known to him long before he is in view by the style of the hunting. If an elk is found, the hounds follow with a burst straight as a line, and at a killing pace, directly up the hill, till he at length turns and bends his headlong course for some stronghold in a deep river to bay. Listening to the hounds till certain of their course, a thorough knowledge of the country at once tells the huntsman of their destination, and away he goes.

He tightens his belt by a hole, and steadily he starts at a long swinging trot, having made up his mind for a day of it. Over hills and valleys, through tangled and pathless forests, but all well known to him, steady he goes at the same pace on the level, easy through the bogs and up the hills, extra steam down hill, and stopping for a moment to listen for the hounds on every elevated spot. At length he hears them! No, it was a bird. Again he fancies that he hears a distant sound — was it the wind? No; there it is — it is old Smut's voice — he is at bay! Yoick to him! he shouts till his lungs are well-nigh cracked, and through thorns and jungles, bogs and ravines, he rushes towards the welcome sound. Thick tangled bushes armed with a thousand hooked thorns suddenly arrest his course; it is the thick fringe of underwood that borders every forest; — the open plain is within a few yards of him. The hounds in a mad chorus are at bay, and the woods ring again with the cheering sound. Nothing can stop him now — thorns, or clothes, or flesh, must go, — something must give way as he bursts through them and stands upon the plain.

There they are in that deep pool formed by the river as it sweeps round the rock. A buck! a noble fellow! Now he charges at the hounds, and strikes the foremost beneath the water with his fore-feet; up they come again to the surface,—they hear their master's well-known shout,—they look round and see his welcome figure on the steep bank. Another moment, a tremendous splash, and he is among his hounds, and all are swimming towards their noble game. At them he comes with a fierce rush. Avoid him as you best can, ye hunters, man, and hounds!

Down the river the buck now swims, sometimes galloping over the shallows, sometimes wading shoulder-deep, sometimes swimming through the deep pools. Now he dashes down the fierce rapids and leaps the opposing rocks between which the torrent rushes at a frightful pace. The hounds are after him; the roaring of the water joins in their wild chorus; the loud holloa of the huntsman is heard above every sound as he cheers the pack on. He runs along the bank of the river, and again the enraged buck turns to bay. He has this time taken a strong position: he stands in a swift rapid about two feet deep; his thin legs cleave the stream as it rushes past, and every hound is swept away as he attempts to stem the current. He is a perfect picture: his nostrils are distended, his mane is bristled up, his eyes flash, and he adds his loud bark of defiance to the din around him. The hounds cannot touch him. Now for the huntsman's part: he calls the stanchest seizers to his side, gives them a cheer on, and steps into the torrent, knife in hand. Quick as lightning the buck springs to the attack; but he has exposed himself, and at that moment the tall lurchers are upon his ears; the huntsman leaps upon one side and plunges the knife behind his shoulder. A tremendous struggle takes place — the whole pack is upon him; still his dying efforts almost free him from their hold: a mass of spray envelopes the whole scene. Suddenly he falls, — he dies, — it is all over. The hounds are called off, and are carefully examined for wounds.

The huntsman is now perhaps some miles from home; he, therefore, cuts a long pole, and tying a large bunch of grass to one end, he sticks the other end into the ground close to the river's edge where the elk is lying. This marks the spot. He calls his hounds together and returns homewards, and afterwards sends men to cut the buck up and bring him home. Elk venison is very good, but is at all times more like beef than English venison.

The foregoing may be considered a general description of elk-hunting, although the incidents of the sport necessarily vary considerably.

The boar is our dangerous adversary, and he is easily known by the character of the run. The hounds seldom open with such a burst upon the scent as they do with an elk. The run is much slower; he runs down this ravine and up that, never going straight away, and he generally comes to bay after a run of ten minutes' duration.

A boar always chooses the very thickest part of the jungle as his position for a bay, and from this he makes continual rushes at the hounds.

The huntsman approaches the scene of the combat, breaking his way with difficulty through the tangled jungle, until within about twenty yards of the bay. He now cheers the hounds on to the attack, and if they are worthy of their name, they instantly rush into the boar regardless of wounds. The huntsman is aware of the seizure by the grunting of the boar and the tremendous confusion in the thick jungle; he immediately rushes to the assistance of the pack knife in hand.

A scene of real warfare meets his view—gaping

wounds upon his best hounds, the boar rushing through the jungle covered with dogs, and he himself becomes the immediate object of his fury when observed.

No time is to be lost. Keeping behind the boar if possible, he rushes to the bloody conflict, and drives the hunting knife between the shoulders in the endeavour to divide the spine. Should he happily effect this, the boar falls stone dead; but if not, he repeats the thrust, keeping a good look out for the animal's tusks.

If the dogs were of not sufficient courage to rush in and seize the boar when halload on, no man could approach him in a thick jungle with only a hunting knife, as he would in all probability have his inside ripped out at the first charge. They are wonderfully active and ferocious, and of immense power, constantly weighing 4 cwt.

The end of nearly every good seizer is being killed by a boar. The better the dog the more likely he is to be killed, as he will be the first to lead the attack, and in thick jungle he has no chance of escaping from a wound.

CHAP. III.

MINNERIA LAKE.—BRUSH WITH A BULL.—AN AWKWARD VIS-À-VIS.—A BRIGHT THOUGHT.—BULL BUFFALO RECEIVES HIS SMALL CHANGE.—WHAT IS MAN?—LONG SHOT WITH THE FOUR-OUNCE.—CHARGED BY A HERD OF BUFFALOS.—THE FOUR-OUNCE DOES SERVICE.—THE "LOLA."—A WOMAN KILLED BY A CROCODILE.—CROCODILE AT BOLGODDÉ LAKE.—A MONSTER CROCODILE.—DEATH OF A CROCODILE.

THE foregoing description may serve as an introduction to the hill sports of Ceylon. One animal, however, yet remains to be described, who surpasses all others in dogged ferocity when once aroused. This is the "Buffalo."

The haunts of this animal are in the hottest parts of Ceylon. In the neighbourhood of lakes, swamps, and extensive plains the buffalo exists in large herds; wallowing in the soft mire, and passing two thirds of his time in the water itself, he may be almost termed amphibious.

He is about the size of a large ox, of immense bone and strength, very active, and his hide is almost free from hair, giving a disgusting appearance to his india-rubber-like skin. He carries his head in a peculiar manner, the horns thrown back, and his nose projecting on a level with his forehead, thus securing himself from a front shot in a fatal part. This renders him a dangerous enemy, as he will receive any number of balls from a small gun in the throat and chest without evincing the least symptom of distress. The shoulder is the acknowledged point to aim at, but from his disposition to face the guns this is a difficult shot to obtain. Should he succeed in catching his antagonist his fury knows no bounds, and he gores his victim to death, trampling and kneeling upon him till he is satisfied that life is extinct.

This sport would not be very dangerous in the forests, where the buffalo could be easily stalked, and where escape would also be rendered less difficult in case of accident; but as he is generally met with upon the open plains free from a single tree, he must be killed when once brought to bay, or he will soon exhibit his qualifications for mischief. There is a degree of uncertainty in their character, which much increases the danger of the pursuit. A buffalo may retreat at first sight with every symptom of cowardice, and thus induce a too eager pursuit, when he will suddenly become the assailant. I cannot explain their character better than by describing the first wild buffalos that I ever saw.

I had not been long in Ceylon, but having arrived in the island for the sake of its wild sports, I had not been idle, and I had already made a considerable bag of large game. Like most novices, however, I was guilty of one great fault. I despised the game, and gave no heed to the many tales of danger and hair-breadth escapes which attended the pursuit of wild animals. This carelessness on my part arose from my first *débût*, having been extremely lucky; most shots had told well, and the animal had been killed with such apparent ease, that I had learnt to place an implicit reliance in the rifle. The real fact was, that I was like many others; I had slaughtered a number of animals without understanding their habits, and I was perfectly ignorant of the sport. This is now many years ago, and it was then my first visit to the island. Some places that were good spots for shooting in those days have since that time been much disturbed, and are now no longer attractive to my eyes. One of these places is Minneria Lake.

I was on a shooting trip accompanied by my brother, whom I will designate as B. We had passed a toilsome day in pushing and dragging our ponies for twenty miles along a narrow path through thick jungle, which half a dozen natives in advance were opening before us with bill-hooks. This had at one time been a good path, but was then overgrown. It is now an acknowledged bridle-road.

At 4 P.M., and eighty miles from Kandy, we emerged from the jungle, and the view of Minneria Lake burst upon us, fully repaying us for our day's march. It was a lovely afternoon. The waters of the lake, which is twenty miles in circumference, were burnished by the setting sun. The surrounding plains were as green as an English meadow, and beautiful forest trees bordered the extreme boundaries of the plains like giant warders of the adjoining jungle. Long promontories densely wooded stretched far into the waters of the lake, forming sheltered nooks and bays teeming with wild-fowl. The deer browsed in herds on the wide extent of plain, or lay beneath the shade of the spreading branches. Every feature of lovely scenery was here presented. In some spots groves of trees grew to the very water's edge; in others, the wide plains free from a single stem or bush stretched for miles along the edge of the lake; thickly wooded hills bordered the extreme end of its waters, and distant blue mountains mingled their dim summits with the clouds.

It was a lovely scene, which we enjoyed in silence, while our ponies feasted upon the rich grass.

The village of Minneria was three miles further on, and our coolies, servants, and baggage were all far behind us. We had, therefore, no rifles or guns at hand, except a couple of shot guns, which were carried by our horsekeepers: for these we had a few balls.

For about half an hour we waited in the impatient expectation of the arrival of our servants with the rifles. The afternoon was wearing away, and they did not appear. We could wait no longer, but determined to take a stroll and examine the country. We therefore left our horses and proceeded.

The grass was most verdant, about the height of a field fit for the scythe in England, but not so thick. From this the snipe arose at every twenty or thirty paces, although the ground was perfectly dry. Crossing a large meadow, and skirting the banks of the lake, from which the ducks and teal rose in large flocks, we entered a long neck of jungle which stretched far into the lake. This was not above two hundred paces in width, and we soon emerged upon an extensive plain bordered by fine forest, the waters of the lake stretching far away upon our left, like a sheet of gold. A few large rocks rose above the surface near the shore; these were covered with various kinds of wild-fowl. The principal tenants of the plain were wild buffalos.

A herd of about a hundred were lying in a swampy hollow about a quarter of a mile from us. Several single bulls were dotted about the green surface of the level plain, and on the opposite shores of the lake were many dark patches undistinguishable in the distance; these were in reality herds of buffalos. There was not a sound in the wide expanse before us, except the harsh cry of the waterfowl that our presence had already disturbed,—not a breath of air moved the leaves of the trees which shadowed us,—and the whole scene was that of undisturbed nature. The sun had now sunk low upon the horizon, and the air was comparatively cool. The multitude of buffalos enchanted us, and with our two light double-barrels we advanced to the attack of the herd before us.

We had not left the obscurity of the forest many seconds before we were observed. The herd started up from their muddy bed, and gazed at us with astonishment. It was a fair open plain of some thousand acres, bounded by the forest that we had just quitted on the one side, and by the lake on the other; thus there was no cover for our advance, and all we could do was to push on.

As we approached the herd they ranged up in a compact body, presenting a very regular line in front. From this line seven large bulls stepped forth, and from their vicious appearance seemed disposed to show fight. In the meantime we were running up, and were soon within thirty paces of them. At this distance the main body of the herd suddenly wheeled round and thundered across the plain in full retreat. One of the bulls at the same moment charged straight at us, but when within twenty paces of the guns he turned to one side and instantly received two balls in the shoulder, B. and I having fired at the same moment. As luck would have it, his blade-bone was thus broken, and he fell upon his knees, but recovering himself in an instant he retreated on three legs to the water.

We now received assistance from a most unexpected quarter. One of the large bulls, his companions, charged after him with great fury, and soon overtaking the wounded beast, he struck him full in the side, throwing him over with a great shock on the muddy border of the lake. Here the wounded animal lay unable to rise, and his conqueror commenced a slow retreat across the plain.

Leaving B. to extinguish the wounded buffalo, I gave chase to the retreating bully. At an easy canter he would gain a hundred paces, and then turning, he would face me; throwing his nose up, and turning his head on one side with a short grunt, he would advance quickly for a few paces, and then again retreat as I continued to approach.

In this manner he led me a chase of about a mile along the banks of the lake, but he appeared determined not to bring the fight to an issue at close quarters. Cursing his cowardice I fired a long shot at him, and reloading with my last spare ball, I continued the chase, led on by ignorance and excitement.

The lake in one part stretched in a narrow creek into the plain, and the bull now directed his course into the angle formed by this turn. I thought that I had him in a corner, and redoubling my exertions I gained upon him considerably. He retreated slowly to the very edge of the creek, and I had gained so fast upon him that I was not thirty paces distant when he plunged into the water and commenced swimming across the creek. This was not more than sixty yards in breadth, and I knew that I could now bring him to action.

Running round the borders of the creek as fast as I could, I arrived at the opposite side on his intended landing-place just as his black form reared from the deep water and gained the shallows, into which I had waded knee-deep to meet him. I now experienced that pleasure as he stood sullenly eyeing me within fifteen paces. Poor stupid fellow! I would willingly, in my ignorance, have betted ten to one upon the shot, so certain was I of his death in another instant.

I took a quick but steady aim at his chest, at the point of connection with the throat. The smoke of the barrel passed to one side; — there he stood, — he had not flinched, he literally had not moved a muscle. The only change that had taken place was in his eye; this, which had hitherto been merely sullen, was now beaming with fury; but his form was as motionless as a statue. A stream of blood poured from a wound within an inch of the spot at which I had aimed; had it not been for this fact, I should not have believed him struck.

Annoyed at the failure of the shot, I tried him with the left-hand barrel at the same hole. The report of the gun echoed over the lake, but there he stood as though he bore a charmed life; — an increased flow of blood from the wound and additional lustre in his eye were the only signs of his being struck.

I was now unloaded, and had not a single ball remaining. It was now his turn. I dared not turn to retreat, as I knew he would immediately charge, and we stared each other out of countenance.

With a short grunt he suddenly sprung forward, but fortunately, as I did not move, he halted: he had, however, decreased his distance, and we now gazed at each other within ten paces. I began to think buffalo-shooting somewhat dangerous, and I would have given something to have been a mile away, but ten times as much to have had my four-ounce rifle in my hand. Oh, how I longed for that rifle in this moment of suspense! Unloaded, without the power of defence, with the absolute certainty of a charge from an overpowering brute, my hand instinctively found the handle of my hunting knife, a useless weapon against such a foe.

Knowing that B. was not aware of my situation at the distance which separated us (about a mile), without taking my eyes from the figure before me, I raised my hand to my mouth and gave a long and loud whistle; this was a signal that I knew would be soon answered if heard.

With a stealthy step, and another short grunt, the bull again advanced a couple of paces towards me. He seemed aware of my helplessness, and he was the picture of rage and fury, pawing the water, and stamping violently with his fore-feet.

This was very pleasant! I gave myself up for lost, but putting as fierce an expression into my features as I could possibly assume, I stared hopelessly at my maddened antagonist.

Suddenly a bright thought flashed through my mind. Without taking my eyes off the animal before me, I put a double charge of powder down the right-hand barrel, and tearing off a piece of my shirt, I took all the money from my pouch, three shillings in sixpenny pieces, and two anna pieces, which I luckily had with me in this small coin for paying coolies. Quickly making them into a rouleau with the piece of rag, I rammed them down the barrel, and they were hardly well home before the bull again sprang forward. So quick was it that I had no time to replace the ramrod, and I threw it in the water, bringing my gun on full cock in the same instant. However, he again halted, being now within about seven paces from me, and we again gazed fixedly at each other, but with altered feelings on my part. I had faced him hopelessly with an empty gun for more than a quarter of an hour, which seemed a century. I now had a charge in my gun, which I knew if reserved till he was within a foot of the muzzle would certainly floor him, and I awaited his onset with comparative carelessness, still keeping my eyes opposed to his gaze.

At this moment I heard a splashing in the water behind me, accompanied by the hard breathing of something evidently distressed. The next moment I heard B.'s voice. He could hardly speak for want of breath, having run the whole way to my rescue, but I could understand that he had only one barrel loaded and no bullets left. I dared not turn my face from the buffalo, but I cautioned B. to reserve his fire till the bull should be close into me, and then to aim at the head.

The words were hardly uttered, when, with the

SKETCHED BY S. W. BAKER.

THE CHARGE OF SIXPENCES

concentrated rage of the last twenty minutes, he rushed straight at me. It was the work of an instant. B. fired without effect. The horns were lowered, their points were on either side of me, and the muzzle of the gun barely touched his forehead when I pulled the trigger, and three shillings' worth of small change rattled into his hard head. Down he went, and rolled over with the suddenly checked momentum of his charge. Away went B. and I as fast as our heels would carry us, through the water and over the plain, knowing that he was not dead but only stunned. There was a large fallen tree about half a mile from us, whose whitened branches rising high above the ground offered a tempting asylum. To this we directed our flying steps, and after a run of a hundred yards, we turned and looked behind us. He had regained his feet and was following us slowly. We now experienced the difference of feeling between hunting and being hunted, and fine sport we must have afforded him.

On he came, but fortunately so stunned by the collision with her Majesty's features upon the coin which he had dared to oppose, that he could only reel forward at a slow canter. By degrees, even this pace slackened, and he fell. We were only too glad to be able to reduce our speed likewise, but we had no sooner stopped to breathe, than he was again up and after us. At length, however, we gained the tree, and we beheld him with satisfaction stretched powerless upon the ground, but not dead, within two hundred yards of us.

We retreated under cover of the forest to the spot at which we had left the horses, fortunately meeting no opposition from wild animals, and we shortly arrived at the village, at which we took up our quarters, vowing vengeance on the following morning for the defeat that we had sustained.

A man is a poor defenceless wretch if left to defend himself against wild animals with the simple natural weapons of arms, legs, and teeth. A tom-cat would almost be a match for him. He has legs which will neither serve him for pursuit or escape if he is forced to trust only in his speed. He has strength of limb which is useless without some artificial weapon. He is an animal, who, without the power of reason, could not even exist in a wild state; his brain alone gives him the strength to support his title of a lord of the creation.

Nevertheless, a lord of the creation does not

appear in much majesty when running for his life from an infuriated buffalo,—the assumed title sits uneasily upon him, when, with scarcely a breath left in his body, he struggles along till he is ready to drop with fatigue, expecting to be overtaken at every step. We must certainly have exhibited poor specimens of the boasted sway of man over the brute creation could a stranger have witnessed our flight on this occasion.

The next morning we were up at day-break, and we returned to the battle-field of the previous evening, in the full expectation of seeing our wounded antagonist lying dead where we had left him. In this we were disappointed,—he was gone, and we never saw him again.

I now had my long two-ounce and my four-ounce rifles with me, and I was fully prepared for a deep revenge for the disgrace of yesterday.

The morning was clear, but cloudy; a heavy thunder-storm during the night had cooled the air, and the whole plain was glistening with bright drops; the peacocks were shrieking from the tree-tops, and spreading their gaudy plumage to the cool breeze; and the whole face of nature seemed refreshed. We felt the same invigorating spirit, and we took a long survey of the many herds of buffalos upon the plain, before we could determine which we should first attack.

A large single bull, who had been lying in a swampy hollow, unobserved by us, suddenly sprang up at about three hundred yards distance, and slowly cantered off. I tried the long two-ounce rifle at him, but, taking too great an elevation, I fired over him. The report, however, had the effect of turning him, and, instead of retreating, he wheeled round and attempted to pass between the guns and the banks of the lake. We were about three hundred yards from the water's edge, and he was soon passing us at full gallop at right-angles about mid-way or a hundred and fifty yards distant.

I had twelve drachms of powder in the four-ounce rifle, and I took a flying shot at his shoulder. No visible effect was produced, and the ball ricochetted completely across the broad surface of the lake (which was no more than a mile wide at this part) in continuous splashes. The gun-bearers said I had fired behind him, but I had distinctly heard the peculiar "fut" which a ball makes upon striking an animal, and although the passage of the ball across the lake appeared remarkable, nevertheless I felt positive that it had first passed through some portion of the animal.

Away the bull sped over the plain at unabated speed, for about two hundred paces, when he suddenly turned and charged towards the guns. On he came for about a hundred yards, but evidently slackening his speed at every stride. At length, he stopped altogether. His mouth was wide open, and I could now distinguish a mass of bloody foam upon his lips and nostrils,—the ball had in reality passed through his lungs, and making its exit from the opposite shoulder it had even then flown across the lake. This was a proof of the effect of twelve drachms of powder.

Having reloaded, I now advanced towards him, and soon arrived within fifty paces. He was the facsimile of the bull that had chased us on the previous day—the same picture of fury and determination; and, crouching low, he advanced a few paces, keeping his eyes fixed upon us, as though we were already his own. A short cough, accompanied by a rush of blood from his mouth, seemed to cause him great uneasiness, and he halted.

Again we advanced till within twenty paces of him. I would not fire, as I saw that he already had enough, and I wished to see how long he could support a wound through the lungs, as my safety in buffalo-shooting might in future depend upon this knowledge.

The fury of his spirit seemed to war with death, and, although reeling with weakness and suffocation, he again attempted to come on. It was his last effort; his eyes rolled convulsively, he gave a short grunt of impotent rage, and the next moment he fell upon his back, with his heels in the air; he was stone dead, and game to the last moment.

I had thus commenced a revenge for the insult of yesterday; I had proved the wonderful power of the four-ounce rifle, a weapon destined to make great havoc amongst the heavy game of Ceylon.

Upon turning from the carcase before us, we observed to our surprise that a large herd of buffalos, that were at a great distance when we had commenced the attack upon the bull, had now approached to within a few hundred yards, and were standing in a dense mass, attentively watching us. Without any delay we advanced towards them, and upon arriving within about a hundred paces, we observed that the herd was headed by two large bulls, one of which was the largest that I had ever seen. The whole herd were bellowing, and pawing the ground. They had winded the blood of the dead bull, and appeared perfectly maddened.

We continued to advance, and we were within about ninety paces of them, when suddenly the whole herd of about two hundred buffalos, headed by the two large bulls before noticed, dashed straight towards us at full gallop. So simultaneous was the onset that it resembled a sudden charge of cavalry, and the ground vibrated beneath their heavy hoofs. Their tails were thrown high above their backs, and the mad and overpowering phalanx of heads and horns came rushing forward as though to sweep us at once from the face of the earth.

There was not an instant to be lost; already but a short space intervened between us and apparently certain destruction. Our gun-bearers were almost in the act of flight; but catching hold of the man who carried the long two-ounce rifle, and keeping him by my side, I awaited the irresistible onset with the four-ounce.

The largest of the bulls was some yards in advance closely followed by his companion, and the herd in a compact mass came thundering down at their heels. Only fifty yards separated us, we literally felt among them, and already experienced a sense of being over-run. I did not look at the herd, but I kept my eye upon the big bull leader. On they flew and were within thirty paces of us when I took a steady shot with the four-ounce, and the leading bull plunged head foremost in the turf turning a complete summersault. Snatching the two-ounce from the petrified gun-bearer, I had just time for a shot as the second bull was within fifteen paces, and at the flash of the rifle his horns ploughed up the turf, and he lay almost at our feet. That lucky shot turned the whole herd. When certain destruction threatened us, they suddenly wheeled to their left when within twenty paces of the guns, and left us astonished victors of the field. We poured an ineffectual volley into the retreating herd from the light guns as they galloped off in full retreat, and reloaded as quickly as possible, as the two bulls, although floored, were still alive. They were, however, completely powerless, and a double-barrelled gun gave each the *coup de grace* by a ball in the forehead. Both rifle-shots had struck at the point of junction of the throat and chest, and the four-ounce ball had passed out of the hind quarter. Our friend of yesterday, although hit in precisely the same spot, had laughed at the light guns.

Although I have since killed about two hundred wild buffalos I have never witnessed another charge by a herd. This was an extraordinary occurrence, and fortunately stands alone in buffalo-shooting. Were it not for the two heavy rifles our career might have terminated in an unpleasant manner. As I before mentioned, this part of the country was seldom or ever disturbed at the time of which I write, and the buffalos were immensely numerous and particularly savage, nearly always turning to bay and showing good sport when attacked.

Having cut out the tongues from the two bulls, we turned homewards to breakfast. Skirting along the edge of the lake, which abounded with small creeks, occasioning as many circuits, we came suddenly upon a single bull, who, springing from his lair of mud and high grass, plunged into a creek, and, swimming across, exposed himself to a dead shot as he landed on the opposite bank about a hundred paces from us. The four-ounce struck him in the hind quarters and broke the hip joint, and, continuing its course along his body, it pierced his lungs and lodged in the skin of the throat. The bull immediately fell, but regaining his feet he took to the water and swam to a small island of high grass about thirty yards from the shore. Upon gaining this he turned and faced us, but in a few seconds he fell unable to rise, and received a merciful shot in the head, which despatched him.

We were just leaving the borders of the lake on our way to the village when two cow buffalos sprung up from one of the numerous inlets, and retreated at full gallop towards the jungle, offering a splendid side shot at about a hundred paces. The leading cow plunged head foremost into the grass as the four-ounce struck her through both shoulders. She was a fine young cow, and we cut some steaks from her in case we should find a scarcity of provisions at Minneria, and, quitting the shores of the lake, we started for breakfast.

It was only 8 A. M. when we arrived. I had bagged five buffalos, four of which were fine bulls. Our revenge was complete, and I had proved that the four-ounce was perfectly irresistible if held straight with the heavy charge of twelve drachms of powder. Since that time I have frequently used sixteen drachms (one ounce) of powder to the charge, but the recoil is then very severe, although the effect upon an animal with a four-ounce steel-tipped conical ball is tremendous.

On our return to the village of Minneria we found a famous breakfast, for which a bath in the neighbouring brook increased an appetite already sharpened by the morning exercise. The buffalo steaks were coarse and bad, as tough as leather, and certainly should never be eaten if better food can be obtained. The tongues are very rich, but require salting.

In those days Minneria was not spoiled by visitors, and supplies were accordingly at a cheap rate, large fowls at one penny each, milk at any price that you chose to give for it. This is now much changed, and the only thing that is still ridiculously cheap is fish.

Give a man sixpence to catch you as many as he can in the morning, and he forthwith starts on his piscatorial errand with a large basket, cone shaped, of two feet diameter at the bottom, and about eight inches at the top. This basket is open at both ends, and is about two feet in length.

The fish that is most sought after is the "lola." He is a ravenous fellow, in appearance between a trout and a carp, having the habits of the former, but the clumsy shoulders of the latter. He averages about three pounds, although he often is caught of nine or ten pounds weight. Delighting in the shallows, he lies among the weeds at the bottom, to which he always retreats when disturbed. Aware of his habits, the fisherman walks knee-deep in the water, and at every step he plunges the broad end of the basket quickly to the bottom. He immediately feels the fish strike against the sides, and putting his hand down through the aperture in the top of the basket he captures him, and deposits him in a basket slung on his back.

These "lola" are delicious eating, being very like an eel in flavour, and I have known one man catch forty in a morning with no other apparatus than his basket.

Minneria Lake, like all others in Ceylon, swarms with crocodiles of a very large size. Early in the morning and late in the evening they may be seen lying upon the banks like logs of trees. I have frequently remarked that a buffalo, shot within a few yards of the lake, has invariably disappeared during the night, leaving an undoubted track where he has been dragged to the water by the crocodiles. These brutes frequently attack the natives when fishing or bathing, but I have never heard of their pursuing any person upon dry land.

I remember an accident having occurred at Madampi, on the west coast of Ceylon, about seven years ago, the day before I passed through the village. A number of women were employed in cutting rushes for mat-making, and were about mid-deep in the water. The horny tail of a large crocodile was suddenly seen above the water among the group of women, and in another instant one of them was seized by the thigh and dragged towards the deeper part of the stream. In vain the terrified creature shrieked for assistance, the horror-stricken group had rushed to the shore, and a crowd of spectators on the bank offered no aid beyond their cries. It was some distance before the water deepened, and the unfortunate creature was dragged for many yards, sometimes beneath the water sometimes above the surface, rending the air with her screams, until at length the deep water hid her from their view. She was never again seen.

Some of these vermin grow to a very large size, attaining the length of twenty feet, and eight feet in girth, but the common size is fourteen feet. They move slowly upon land, but are wonderfully fast and active in the water. They commonly lie in wait for their prey under some hollow bank in a deep pool, and when the unsuspecting deer or even buffalo stoops his head to drink he is suddenly seized by the nose and dragged beneath the water. Here he is speedily drowned and consumed at leisure.

The two lower and front teeth of a crocodile project through the upper jaw, and their white points attract immediate notice as they protrude through the brown scales on the upper lip. When the mouth is closed the jaws are thus absolutely locked together.

It is a common opinion that the scales on the back of a crocodile will turn a ball; this is a vulgar error. The scales are very tough and hard, but a ball from a common fowling-piece will pass right through the body. I have even seen a hunting knife driven at one blow deep into the hardest part of the back; and this was a crocodile of a large size, about fourteen feet long, that I shot at a place called Bolgoddé, twenty-two miles from Colombo.

A man had been setting nets for fish, and was in the act of swimming to the shore, when he was seized and drowned by a crocodile. The next morning two buffalos were dragged into the water close to the spot, and it was supposed that these murders were committed by the same crocodile. I was at Colombo at the time, and hearing of the accident, I rode off to Bolgoddé to try my hand at catching him.

Bolgoddé is a very large lake of many miles in circumference, abounding with crocodiles, widgeon, teal, and ducks.

On arrival that evening, the moodeliar (headman) pointed out the spot where the man had been destroyed, and where the buffalos had been dragged in by the crocodile. One buffalo had been entirely devoured, but the other had merely lost his head, and his carcase was floating in a horrible state of decomposition near the bank. It was nearly dark, so I engaged a small canoe to be in readiness by break of day.

Just as the light streaked the horizon I stepped into the canoe. This required some caution, as it was the smallest thing that can be conceived to support two persons. It consisted of the hollow trunk of a tree six feet in length and about one foot in diameter. A small outrigger prevented it from upsetting, but it was not an inch from the surface of the water when I took my narrow seat, and the native in the stern paddled carefully towards the carcase of the buffalo.

Upon approaching within a hundred yards of the floating carcase, I counted five forms within a few yards of the flesh. These objects were not above nine inches square, and appeared like detached pieces of rough bark. I knew them to be the foreheads of different crocodiles, and presently one moved towards the half-consumed buffalo. His long head and shoulders projected from the water as he attempted to fix his fore-claws into the putrid flesh; this, however, rolled over towards him, and prevented him from getting a hold; but the gaping jaws nevertheless made a wide breach in the buffalo's flank. I was now within thirty yards of them, and, being observed, they all dived immediately to the bottom.

The carcase was lying within a few yards of the bank, where the water was extremely deep and clear. Several large trees grew close to the edge and formed a good hiding-place; I therefore landed, and, sending the canoe to a distance, I watched the water.

I had not been five minutes in this position before I saw in the water at my feet, in a deep hole close to the bank, the immense form of a crocodile as he was slowly rising from his hiding place to the surface. He appeared to be about eighteen feet long, and he projected his horny head from the surface, bubbled, and then floated with only his forehead and large eyes above the water. He was a horrible-looking monster, and from his size I hoped he was the villain that had committed the late depredations. He was within three yards of me; and, although I stood upon the bank, his great round eyes gazed at me without a symptom of fear. The next moment I put a two-ounce ball exactly between them and killed him stone dead. He gave a convulsive slap with his tail, which made the water foam, and, turning upon his back, he gradually sunk till at length I could only distinguish the long line of his white belly twenty feet below me.

Not having any apparatus for bringing him to the surface, I again took to the canoe, as a light breeze that had sprung up was gradually moving the carcase of the buffalo away. This I slowly followed until it at length rested in a wide belt of rushes which grew upon the shallows near the shore. I pushed the canoe into the rushes within four yards of the carcase, keeping to windward to avoid the sickening smell.

I had not been long in this position before the body suddenly rolled over as though attacked by something underneath the water, and the next moment the tall reeds brushed against the sides of the canoe, being violently agitated in a long line evidently by a crocodile at the bottom.

The native in the stern grew as pale as a black can turn with fright, and instantly began to paddle the canoe away. This, however, I soon replaced in its former position, and then took his paddle away to prevent further accidents. There sat the captain of the fragile vessel in the most abject state of terror. We were close to the shore, and the water was not more than three feet deep, and yet he dared not jump out of the canoe, as the rushes were again brushing against its sides, being moved by the hidden beast at the bottom. There was no help for him, so, after vainly imploring me to shove the canoe into deep water, he at length sat still.

In a few minutes the body of the buffalo again moved, and the head and shoulders of a crocodile appeared above water and took a bite of some pounds of flesh. I could not get a shot at the head from his peculiar position, but I put a ball through his shoulders, and immediately shoved the canoe astern. Had I not done this we should most likely have been upset, as the wounded brute began to lash out with his tail in all directions, till he at length retired to the bottom among the rushes. Here I could easily track him, as he slowly moved along, by the movement of the reeds. Giving the native the paddle, I now by threats induced him to keep the canoe over the very spot where the rushes were moving, and we slowly followed on the track while I kept watch in the bow of the canoe with a rifle. Suddenly the movement in the rushes ceased, and the canoe stopped accordingly. I leaned slightly over the side to look into the water, when up came a large air-bubble, and directly after an apparition in the shape of some fifteen pounds of putrid flesh. The stench was frightful, but I knew my friend must be very bad down below to disgorge so sweet a morsel. I therefore took the paddle and poked for him; the water being shallow I felt him immediately. Again the rushes moved; I felt the paddle twist as his scaly back glided under it, and a pair of gaping jaws appeared above the water, wide open within two feet of the canoe. The next moment his head appeared, and the two-ounce ball shattered his brain. He sunk to the bottom, the rushes moved slightly and were then still.

I now put the canoe ashore, and cutting a strong stick with a crook at one end, I again put out to the spot and dragged for him. He was quite dead; and catching him under the fore-leg, I soon brought him gently to the surface of the water. I now made fast a line to his fore-leg, and we towed him slowly to the village, the canoe being level with the water's edge.

His weight in the water was a mere trifle, but on arrival at the village on the banks of the lake, the villagers turned out with great glee and fastened ropes to different parts of his body to drag him out. This operation employed about twenty men. The beast was about fourteen feet long; and he was no sooner on shore than the natives cut him to pieces with axes, and threw the sections into the lake to be devoured by his own species. This was a savage kind of revenge which appeared to afford them great satisfaction.

Taking a large canoe, I paddled along the shores of the lake with a short gun, and made a good bag of ducks and teal, and returned to breakfast. The fatness and flavour of the wild ducks in Ceylon is quite equal to the best in England.

CHAP. IV.

EQUIPMENT FOR A HUNTING TRIP. — IN CHASE OF A HERD OF ELEPHANTS. — HARD WORK. — CLOSE QUARTERS. — SIX FEET FROM THE MUZZLE. — A BLACK WITH A DEVIL.

There is one thing necessary to the enjoyment of sport in Ceylon, and without which no amount of game can afford thorough pleasure; this is personal comfort. Unlike a temperate climate, where mere attendance becomes a luxury, the pursuit of game in a tropical country is attended with immense fatigue and exhaustion. The intense heat of the sun, the dense and suffocating exhalations from swampy districts, the constant and irritating attacks from insects, all form drawbacks to sport that can only be lessened by excellent servants and by the most perfect arrangements for shelter and supplies. I have tried all methods of travelling, and I generally manage to combine good sport with every comfort and convenience.

A good tent, perfectly waterproof, and of so light a construction as to travel with only two bearers, is absolutely indispensable. My tent is on the principle of an umbrella, fifteen feet in diameter, and will house three persons comfortably. A round table fits in two halves round the tent pole; three folding chairs have ample space; three beds can be arranged round the tent walls; the boxes of clothes, &c., stow under the beds; and a dressing-table and gun-rack complete the furniture.

Next in importance to the tent is a good canteen. Mine is made of japanned block tin, and contains in close-fitting compartments an entire dinner and breakfast service for three persons, including everything that can be required in an ordinary establishment. This is slung upon a bamboo, carried by two coolies.

Clothes must always be packed in tin boxes, or the whole case will most likely be devoured by white ants. Cooking utensils must be carried in abundance, together with a lanthorn, an axe, a bill-hook, a tinder-box, matches, candles, oil, tea, coffee, sugar, biscuits, wine, brandy, sauces, &c., a few hams, some tins of preserved meats and soups, and a few bottles of curaçoa, a glass of which, in the early dawn after a cup of hot coffee and a biscuit, is a fine preparation for a day's work.

I once tried the rough system of travelling, and started off with nothing but my guns, clothes, a box of biscuits, and a few bottles of brandy — no bed, no pillow, no tent or chairs or table, but, as my distressed servant said, "no nothing." This was many years ago, when the excitement of wild sports was sufficient to laugh at discomfort. I literally depended upon my gun for food, and my cooking utensils consisted of one saucepan and a gridiron, a "stew" and a "fry" being all that I looked forward to in the way of gourmandism. Sleeping on the bare ground in native huts, dining cross-legged upon mother earth with a large leaf as a substitute for a plate, a cocoa-nut shell for a glass, my hunting knife comprising all my cutlery, I thus passed through a large district of wild country, accompanied by B., and I never had more exciting sport.

It was on this occasion that I had a memorable hunt in the neighbourhood of Narlandé, within thirty miles of Kandy. It was our first day's stage, and, upon our arrival at about 2 P. M., we left our guns at the post-holder's hut, while we proceeded to the river to bathe.

We were hardly dressed before a native came running to tell us that several elephants were devouring his crop of korrakan, a grain something like clover seed, upon which the people in this part almost entirely subsist.

Without a moment's delay we sent for the guns. The post-holder was a good tracker, and a few minutes of sharp walking through a path bordered on either side by dense thorny jungle brought us to a chéna ground or cultivated field. The different watch-houses erected in the large trees were full of people, who were shrieking and yelling at the top of their voices, having just succeeded in scaring the elephants into the jungle.

The whole of the country in this neighbourhood has, in successive ages, been cleared and cultivated: the forest has been felled. The poverty of the soil yields only one crop, and the lately cleared field is again restored to nature. Dense thorny jungle immediately springs up, which a man cannot penetrate without being torn to pieces by the briars. This is called chéna jungle, and is always the favourite resort of elephants and all wild animals, the impervious character of the bush forming a secure retreat.

From these haunts, the elephants commit nocturnal descents upon the crops of the natives. The korrakan is a sweet grass, growing about two feet high, and so partial are the elephants to this food, that they will invade the isolated field even during the day-time. Driven out by shouts, and by shots fired by the natives from their secure watch-houses, they will retreat to their cover, but in a few minutes they will reappear from another part of the jungle, and again commence their depredations.

The havoc committed by a large herd of elephants can well be imagined.

In this instance, there were only three elephants, a large bull with a mother and her young one, or what we call a "poonchy." On entering the korrakan field we distinctly heard them breaking the boughs at no great distance. We waited for some time to see if they would return to the field; but they apparently were aware of some impending danger, as they did not move from their strong position. This was a cunning family of elephants, as they had retreated "down wind," and the jungle being so thick that we could with difficulty follow even upon their track made it very doubtful whether we should kill them.

We cautiously entered. It was one mass of thorns, and we were shortly compelled to crawl upon our hands and knees. This was arduous work, as we had great difficulty in carrying the guns so as to avoid the slightest noise. I was leading the way, and could distinctly hear the rustling of the leaves as the elephants moved their ears. We were now within a few feet of them, but not an inch of their bodies could be seen, so effectually were they hidden by the thick jungle. Suddenly we heard the prolonged wh-r-r, wh-r-r-r-r, as one of the elephants winded us; the shrill trumpet sounded in another direction, and the crash through the jungle took place which nothing but an elephant can produce. In such dense jungle, where the elephants are invisible, this crash is most exciting if close at hand, as in the present instance. It is at the first burst impossible to tell whether the elephant is coming at you or rushing away. In either case it is extremely dangerous, as these chéna jungles are almost devoid of trees; thus there is no cover of sufficient strength to protect a man should he attempt to jump on one side, and he may even be run over by accident.

A few moments assured us of their retreat, and we instantly followed upon their track, running at full speed along the lane which they had crushed in their headlong flight. This was no easy matter; the jungle itself was certainly broken down, but innumerable hooked thorns, hanging from rope-like creepers which had been torn down by the rush of the elephants, caught us upon every side. In a few minutes our clothes were in rags, and we were bleeding from countless scratches; but we continued the chase as fast as we could run upon the track. The prickly cactus, which abounds in these jungles and grows to the height of twenty feet, in some places checked us for a few moments, being crushed into a heap by the horny-footed beasts before us. These obstacles overcome, we again pushed on at a rapid pace, occasionally listening for a sound of the retreating game.

We now observed that the herd had separated; the bull had gone off in one direction, and the female with her half-grown poonchy in another. Following the latter, we again pushed on at a quick run, as the elephants had evidently gone off at a great pace, and were far in advance. For about half an hour we had continued the pursuit at the same speed, when we suddenly heard the warning wh-r-r-r as the elephants winded us at a distance of 200 yards, and the crash instantly following this sound told us too plainly that the game was fearfully on the alert, and gave us little hopes of overtaking them, as they were travelling directly down wind.

Speed was our only chance, and again we rushed forward in hot pursuit through the tangled briars, which yielded to our weight, although we were almost stripped of clothes. Another half hour passed, and we had heard no further signs of the game. We stopped to breathe, and we listened attentively for the slightest sound. A sudden crash in the jungle at a great distance assured us that we were once more discovered. The chase seemed hopeless; the heat was most oppressive; and we had been running for the last hour at a killing pace through a most distressing country. Once more, however, we started off, determined to keep up the pursuit as long as daylight would permit. It was now 5 P.M., and we had one hour left before darkness would set in. The wind had entirely ceased, leaving a perfect calm; the air was thick and heavy, and the heat was thus rendered doubly fatiguing. We noticed, however, that the track of the elephants had doubled back instead of continuing in the direct line that we had followed so long. This gave us hope, as the elephants no longer had the advantage of wind, and we pushed on as fast as we could go.

It was about half an hour before dusk, and our patience and hopes were alike exhausted, when we suddenly once more heard the wh-r-r-r of the elephants winding us within a hundred yards. It was our last chance, and with redoubled speed we rushed after them.

Suddenly we broke from the high jungle in which we had been for the last two hours, and we found ourselves in a chéna jungle of two years' growth, about five feet high, but so thick and thorny, that it resembled one vast blackthorn hedge, through which no man could move except in the track of the retreating elephants.

To my delight, on entering this low jungle, I saw the female at about forty yards' distance, making off at a great pace. I had a light double-barrelled gun in my hand, and, in the hopes of checking her pace, I fired a flying shot at her ear. She had been hunted so long that she was well inclined to fight, and she immediately slackened her speed so much that in a few instants I was at her tail, so close that I could have slapped her. Still she ploughed her way through the thick thorns, and, not being able to pass her owing to the barrier of jungle, I could only follow close at her heels and take my chance of a shot. At length, losing all patience, I fired my remaining barrel under her tail, giving it an upward direction in the hope of disabling her spine.

A cloud of smoke hung over me for a second, and, throwing my empty gun on one side, I put my hand behind me for a spare gun. I felt the welcome barrel pushed into my hand, at the same moment that I saw the infuriated head of the elephant with

SIX FEET FROM THE MUZZLE.

ears cocked charging through the smoke. It was the work of an instant. I had just time to cock the two-ounce rifle and take a steady aim. The next moment we were in a cloud of smoke, but as I fired I felt certain of her. The smoke cleared from the thick bushes, and she lay dead at *six feet* from the spot where I stood. The ball was in the centre of her forehead, and B., who had fired over my shoulder so instantaneously with me, that I was not aware of it, had placed his ball within three inches of mine. Had she been missed I should have fired my last shot.

This had been a glorious hunt; many miles had been gone over, but by great luck when the wind dropped, and the elephant altered her course, she had been making a circuit for the very field of korrakan at which we had first found her. We were thus not more than three miles from our resting place, and the trackers, who know every inch of the country, soon brought us to the main road.

The poonchy and the bull elephant, having both separated from the female, escaped.

One great cause of danger in shooting in thick jungles is the obscurity occasioned by the smoke of the first barrel; this cannot escape from the surrounding bushes for some time, and effectually prevents a certain aim with the remaining barrel. In wet weather this is much increased.

For my own part I dislike shooting in thick jungles, and I very seldom do so. It is extremely dangerous, and is like shooting in the dark; you never see the game until you can almost touch it, and the labour and pain of following up elephants through thorny jungle is beyond description.

On our return to the post-holder's hut we dined and prepared for sleep. It was a calm night, and not a sound disturbed the stillness of the air. The tired coolies and servants were fast asleep, the lamp burnt dimly, being scantily fed with oil, and we were in the act of lying down to rest, when a frightful scream made us spring to our feet. There was something so unearthly in the yell that we could hardly believe it human. The next moment a figure bounded into the little room that we occupied. It was a black, stark naked. His tongue, half bitten through, protruded from his mouth; his bloodshot eyes, with a ghastly stare, were straining from their sockets, and he stood gazing at us with his arms extended wide apart. Another horrible scream burst from him, and he fell flat upon his back.

The post-holder and a whole crowd of awakened coolies now assembled, and they all at once declared that the man had a devil. The fact is, he had a fit of epilepsy, and his convulsions were terrible. Without moving a limb he flapped here and there like a salmon when just landed. I had nothing with me that would relieve him, and I therefore left him to the hands of the post-holder, who prided himself upon his skill in exorcising devils. All his incantations produced no effect, and the unfortunate patient suddenly sprung to his feet and rushed madly into the thorny jungle. In this we heard him crashing through like a wild beast, and I do not know to this day whether he was ever heard of afterwards.

The Cingalese have a thorough belief in the presence of devils; one sect are actually "devil *worshippers*," but the greater portion of the natives are Bhuddists. Among this nation the missionaries make very slow progress. There is no character to work upon in the Cingalese: they are faithless, cunning, treacherous, and abject cowards; superstitious in the extreme, and yet unbelieving in any one God. A converted Bhuddist will address his prayers to our God if he thinks he can obtain any temporal benefit by so doing; but, if not, he would be just as likely to pray to Bhudda, or to the Devil.

I once saw a sample of heathen conversion in Ceylon, that was enough to dishearten a missionary. A Roman Catholic chapel had been erected in a wild part of the country by some zealous missionary, who prided himself upon the number of his converts. He left his chapel during a few weeks' absence in some other district, during which time his converts paid their devotion at the Christian altar. They had made a few little additions to the ornaments of the altar, which must have astonished the priest on his return.

There was an image of our Saviour, and the Virgin;—this was all according to custom. But there were also "*three images of Bhudda*," a coloured plaster-of-paris image of the *Queen and Prince Albert* upon the altar, and a very questionable penny print in vivid colours hanging over the altar, entitled the "Stolen Kiss." So much for the conversion of the heathen in Ceylon. The attempt should only be made in the schools, where the children may be brought up as Christians; but the idea of converting the grown-up heathen is a fallacy.

CHAP. V.

THE FOUR-OUNCE AGAIN.—TIDINGS OF A ROGUE.—APPROACHING A TANK ROGUE.—AN EXCITING MOMENT.—RUINS OF POLLANARUA.—ANCIENT RUINS.—ROGUES AT DOOLANA.—B. CHARGED BY A ROGUE.—PLANNING AN ATTACK.—A CHECK.—NARROW ESCAPE.—ROGUE-STALKING.—A BAD ROGUE.—DANGERS OF ELEPHANT-SHOOTING.—THE RHATAMAHATMEYA'S TALE.

A BROKEN nipple in my long two-ounce rifle took me to Trincomalee, about seventy miles out of my proposed route. Here I had it punched out, and replaced with a new one, which I fortunately had with me. No one who has not experienced the loss, can imagine the disgust occasioned by an accident to a favourite rifle in a wild country. A spare nipple and mainspring for each barrel and lock should always be taken on a shooting trip.

In passing by Kandelly, on my return from Trincomalee, I paid a second visit to the lake. This is very similar to that of Minneria; but the shooting at that time was destroyed from the same cause which has since ruined Minneria, " too many guns." The buffalos were not worthy of the name; I could not make one show fight, nor could I even get within three hundred yards of them. I returned from the plain with disgust; but just as I was quitting the shores of the lake, I noticed three buffalos in the shallows about knee-deep in the water, nearly half a mile from me. They did not look bigger than dogs, the distance was so great.

There is nothing like a sheet of water for trying a rifle; the splash of the ball shows with such distinctness the accuracy, or the defect, in the shooting. It was necessary that I should fire my guns off in order to clean them that evening; I therefore tried their power at this immense distance.

The long two-ounce fell short, but in a good line. I took a rest upon a man's shoulder with the four-ounce rifle, and, putting up the last sight, I aimed at the leading buffalo, who was walking through the water parallel with us. I aimed at the outline of the throat, to allow for his pace at this great distance. The recoil of the rifle cut the man's ear open, as there were sixteen drachms of powder in this charge.

We watched the smooth surface of the water as

the invisible messenger whistled over the lake. Certainly three seconds elapsed before we saw the slightest effect. At the expiration of that time the buffalo fell suddenly in a sitting position, and there he remained fixed: many seconds after, a dull sound returned to our ears; it was the "futt" of the ball, which had positively struck him at this immense range. What the distance was I cannot say; it may have been 600 yards, or 800, or more. It was shallow water the whole way; we, therefore, mounted our horses and rode up to him. Upon reaching him, I gave him a settling ball in the head, and we examined him. The heavy ball had passed completely through his hips, crushing both joints, and, of course, rendering him powerless at once.

The shore appeared full half a mile from us on our return, and I could hardly credit my own eyes, the distance was so immense, and yet the ball had passed clean through the animal's body.

It was of course a chance shot, and, even with this acknowledgment, it must appear rather like the "marvellous" to a stranger;—that is my misfortune, not my fault. I certainly never made such a shot before, or since; it was a sheer lucky hit, say at 600 yards; and the wonderful power of the rifle was thus displayed in the ball perforating the large body of the buffalo at this range. This shot was made with a round ball, not a cone. The round belted ball for this heavy two-grooved rifle weighs three ounces. The conical ball weighs a little more than four ounces.

While describing the long shots performed by this particular rifle, I cannot help recounting a curious chance with a large rogue elephant in Topari tank. This tank or lake is, like most others in Ceylon, the result of immense labour in past ages. Valleys were closed in by immense dams of solid masonry, which, checking the course of the rivers, formed lakes of many miles in extent. These were used as reservoirs for the water required for the irrigation of rice lands. The population who effected these extensive works have long since passed away; their fate is involved in mystery. The records of their ancient cities still exist, but we have no account of their destruction. The ruins of one of these cities, Pollanarua, are within half a mile of the village of Topari, and the waters of the adjacent lake are still confined by a dam of two miles in length, composed of solid masonry. When the lake is full it is about eight miles in circumference.

I had only just arrived at the village, and my horsekeeper had taken the horse to drink at the lake, when he suddenly came running back to say that a rogue elephant was bathing himself on the opposite shore, at about two miles' distance.

I immediately took my guns and went after him. My path lay along the top of the great dam, which formed a causeway covered with jungle. This causeway was about sixty feet in breadth, and two miles in length; the lake washed its base about twenty feet below the summit. The opposite shore was a fine plain bordered by open forest, and the lake spread into the grassy surface in wide and irregular bays.

I continued my course along the causeway at a fast walk, and on arriving at the extremity of the lake I noticed that the ancient dam continued for a much greater distance. This, together with the great height of the masonry from the level of the water, proved that the dimensions of the lake had formerly been of much greater extent.

Descending by the rugged stones which formed the dam wall, I reached the plain, and, keeping close to the water's edge, I rounded a large neck of land covered with trees, which projected for some distance into the lake. I knew, by the position of the elephant when I first saw him, that he was not far beyond this promontory, and I carefully advanced through the open forest, hoping that I might meet him there, on his exit from his bath. In this I was mistaken, for on passing through this little belt of trees I saw the elephant still in the lake, belly deep, about three hundred paces from me. He was full a hundred and twenty yards from the shore, and I was puzzled how to act. He was an immense brute, being a fine specimen of a tank "rogue." This class are generally the worst description of rogue elephants, who seldom move far from the lakes, but infest the shores of the tanks for many years. Being quite alone with the exception of two worthless gun-bearers, the plan of attack required some consideration.

The belt of trees in which I stood was the nearest piece of cover to the elephant, the main jungle being about a quarter of a mile from the shore of the lake. In the event of a retreat being necessary, this cover would therefore be my point. There was a large tamarind-tree growing alone upon the plain about a hundred and fifty paces from the water's edge, exactly in a line with the position of the elephant. The mud plastered to a great height upon the stem showed this to be his favourite rubbing-post after bathing.

Having determined upon my plan of attack, I took the guns from the gun-bearers and sent the men up the tree, as I knew they would run away in the event of danger, and would most probably take the guns with them in their flight. Having thus secured the guns, I placed the long two-ounce against a large and conspicuous tree that grew upon the extreme edge of the forest, and I cautiously advanced over the open plain with my two remaining guns, one of which I deposited against the stem of the single tamarind-tree. I had thus two points for a defensive retreat, should it be necessary.

I had experienced considerable difficulty in attaining my position at the tamarind-tree without being observed by the elephant; fortunately, I had both the wind and the sun favourable, the latter shining from my back full into the lake.

The elephant was standing with his back to the shore exactly in a line with me, and he was swinging his great head from side to side, and flapping his ears in the enjoyment of his bath. I left the tree with my four-ounce rifle, and, keeping in a direct line for his hind-quarters,

I walked towards him. The grass was soft and short; I could therefore approach without the slightest noise: the only danger in being discovered was in the chance that I might be seen as he swung his head continually on either side. This I avoided by altering my course as I saw his head in the act of coming round, and I soon stood on the edge of the lake exactly behind him, at about a hundred and twenty yards. He was a noble-looking fellow, every inch a rogue, his head almost white with numerous flesh-coloured spots. These give a savage and disgusting appearance to an elephant, and altogether he looked a formidable opponent. I had intended to shout on arriving at my present position, and then to wait for the front shot as he charged; but on looking back to the tamarind-tree, and my proposed course for retreat, the distance appeared so great, rendered still more difficult by a gradual ascent, that I felt it would be impossible to escape if my chance lay in running. I hardly knew what to do; I had evidently caught a "Tartar."

His head was perpetually swinging to and fro, and I was of course accordingly altering my position to avoid his eye. At one of these half-turns he flapped his right ear just as his head came round, and I observed a perfectly white mark, the size of a saucer, behind the ear, in the exact spot for a fatal shot. I at once determined to try it even at this distance; at all events if it failed and he should charge, I had a fair start, and by getting the spare gun from the tamarind-tree I could make a defence at the cover.

His attention was completely absorbed in a luxurious repast upon a bed of the succulent lotus. He tore up bunches of the broad leaves and snaky stalks, and, washing them carefully with his trunk, he crushed the juicy stems, stuffing the tangled mass into his mouth as a savage would eat macaroni. Round swung his head once more, the ear flapped, the mark was exposed, but the ear again concealed it just as I had raised the rifle. This happened several times, but I waited patiently for a good chance, being prepared for a run the moment after firing.

Once more his head swung towards me; the sun shone full upon him; and I raised the rifle to be ready for him if he gave me the chance. His ear flapped forward just as his head was at a proper angle for a shot. The mark shone brightly along the sights of the rifle as I took a steady aim, and the answer to the report of the gun was a dull splash.

He had sunk upon his knees stone dead. I could hardly believe my eyes. The sight of so large an animal being killed at such a distance by one shot had an extraordinary effect. I heard a heathenish scream of joy behind me, and upon turning round I perceived the now courageous gun-bearers running towards me at their best pace. They were two of the Topari villagers, and had been perfectly aghast at the idea of one person, with only one single-barrelled rifle, attacking a tank rogue in the open plain. The sequel had turned their fear into astonishment. They now had the laugh at me, however, as they swam fearlessly up to the dead elephant to cut off his tail, which I would not have done for any reward, for fear of crocodiles, which abound in the tank. The ball had struck the white mark exactly in the centre, which pleased these natives exceedingly, and they returned in safety with the tail.

I have frequently tried these long shots since, but I never succeeded again except once, and that was not satisfactory, as the elephant did not die upon the spot, but was found by the natives on the following day.

On my return to the village I took a short gun and strolled along the banks of the lake. The snipe were innumerable, and I killed them till my head ached with the constant recoil of the gun in addition to the heat. I also killed several couple of ducks and teal, in addition to twenty-eight couple of snipe. This was the Paradise for sport at the time of which I write. It had never been disturbed; but it has since shared the fate of many other places.

The open forest in the vicinity of the lake abounded with deer. Grassy glades beneath the shady trees give a park-like appearance to the scene, and afford a delightful resort for the deer.

In strolling through these shady glades, you suddenly arrive among the ruins of ancient Pollanarua. The palaces are crumbled into shapeless mounds of bricks. Massive pillars, formed of a single stone some twelve feet high, stand in upright rows throughout the jungle here and there over an extent of miles of country. The buildings which they once supported have long since fallen, and the pillars now stand like tombstones over vanished magnificence. Some buildings are still standing; among these are two dagobas, huge monuments of bricks, formerly covered with white cement and elaborately decorated with different devices. These are shaped like an egg which has been cut nearly in half and then placed upon its base; but the cement has perished, and they are mounds of jungle and rank grass which has overgrown them, although the large dagoba is upwards of a hundred feet high.

A curious temple, formed on the imperishable principle of excavating in the solid rock, is in perfect preservation, and is still used by the natives as a place of worship: this is presided over by a priest. Three large images of Bhudda, carved out of solid rock, occupy the positions in which he is always represented; that in the recumbent posture is fifty-six feet long, cut from one solid stone.

I was strolling through these ruins when I suddenly saw a spotted doe feeding among the upright pillars before mentioned. I was within twenty yards of her before she was aware of my vicinity, and I bagged her by a shot with a double-barrelled gun. At the report of the gun a herd of about thirty deer, which were concealed among the ruins, rushed close by me, and I bagged another doe with the remaining barrel.

The whole of this country must at one time

have been densely populated; perhaps this very density may have produced pestilence, which swept away the inhabitants. The city has been in ruins for about 600 years, and was founded about 300 years before Christ. Some idea of the former extent of these Ceylon antiquities may be formed from the present size of the ruins. Those of Anarajapoora are 16 miles square, comprising a surface of 256 square miles. Those of Pollanarua are much smaller, but they are nevertheless of great extent.

The inhabitants of the present village of Toparí are a poor squalid race; and if they are descended in a direct line from the ancient occupants of the city, they are as much degenerated in character and habits as the city itself is ruined in architecture. Few countries can be more thinly populated than Ceylon, and yet we have these numerous proofs of a powerful nation having once existed. Whereever these lakes or tanks exist in the present day, a populous country once flourished. In all countries which are subject to months of drought, a supply of water is the first consideration, or cultivation must cease. This was the object in forming the tanks, which are especially numerous throughout the Tambancadua district. These tank countries afford a great diversity of sport, as they all abound with wild-fowl and with snipe in their season (from November to May). During the time of drought they are always the resort of every kind of wild animal, who are forced to the neighbourhood for a supply of water.

The next tank to Toparí is that of Doolana; this is eight miles from the former, and is of about the same extent. In this district there are no less than eight of these large lakes. Their attractions to rogue elephants having been explained, it may be readily understood that these gentry abound throughout the district. I shall, therefore, select a few incidents which have happened to me in these localities, which will afford excellent illustrations of the habits of "rogues."

Having arrived at Doolana, on the 5th April, 1847, with excellent Moormen trackers, who were elephant-catchers by profession, I started for a day's sport in company with my brother B. This particular portion of the district is inhabited entirely by Moormen. They are a fine race of people, far superior to the Cingalese. They are supposed to be descended from Arabian origin, and they hold the Mahometan religion. The Rhatamahatmeya, or head-man of the district, resides at

Doolana, and he had received us in a most hospitable manner. We, therefore, started direct from his house.

Passing through a belt of low thick jungle, exactly in front of the village, we entered upon the plain which formed the border of the tank. This lake is about three miles in length, but is not more than a mile in width in its widest part, and in some places is very much less. The opposite side of the tank is fine open forest, which grows to the water-edge, and is in some parts flooded during the wet season. At this time the soil was deep and muddy.

This was not a place visited by sportsmen at that period; and upon arriving at the margin of the lake, an exciting view presented itself. Scattered over the extent of the lake, were "thirteen rogue elephants,"—one was not a quarter of a mile from us; another was so far off he could hardly be distinguished; another was close to the opposite jungle; and they were, in fact, all single elephants. There was an exception to this, however, in one pair of elephants who stood in the very centre of the tank, side by side; they were as black as ebony, and, although in view with many brother rogues, they appeared giants even among giants. The Moormen immediately informed us that they were a notorious pair, who always associated together, and were the dread of the neighbourhood. There were many tales of their ferocity and daring, which at the time we gave little heed to.

Crossing the tank in a large canoe, we arrived in the open forest upon the opposite shore. It was a mass of elephant tracks which sunk deep in the soft earth. They were all so fresh and so confused, that tracking was very difficult. However, we at length fixed upon the tracks of a pair of elephants, and followed them up. This was a work of considerable time, but the distant cracking of a bough at length attracted us to their position, and we shortly came up with them, just as they had winded us, and were moving off. I fired an ineffectual shot at the temple of one, which separated him from the other, after whom we started in chase at full speed. Full speed soon ended in a stand-still in such ground; it was deep stiff clay, in which we sunk over our ankles at every step, and varied our struggles by occasionally flying sprawling over the slippery roots of the trees.

The elephants ran clean away from us, and the elephant-catchers, who knew nothing of the rules for carrying spare guns, entering into the excitement of the chase, and, free from the impediments of shoes, ran lightly along the muddy ground, and were soon out of sight as well as the elephants. Still we struggled on, when, presently, we heard a shout, and then a shot; then another shout; then the trumpet of an elephant. Shot after shot then followed with a chorus of shouts; they were actually firing all our spare guns!

In a few moments we were up with them. In a beautifully open piece of forest, upon good hard ground, these fellows were having a regular battle with the rogue. He was charging them with the greatest fury, but he no sooner selected one man for his object, than these active fellows diverted his rage by firing into his hind-quarters, and yelling at him. At this, he would immediately turn and charge another man, when he would again be assailed as before. When we arrived, he immediately selected B., and came straight at him, but offered a beautiful shot in doing so, and B. dropped him dead.

The firing had disturbed a herd of elephants from the forest, and they had swum the large river in the neighbourhood, which was at that time so swollen that we could not cross it. We, therefore, struck off to the edge of the forest where the waters of the lake washed the roots of the trees, and from this point we had a fine view of the greater portion of the lake.

All the rogues that we had at first counted had retired to their several entrances in the forest, except the pair of desperadoes already mentioned,—they knew no fear, and had not heeded the shots fired. They were tempting baits, and we determined to get them if possible. These two villains were standing belly-deep in the water, about a quarter of a mile from the shore; and the question was, "How were we to get near them?" Having observed that the other rogues had retreated to the forest at the noise of the firing, it struck me that we might by some ruse induce these two champions to follow their example, and, by meeting them on their entrance, we might bring them to action.

Not far upon our left, a long shallow bank, covered with reeds, stretched far into the tank. By wading knee-deep along this shoal, a man might approach to within two hundred paces of the elephants, and would be nearly abreast of them. I, therefore, gave a man a gun, and instructed him to advance to the extreme end of the shallows, taking care to conceal himself in the rushes, and when at the nearest point he was to fire at the elephants. This, I hoped, would drive them to the jungle, where we should endeavour to meet them.

The Moorman intrusted upon this mission was a plucky fellow, and he started off, taking a double gun and a few charges of powder and ball. The elephant-catchers were delighted with the idea, and we patiently awaited the result. About a quarter of an hour passed away, when we suddenly saw a puff of white smoke spring from the green rushes at the point of the sandbank. A few moments after we heard the report of the gun, and we saw the ball splash in the water close to the elephants. They immediately cocked their ears, and throwing their trunks high in the air, they endeavoured to wind the enemy; but they did not move, and they shortly again commenced feeding upon the water-lilies. Another shot from the same place once more disturbed them, and, while they winded the unseen enemy, two more shots in quick succession from the old quarter decided their opinion, and they stalked proudly through the water towards the shore.

Our satisfaction was great, but the delight of the elephant-catchers knew no bounds. Away they started along the shores of the lake, hopping from root to root, skipping through the mud, which was more than a foot deep, their light forms hardly sinking in the tough surface. A nine-stone man certainly has an advantage over one of twelve in this ground; added to this, I was carrying the long two-ounce rifle of sixteen pounds, which, with ammunition, &c., made up about thirteen and a half stone, in deep stiff clay. I was literally half-way up the calf of my leg in mud at every step, while these light naked fellows tripped like snipe over the sodden ground. Vainly I called upon them to go easily; their moment of excitement was at its full pitch, and they were soon out of sight among the trees and underwood, taking all the spare guns, except the four-ounce rifle, which, weighing twenty-one pounds, effectually prevented the bearer from leaving us behind.

What added materially to the annoyance of losing the spare guns, was the thoughtless character of the advance. I felt sure that these fellows would outrun the position of the elephants, which, if they had continued in a direct route, should have entered the jungle within three hundred yards of our first station.

We had slipped, and plunged, and struggled

over this distance, when we suddenly were checked in our advance. We had entered a small plot of deep mud and rank grass surrounded upon all sides by dense rattan jungle. This stuff is one woven mass of hooked thorns: long tendrils, armed in the same manner, although not thicker than whip-cord, wind themselves round the parent canes, and form a jungle which even elephants dislike to enter. To man, these jungles are perfectly impervious.

Half-way to our knees in mud, we stood in this small open space of about thirty feet by twenty. Around us was an opaque screen of this impenetrable jungle; the lake lay about fifty yards upon our left, behind the thick rattan. The gun-bearers were gone ahead somewhere, and were far in advance. We were at a stand-still. Leaning upon my long rifle, I stood within four feet of the wall of jungle which divided us from the lake. I said to B., "The trackers are all wrong, and have gone too far. I am convinced that the elephants must have entered somewhere near this place."

Little did I think that at that very moment they were within a few feet of us. B. was standing behind me on the opposite side of the small open, or about seven yards from the jungle.

I suddenly heard a deep guttural sound in the thick rattan within four feet of me; in the same instant the whole tangled fabric bent over me, and bursting asunder showed the furious head of an elephant with uplifted trunk in full charge upon me.

I had barely time to cock my rifle, and the barrel almost touched him as I fired. I knew it was in vain as his trunk was raised. B. fired his right-hand barrel at the same moment without effect from the same cause. I jumped on one side and attempted to spring through the deep mud: it was of no use, the long grass entangled my

NARROW ESCAPE.

feet, and in another instant I lay sprawling in the enraged elephant's path within *a foot* of him. In that moment of suspense I expected to hear the crack of my own bones as his massive foot would be upon me. It was an atom of time. I heard the crack of a gun; it was B.'s last barrel. I felt a spongy weight strike my heel, and, turning quickly heels over head, I rolled a few paces and regained my feet. That last shot had floored him just as he was upon me; the end of his trunk had fallen upon my heel. Still he was not dead, but he struck at me with his trunk as I passed round his head to give him a finisher with the four-ounce rifle, which I had snatched from our solitary gun-bearer.

My back was touching the jungle from which the rogue had just charged, and I was almost in the act of firing through the temple of the still struggling elephant when I heard a tremendous crash in the jungle behind me similar to the first, and the savage scream of an elephant. I saw the ponderous fore-leg cleave its way through the jungle directly upon me. I threw my whole weight back against the thick rattans to avoid him, and the next moment his foot was planted within an inch of mine. His lofty head was passing over me in full charge at B., who was unloaded, when, holding the four-ounce rifle perpendicularly, I fired exactly under his throat. I thought he would fall upon me and crush me, but this shot was the only chance, as B. was perfectly helpless.

A dense cloud of smoke from the heavy charge of powder for the moment obscured everything. I had jumped out of the way the instant after firing. The elephant did not fall, but he had his death wound: the ball had severed his jugular, and the blood poured from the wound. He stopped, but collecting his stunned energies he still blundered forward towards B. He, however, avoided him by running to one side, and the wounded brute staggered on through the jungle. We now loaded the guns; the first rogue was quite dead, and we followed in pursuit of rogue number two. We heard distant shots, and upon arriving at the spot we found the gun-bearers. They had heard the wounded elephant crashing through the jungle, and they had given him a volley just as he was crossing the river, over which the herd had escaped in the morning. They described the elephant as perfectly helpless from his wound, and they imagined that he had fallen in the thick bushes on the opposite bank of the river. As I before mentioned we could not cross the river on account of the torrent, but in a few days it subsided, and the elephant was found lying dead in the spot where they supposed he had fallen.

Thus happily ended the destruction of this notable pair; they had proved themselves all that we had heard of them, and by their cunning dodge of hiding in the thick jungle they had nearly made sure of us. We had killed three rogues that morning, and we returned to our quarters well satisfied.

Since that period I have somewhat thinned the number of rogues in this neighbourhood. I had a careful and almost certain plan of shooting them. Quite alone, with the exception of two faithful gun-bearers, I used to wait at the edge of the jungle at their feeding time, and watch their exit from the forest. The most cautious stalking then generally enabled me to get a fatal shot before my presence was discovered. This is the proper way to succeed with rogue elephants, although of course it is attended with considerable danger. I was once very nearly caught near this spot, where the elephants are always particularly savage. The lake was then much diminished in size by dry weather, and the water had retired for about a hundred yards from the edge of the forest, leaving a deep bed of mud covered with slime and decayed vegetable matter. This slime had hardened in the sun and formed a cake over the soft mud beneath. Upon this treacherous surface a man could walk with great care. Should the thin covering break through he would be immediately waist-deep in the soft mud. To plod through this was the elephants' delight. Smearing a thick coat of the black mud over their whole bodies, they formed a defensive armour against the attacks of musquitos, which are the greatest tormenters that an elephant has to contend with.

I was watching the edge of the forest one afternoon at about four o'clock, when I noticed the massive form of one of these tank rogues stalk majestically from the jungle, and proceed through the deep mud towards the lake. I had the wind, and I commenced stalking him.

Advancing with my two gun-bearers in single file, I crept carefully from tree to tree along the edge of the forest for about a quarter of a mile, until I arrived at the very spot at which he had made his exit from the jungle.

I was now within eighty yards of him as he stood with his head towards the lake, and his hind-quarters exactly facing me. His deep tracks in the mud were about five feet apart, so great was his stride and length of limb, and, although the soft bog was at least three and a half feet deep, his belly was full two feet above the surface. He was a fine fellow, and, with intense caution, I advanced towards him over the trembling surface of baked slime. His tracks had nearly filled with water, and looked like little wells. The bog waved as I walked carefully over it, and I stopped once or twice, hesitating whether I should continue: I feared the crusty surface would not support me, as the nearer I approached the water's edge, the weaker the coating of slime became, not having been exposed for so long a time to the sun as that at a greater distance.

He was making so much noise in splashing the mud over his body that I had a fine chance for getting up to him. I could not stand the temptation, and I crept up as fast as I could.

I got within eight paces of him unperceived; the mud that he threw over his back spattered round me as it fell. I was carrying a light double-barrelled gun, but I now reached back my hand to exchange it for my four-ounce rifle. Little did I expect the sudden effect produced by the additional weight of the heavy weapon. The treacherous surface suddenly gave way, and in an instant I was waist deep in mud. The noise that I had made in falling had at once aroused the elephant, and, true to his character of a rogue, he immediately advanced with a shrill trumpet towards me. His ears were cocked, and his tail was well up; but, instead of charging, as rogues generally do, with his head thrown rather back and held high, which renders a front shot very uncertain, he rather lowered his head, and splashed towards me through the mud, apparently despising my diminutive appearance.

I thought it was all up with me this time: I was immovable in my bed of mud, and, instead of the clean brown barrel that I could usually trust to in an extremity, I raised a mass of mud to my shoulder, which encased my rifle like a flannel bag. I fully expected it to miss fire; no sights were visible, and I had to guess the aim with the advancing elephant within five yards of me. Hopelessly I pulled the slippery trigger. The rifle did not even hang fire, and the rogue fell into the deep bed of mud, stone dead. If the rifle had missed fire, I must have been killed, as escape would have been impossible. It was with great difficulty that I was extricated from my muddy position by the joint exertions of myself and gun-bearers.

Elephants, buffalos, and hogs are equally fond of wallowing in the mud. A buffalo will gallop through a swamp, hock deep, in which a horse would be utterly powerless, even without a rider. Elephants can also make wonderful progress through deep mud, the formation of the hind legs with knees instead of hocks giving them an increased facility for moving through heavy ground.

The great risk in attacking rogue elephants consists in the impracticability of quick movements upon such ground as they generally frequent. The speed and activity of a man, although considerable upon a smooth surface, is as nothing upon rough stumpy grass wilds, where even walking is laborious. What is comparatively level to an elephant's foot is as a ploughed field to that of a man. This renders escape from pursuit next to impossible, unless some welcome tree should be near, round which the hunter could dodge, and even then he stands but a poor chance, unless assistance is at hand. I have never seen any one who could run at full speed in rough ground without falling, if pursued. Large stones, tufts of rank grass, holes, fallen boughs, gullies, are all impediments to rapid locomotion when the pursued is forced to be constantly looking back to watch the progress of his foe, and to be the judge of his own race.

There is a great art in running away. It requires the perfection of coolness and presence of mind, without which a man is most likely to run into the very danger that he is trying to avoid. This was the cause of Major Haddock's death in Ceylon, some years ago. He had attacked a "rogue," and, being immediately charged, he failed to stop him, although he gave him both barrels. Being forced to run, he went off at full speed, and turning quickly round a tree, he hoped the elephant would pass him. Unfortunately, he did not look behind him before he turned, and the elephant passed round the opposite side of the tree, and, of course, met him face to face. He was instantly trampled to death.

Mr. Wallet was also killed by a rogue elephant: this animal was shot a few days afterwards, after a spirited contest, by Captain Galway and Ensign Scroggs, both of whom were very nearly caught in the encounter. A gentleman of the name of Keane was added to the list of victims a few years ago. He had fired without effect, and was almost immediately overtaken by the elephant, and crushed to death. The most extraordinary tale that I have ever heard of rogue elephants in Ceylon, was told me by the Rhatamahatmeya of Doolana, who was present at the scene, when a lad. I do not profess to credit it entirely; but I will give it in his own words, and, to avoid the onus of an improbable story, I will entitle it the "Rhatamahatmeya's Tale." In justice to him, I must acknowledge that his account was corroborated by all the old men of the village.

THE RHATAMAHATMEYA'S TALE.

"There was a notorious rogue elephant at Doolana about thirty years ago, whose ferocity was so extreme that he took complete possession of a certain part of the country adjoining the lake. He had killed eight or nine persons, and his whole object in existence appeared to be the waylaying and destruction of the natives. He was of enormous size, and was well known by a peculiar flesh-coloured forehead.

"In those days there were no fire-arms in this part of the country; therefore there was no protection for either life or property from this monster, who would invade the paddy-fields at night, and actually pull down the watch-houses, regardless of the blazing fires which are lighted on the hearth of sand on the summit; these he used to scatter about and extinguish. He had killed several natives in this manner, involving them in the common ruin with their watch-houses. The terror created by this elephant was so extreme that the natives deserted the neighbourhood that he infested.

"At length many months passed away without his being either seen or heard of: the people began to hope that he had died from the effect of poisoned arrows, which had frequently been shot at him from the watch-houses in high trees; and, by degrees, the terror of his name had lost its power, and he ceased to be thought of.

"It was in the cool of the evening, about an hour before sunset, that about twenty of the women from the village were upon the grassy borders of the lake, engaged in sorting and tying into bundles the rushes which they had been gathering during the day for making mats. They were on the point of starting homewards with their loads, when the sudden trumpet of an elephant was heard, and to their horror they saw the well known rogue, with the unmistakable mark upon his forehead, coming down in full charge upon them. The ground was perfectly open; there were no trees for some hundred yards, except the jungle from which he was advancing at a frightful speed. An indiscriminate flight of course took place, and a race of terror commenced. In a few seconds the monster was among them, and, seizing a young girl in his trunk, he held her high in the air, and halted, as though uncertain how to dispose of his helpless victim. The girl, meanwhile, was vainly shrieking for assistance, and the petrified troop of women having gained the shelter of some jungle, gazed panic-stricken upon the impending fate of their companion.

"To their horror the elephant slowly lowered her in his trunk till near the ground, when he gradually again raised her, and, bringing her head into his mouth, a report was heard like the crack of a whip;—it was the sudden crushing of her skull. Tearing the head off by the neck, he devoured it; and, placing his fore-foot upon the body, he tore the arms and legs from their sockets with his trunk, and devoured every portion of her.

"The women rushed to the village with the news of this unnatural carnage.

"Doolana and the neighbourhood has always been famous for its elephant-hunters, and the husband of this unfortunate girl was one of the most active in their pursuit. The animals are caught in this country, and sold to the Arabs, for the use of the Indian government.

"The news of this bloody deed flew from village to village; war to the knife was declared against the perpetrator, and preparations were accordingly made.

"Since the murder of this girl he had taken up his abode in a small isolated jungle adjoining, surrounded by a small open plain of fine soft grass, upon a level sandy soil.

"A few days after this act, a hundred men assembled at Doolana, determined upon his destruction. They were all picked elephant-hunters—Moormen; active and sinewy fellows, accustomed to danger from their childhood. Some were armed with axes, sharpened to the keenest edge; some with long spears; and others with regular elephant ropes, formed of the thongs of raw deer's hide, beautifully twisted. Each division of men had a separate duty allotted.

"They marched towards the small jungle in which the rogue was known to be; but he anticipated their wishes, and before they were within a hundred paces of his lair, he charged furiously out. The conflict began in good earnest. The spearmen were in advance, and the axemen were divided into two parties, one on either flank, with an equal number of ropemen. The instant that he charged, the whole body of men ran forward at full speed to meet him; still he continued his furious onset, undismayed by the yells of a hundred men. The spearmen halted when within twenty yards, then turned and fled; this had been agreed upon beforehand. The elephant passed the two flanks of axemen in pursuit of the flying enemy; the axemen immediately closed in behind him, led by the husband of the murdered girl. By a well-directed blow upon the hind leg, full of revenge, this active fellow divided the sinew in the first joint above the foot. That instant the elephant fell upon his knees, but recovered himself directly, and endeavoured to turn upon his pursuers; a dozen axes flashed in the sun-beams, as the strokes were aimed at the other hind leg. It was the work of an instant: the massive limb bent powerless under him, and he fell in a sitting posture, utterly helpless, but roaring with mad and impotent fury. The ropemen now threw nooses over his trunk and head; his struggles, although tremendous, were in vain; fifty men, hanging their weight upon several ropes attached to his trunk, rendered that dreaded weapon powerless. The sharp lances were repeatedly driven into his side, and several of the boldest hunters climbing up the steep ascent of his back, an axe was seen to fall swiftly and repeatedly upon his spine, on the nape of his tough neck. The giant form suddenly sunk; the spine was divided, and the avenging blow was dealt by the husband of his late victim. The destroyer was no more. The victory was gained without the loss of a man."

The natives said that this elephant was mad; if so, it may account in some measure for the unheard-of occurrence of an elephant devouring flesh. Both elephants and buffalos attack man from malice alone, without the slightest idea of making a meal of him. This portion of the Headman's story I cannot possibly believe, although he swears to it. The elephant may, perhaps, have cracked her head, and torn his victim to pieces in the manner described, but the actual "*eating*" is incredible.

CHAP. VI.

CHARACTER OF THE VEDDAHS. — DESCRIPTION OF THE VEDDAHS. —A MONAMPITYA ROGUE.—ATTACKING THE ROGUE.—BREATHLESS EXCITEMENT. — DEATH OF A LARGE ROGUE. — UTILITY OF THE FOUR-OUNCE. — A CURIOUS SHOT.—FURY OF A BULL BUFFALO. — CHARACTER OF THE WILD BUFFALO. — BUFFALO SHOOTING AT MINNERIA LAKE. — CHARGE IN HIGH REEDS. — CLOSE OF A GOOD DAY'S SPORT.—LAST DAY AT MINNERIA.— A LARGE SNAKE.—AN UNPLEASANT BEDFELLOW.

Doolana is upon the very verge of the most northern point of the Veddah country, the whole of which wild district is the finest part of Ceylon for sport. Even to this day few Europeans have hunted these secluded wilds. The wandering Veddah, with his bow and arrows, is occasionally seen roaming through his wilderness in search of deer, but the report of a native's gun is never heard; the game is therefore comparatively undisturbed. I have visited every portion of this fine sporting country, and since I have acquired the thorough knowledge of its attractions, I have made up my mind never to shoot anywhere but there. The country is more open than in most parts of Ceylon, and the perfect wildness of the whole district is an additional charm.

The dimensions of the Veddah country are about eighty miles from north to south, by forty in width. A fine mountain, known as the "Gunner's Coin," is an unmistakable landmark upon the northern boundary. From this point a person may ride for forty miles without seeing a sign of a habitation; the whole country is perfectly uncivilised, and its scanty occupants, the "Veddahs," wander about like animals, without either home, laws, or religion.

I have frequently read absurd descriptions of their manners and customs, which must evidently have been gathered from hearsay, and not from a knowledge of the people. It is a commonly believed report that the Veddahs "*live in the trees*," and a stranger immediately confuses them with rooks and monkeys. Whoever first saw Veddah huts in the trees, would have discovered, upon inquiry, that they were temporary watch-houses, from which they guard a little plot of korrakan from the attacks of elephants and other wild beasts. Far from *living* in the trees, they live nowhere; they wander over the face of their beautiful country, and migrate to different parts at different seasons, with the game which they are always pursuing. The seasons in Ceylon vary in an extraordinary manner, considering the small size of the island. The wet season, in one district, is the dry season in another, and *vice versa*. Wherever the dry weather prevails, the pasturage is dried up; the brooks and pools are mere sandy gullies and pits. The Veddahs watch at some solitary hole which still contains a little water, and to this the deer and every species of Ceylon game resorts. Here his broad-headed arrow finds a supply. He dries the meat in long strips in the sun, and cleaning out some hollow tree, he packs away his savoury mass of sun-cooked flesh, and fills up the reservoir with wild honey; he then stops up the aperture with clay.

The last drop of water evaporates, the deer leave the country, and migrate into other parts where mountains attract the rain and the pasturage is abundant. The Veddah burns the parched grass wherever he passes, and the country is soon a blackened surface; not a blade of pasture remains; but the act of burning ensures a sweet supply shortly after the rains commence, to which the game and the Veddahs will then return. In the meantime he follows the game to other districts, living in caves where they happen to abound, or making a temporary hut with grass and sticks.

Every deer-path, every rock, every peculiar feature in the country, every pool of water, is known to these hunting Veddahs; they are consequently the best assistants in the world in elephant-hunting. They will run at top speed over hard ground upon an elephant's track, which is barely discernible even to the practised eye of a white man. Fortunately, the number of these people is very trifling, or the game would be scarce. They hunt like the leopard; — noiselessly stalking till within ten paces of their game, they let the broad arrow fly. At this distance who could miss? Should the game be simply wounded, it is quite enough; they never lose him, but hunt him up, like hounds upon a blood track.

Nevertheless, they are very bad shots with the bow and arrow, and they never can improve while they restrict their practice to such short ranges.

I have often tried them at a mark at sixty yards, and, although a very bad hand with a bow myself, I have invariably beaten them with their own weapons. These bows are six feet long, made of a light supple wood, and the strings are made of the fibrous bark of a tree, greased and twisted. The arrows are three feet long, formed of the same wood as the bows. The blades are themselves seven inches of this length, and are flat, like the blade of a dinner-knife brought to a point. Three short feathers from the peacock's wing are roughly lashed to the other end of the arrow.

The Veddah in person is extremely ugly; short, but sinewy; his long uncombed locks fall to his waist, looking more like a horse's tail than human hair. He despises money; but is thankful for a knife, a hatchet, or a gaudy-coloured cloth, or brass pot for cooking.

The women are horribly ugly, and are almost entirely naked. They have no matrimonial regulations, and the children are squalid and miserable. Still these people are perfectly happy, and would prefer their present wandering life to the most luxurious restraint. Speaking a language of their own, with habits akin to those of wild animals, they keep entirely apart from the Cingalese. They barter deer-horns and bees'-wax with the travelling Moormen pedlars in exchange for their trifling requirements. If they have food they eat it; if they have none they go without until by some chance they procure it. In the meantime they chew the bark of various trees, and search for berries, while they wend their way for many miles to some remembered store of deer's flesh and honey, laid by in a hollow tree.

The first time that I ever saw a Veddah was in the north of the country. A rogue elephant was bathing in a little pool of deep mud and water near the tank of Monampitya, about six miles from the "Gunner's Coin." This Veddah had killed a wild pig, and was smoking the flesh within a few yards of the spot, when he suddenly heard the elephant splashing in the water. My tent was pitched within a mile of the place, and he accordingly brought me the intelligence.

Upon arrival at the pool I found the elephant so deep in the mud that he could barely move. His hind-quarters were towards me; and the pool not being more than thirty yards in diameter, and surrounded by impenetrable rattan jungle on all sides but one small opening, in which I stood, I was obliged to clap my hands to excite his attention. This had the desired effect; he turned slowly round, and I shot him immediately. This was one of the Monampitya tank rogues, but in his muddy position he had no chance.

The largest elephant that I have ever seen was in this neighbourhood. I had arrived one afternoon at about five o'clock in a fine plain, about twelve miles from Monampitya, where the presence of a beautiful lake and high grass promised an abundance of game. It was a most secluded spot, and my tent and coolies being well up with my horse, I fixed upon a shady nook for the tent, and I strolled out to look for tracks while it was being pitched.

A long promontory stretched some hundred yards into the lake, exactly opposite the spot I had fixed upon for the encampment, and, knowing that elephants when bathing generally land upon the nearest shore, I walked out towards the point of this projecting neck of land.

The weather was very dry, and the ground was a mass of little pitfalls, about two feet deep, which had been made by the feet of the elephants in the wet weather, when this spot was soft mud, and evidently the favourite resort of the heavy game. The ground was now baked by the sun as hard as though it were frozen, and the numerous deep ruts made walking very difficult. Several large trees and a few bushes grew upon the surface, but for the most part it was covered by a short though luxuriant grass. One large tree grew within fifty yards of the extreme point of the promontory, and another of the same kind grew at an equal distance from it, but nearer to the main land. Upon both these trees was a coat of thick mud not many hours old. The bark was rubbed completely away, and this appeared to have been used for years as a favourite rubbing-post by some immense elephant. The mud reached full twelve feet up the trunk of the tree, and there were old marks far above this which had been scored by his tushes. There was no doubt that one of these tank rogues of extraordinary size had frequented this spot for years, and still continued to do so, the mud upon the tree being still soft, as though it had been left there that morning. I already coveted him, and having my telescope with me, I took a minute survey of the opposite shore, which was about half a mile distant, and was lined with fine open forest to the water's edge. Nothing was visible. I examined the other side of the lake with the same want of success. Although it was such a quiet spot, with beautiful grass and water, there was not a single head of game to be seen. Again I scrutinised the opposite shore. The glass was no sooner raised to my eye than I started at the unexpected apparition. There was no mistaking him; he had appeared as though by magic — an elephant of the most extraordinary size that I have ever seen. He was not still for an instant, but was stalking quickly up and down the edge of the lake as though in great agitation. This restlessness is one of the chief characteristics of a bad rogue. I watched him for a few minutes, until he at length took to the water, and after blowing several streams over his shoulders, he advanced to the middle of the tank, where he commenced feeding upon the lotus-leaves and sedges.

It was a calm afternoon, and not a breath of air was stirring; and fearing lest the noise of the coolies, who were arranging the encampment, should disturb him, I hastened back. I soon restored quiet, and ordering the horses to be led into the jungle lest he should discover them, I made the people conceal themselves; and taking my two Moormen gun-bearers, who were trusty fellows that I had frequently shot with, I crept cautiously back to my former position, and took my station behind the large tree farthest from the point which commanded the favourite rubbing-post and within fifty yards of it. From this place

I attentively watched his movements. He was wandering about in the water, alternately feeding and bathing; and there was a peculiar devilry in his movements that marked him as a rogue of the first class. He at length made up his mind to cross the tank, and he advanced at quick strides through the water straight for the point upon which I hoped to meet him.

This was an exciting moment. I had no companion, but depended upon my own gun, and the rutty nature of the ground precluded any quick movements. The watching of the game is the intense excitement of elephant-shooting,—a feeling which only lasts until the animal is within shot, when it suddenly vanishes and gives place to perfect calmness. At this time I could distinctly hear the beating of my own heart, and my two gun-bearers, who did not know what fear was, were literally trembling with excitement.

He was certainly a king of beasts, and proudly he advanced towards the point. Suddenly he disappeared; nothing could be seen but his trunk above the water as he waded through the deep channel for a few yards, and then reared his majestic form dripping from the lake. He stood upon "the point." I never saw so grand an animal; it seemed as though no single ball could kill him; and although his head and carcase were enormous, still his length of leg appeared disproportionately great. With quick springy paces he advanced directly for his favourite tree, and began his process of rubbing, perfectly unaware of the hidden foes so near him.

Having finished his rubbing, he tore up several bunches of grass, but, without eating them, he threw them pettishly over his back, and tossed some from side to side. I was in momentary dread lest a horse should neigh and disturb him, as they were within two hundred paces of where he stood. Everything was, however, quiet in that direction, where the hiding coolies were watching the impending event with breathless interest.

Having amused himself for some moments by kicking up the turf and dirt and throwing the sand over his back, he took it into his head to visit the main shore, and for this purpose he strode quickly in the direction of the encampment. I moved round the tree to secrete myself as he advanced. He was soon exactly at right angles with me as he was passing the tree, when he suddenly stopped: his whole demeanour changed in an instant; his ears cocked, his eyes gleamed, his tail on end, and his trunk raised high in the air, he turned the distended tip towards the tree from

A BREATHLESS MOMENT.

behind which I was watching him. He was perfectly motionless and silent in this attitude for some moments. He was thirty yards from me, as I supposed, at the time, and I reserved my fire, having the four-ounce rifle ready. Suddenly, with his trunk still raised, his long legs swung forward towards me. There was no time to lose;—I was discovered, and a front shot would be useless with his trunk in that position. Just as his head was in the act of turning towards me I took a steady shot at his temple. He sunk gently upon his knees, and never afterwards moved a muscle. His eyes were open, and so bright that I pushed my finger in them to assure myself that life was perfectly extinct. He was exactly thirty-two paces from the rifle, and the ball had passed in at one temple and out at the other. His height may be imagined from this rough method of measuring. A gun-bearer climbed upon his back as the elephant lay upon all-fours, and holding a long stick across his spine at right angles, I could just touch it with the points of my fingers by reaching to my utmost height. Thus, as he lay, his back was seven feet two inches, perpendicular height, from the ground. This would make his height, when erect, about twelve feet on the spine —an enormous height for an elephant, as twelve feet on the top of the back is about equal to eleven feet six inches at the shoulder. If I had not fortunately killed this elephant at the first shot, I should have had enough to do to take care of myself; as he was one of the most vicious-looking brutes that I ever saw, and he was in the very act of charging when I shot him.

With these elephants the four-ounce rifle is an invaluable weapon; even if the animal is not struck in the mortal spot, the force of the blow upon the head is so great that it will generally bring him upon his knees, or at least stop him. It has failed once or twice in this, but not often; and upon those occasions I had loaded with the conical ball. This, although it will penetrate much farther through a thick substance than a round ball, is not so effective in elephant-shooting as the latter. The reason is plain enough. No shot in the head will kill an elephant dead, unless it passes through the brain; an ounce ball will effect this as well as a six-pound shot; but there are many cases where the brain cannot be touched, by a peculiar method of carrying the head and trunk in charging, &c.; a power is then required that by the concussion will knock him down, or turn him; this power is greater in the round ball than in the conical, as a larger surface is suddenly struck. The effect is similar to a man being run through the arm with a rapier, or thrust at with a poker,—the rapier will pass through him almost without his knowledge, but the poker will knock him down. Thus the pointed conical ball will, perhaps, pass through an elephant's forehead, and penetrate as far as his shoulders, but it will produce no immediate effect. For buffalo-shooting, the conical ball is preferable, as, with the heavy charge of powder that I use, it will pass completely through him from end to end. A four-ounce ball, raking an animal from stem to stern, must settle him at once. This is a desirable thing to accomplish with wild buffalos; as they may frequently prove awkward customers, even after receiving several mortal wounds from light guns.

The four-ounce conical ball should be an excellent weapon for African shooting, where the usual shot at an elephant is at the shoulder. This shot would never answer in Ceylon: the country is not sufficiently open to watch the effects produced upon the animal, and although he may have a mortal wound, he carries it away with him, and is not bagged. I have frequently tried this shot; and, although I have seen the elephants go away with ears and trunk drooping, still I have never bagged more than one by any but the head-shot. This fellow was a small "tusker," who formed one of a herd in thick thorny jungle. There were several rocks in this low jungle which overtopped the highest bushes; and having taken my station upon one of these, I got a downward shot between the shoulders at the tusker, and dropped him immediately as the herd passed beneath. The jungle was so thick that I could not see his head, or, of course, I should have chosen the usual shot. This shot was not a fair criterion for the shoulder, as I happened to be in a position that enabled me to fire down upon him, and the ball most likely passed completely through him.

I remember a curious and unexpected shot that I once made with the four-ounce rifle, which illustrates its immense power. I was shooting at Minneria, and was returning to the tent in the afternoon, having had a great day's sport with buffalos, when I saw a large herd in the distance, ranged up together, and gazing intently at some object near them. Being on horseback, I rode up to them, carrying my heavy rifle; and, upon a near approach, I discovered two large bulls, fighting furiously. This combat was exciting the attention of the herd, who retreated upon my approach. The two bulls were so engaged in their duel, that they did not notice me until I was within fifty yards of them. First one, then the other, was borne to the ground, when presently their horns became locked together, as though arm in arm. The more they tugged to separate themselves, the tighter they held together, and at length they ranged side by side. Taking a shot at the shoulder of the nearest bull, they both fell suddenly to the ground. The fall unlocked their horns, and one bull, recovering his legs, retreated at a slow pace, and dead lame. The nearest bull was killed; and mounting my

TWO BULLS AT ONE SHOT.

horse, I galloped after the wounded buffalo. The chase did not last long. Upon arriving within fifty yards of his flank, I noticed the blood streaming from his mouth, and he presently rolled over and died. The ball, having passed through his antagonist, had entered his shoulder, and, smashing the shoulder-blade, had passed through the body, lodging in the tough hide upon his opposite side, from which I extracted it, by simply cutting the skin which covered it.

I have frequently seen the bull buffalos fight each other with great fury. Upon these occasions they are generally the most dangerous, all their natural ferocity being increased by the heat of the combat. I was once in pursuit of an elephant which led me across the plain at Minneria, when I suddenly observed a large bull buffalo making towards me, as though to cut me off in the very direction in which I was advancing. Upon his near approach, I noticed numerous bloody cuts and scratches upon his neck and shoulders, which were evidently only just made by the horns of some bull with whom he had been fighting. Not wishing to fire, lest I should alarm the elephant, I endeavoured to avoid him; but this was no easy task. He advanced to within fifty paces of me, and ploughing up the ground with his horns, and roaring, he seemed determined to make an attack. However, I managed to pass him at length, being determined to pay him off on my return, if he were still in the same spot.

On arriving near the position of the elephant, I saw at once that it was impossible to get him; —he was standing in a deep morass of great extent, backed by thick jungles, and I could not approach nearer than a hundred and fifty paces.

After trying several ruses to induce him to quit his mud-bath, and come on, I found it was of no use; he was not disposed to be a fighter, as he saw my strong position upon some open rising ground among some large trees. I therefore took a rest upon the branch of a tree, and gave him a shot from the four-ounce rifle, through the shoulder. This sent him to the thick jungle with ears and trunk drooping, but produced no other effect. I therefore returned towards the tent, fully expecting to meet my old enemy, the bull, whom I had left master of the field. In this I was not disappointed; he was standing within a few yards of the same spot, and, upon seeing me, he immediately advanced, having a very poor opinion of an enemy who had retreated from him an hour previous.

Instead of charging at a rapid pace, he trotted slowly up, and I gave him the four-ounce when within fifty yards. This knocked him over; but, to my astonishment, he recovered himself instantly, and galloped towards me. Again he stopped within twenty yards of me, and it was fortunate for me that he did; for a servant, who was carrying my long two-ounce rifle, had, in his excitement, cocked it, and actually set the hair-trigger. This he managed to touch as he handed it to me, and it exploded close to my head. I had only a light double-gun loaded, and the buffalo was evidently prepared to charge in a few seconds.

To my great satisfaction, I saw the bloody foam gathering upon his lips, and I knew that he was struck through the lungs; but, nevertheless, the distance was so short between us that he could reach me in two or three bounds. Keeping my Moorman with the light gun close to me, in readiness, I began to load my two big rifles. In the mean time, the bull was advancing step by step with an expression of determined malice, and my Cingalese servant, in an abject state of fright, was imploring me to run,—simply as an excuse for his own flight. "Buffalo's coming, sar! Master, run plenty, quick! Buffalo's coming, sar! Master, get big tree!" I could not turn to silence the fellow, but I caught him a fine backward kick upon the shins with my heel, which stopped him, and in a few seconds I was loaded, and the four-ounce was in my hand. The bull, at this time, was not fifteen yards from me; but, just as I was going to fire, I saw him reel to one side; and, in another moment, he rolled upon his back, a dead buffalo; although I had not fired after my first shot. The ball, having entered his chest, was sticking in the skin of his haunch, having passed through his lungs. His wonderful pluck had kept him upon his legs until life was extinct.

I am almost tired of recounting so many instances of the courage of these beasts. When I look back to those scenes, so many ghosts of victims rise up before me, that, were I to relate one half their histories, it would fill a volume. The object, in describing these encounters, is to show the style of animal that the buffalo is in his natural state. I could relate a hundred instances where they have died like curs, and have afforded no more sport than tame cows; but I merely enumerate those scenes worth relating that I have witnessed. This will show that the character of a wild buffalo can never be depended upon; and if their pursuit is followed up as a sport by itself, the nature of the animal cannot be judged by the individual behaviour of any particular beast. Some will fight, and some will fly, and no one can tell which will take place: it is at the option of the beast. Caution and good shooting, combined with heavy rifles, are necessary. Without heavy metal, the sport would be superlatively dangerous, if regularly followed up. Many persons kill a wild buffalo every now and then; but I have never met with a single sportsman in Ceylon who has devoted himself to the pursuit as a separate sport. Unless this is done, the real character of buffalos in general must remain unknown. It may, however, be considered as a rule with few exceptions, that the buffalo seldom commences the attack unless pursued. Their instinct at once tells them whether the man advancing towards them over the plain comes as an enemy. They may then attack; but if unmolested they will generally retreat, and, like all men of true courage, they will never seek a quarrel, and never give in when it is forced upon them. Many descriptions of my encounters with these animals may appear to militate against this theory, but they are the exceptions that I have met with: the fierce look of defiance, and the quick tossing of the head, may appear to portend a charge; but the animals are generally satisfied with this demonstration, and retreat.

Attack the single bulls and follow them up, and they will soon show their real character. Heavy rifles then make a good sport of what would otherwise be a chance of ten to one against the man. It must be remembered that the attack is generally upon an extensive plain, without a single sheltering tree; escape by speed is therefore impossible, and even a horse must be a good one, or a buffalo will catch him.

Without wading through the many scenes of carnage that I have witnessed in this branch of sport, I will sum up the account of buffalo-shooting by a description of one day's work at Minneria.

The tent was pitched in a secluded spot, beneath some shady trees, through which no ray of sun could penetrate; the open forest surrounded it on all sides, but through the vistas of dark stems the beautiful green plain and glassy lake could be seen stretching into an undefined distance. The blue hills, apparently springing from the bosom of the lake, lined the horizon, and the shadowy forms of the Kandian mountains mingled indistinctly with the distant clouds. From this spot, with a good telescope, I could watch the greater part of the plain, which was at this time enlivened by the numerous herds of wild buffalos scattered over the surface. A large bull was standing alone about half a mile from the tent, and I thought him a fine beast to begin with.

I started with two well-known and trusty gun-bearers. This bull apparently did not wish to fight, and when at nearly four hundred yards distance, he turned and galloped off. I put up all the sights of the long two-ounce rifle, and for an instant he dropped to the shot at this distance, but recovering immediately, he turned round, and, although upon only three legs, he charged towards me. At this distance I should have had ample time to reload before he could have come near me, so I took a quiet shot at him with my four-ounce rifle. A second passed, and he pitched upon his head, and lay upon the ground, struggling in vain to rise. This wâs an immensely long shot to produce so immediate an effect, so reloading quickly I stepped the distance. I measured three hundred and fifty-two paces, and I then stood within ten yards of him, as he still lay upon the ground, endeavouring vainly to rush at me. A ball in his head settled him. The first shot had broken his hind leg—and the shot with the big rifle had hit him on the nose, and, tearing away the upper jaw, it had passed along his neck, and escaped from behind his shoulder. This was a great chance to hit him so exactly at such a range. His skull is now in England, exhibiting the terrific effect of the heavy ball.

I had made up my mind for a long day's work, and I therefore mounted my horse and rode over the plain. The buffalos were very wild, as I had been shooting here for some days, and there were no less than forty-two carcases scattered about the plain in different directions. I fired several ineffectual shots at immense ranges; at length I even fired at random into a large herd, which seemed determined to take to the jungle. After they had galloped for a quarter of a mile, a cow dropped to the rear and presently fell. Upon riding up to her, I found her in the last gasp; the random shot had struck her behind the shoulder, and I finished her by a ball in the head. One of the bulls from this herd had separated from the troop, and had taken to the lake; he had waded out for about four hundred yards, and was standing shoulder deep. This was a fine target; a black spot upon the bright surface of the lake, although there was not more than eighteen inches of his body above the water. I rode to the very edge of the lake, and then dismounting, I took a rest upon my saddle. My horse, being well accustomed to this work, stood like a statue, but the ball dapped in the water just beyond the mark. The buffalo did not move an inch until the third shot. This hit him, and he swam still further off; but he soon got his footing, and again gave a fair mark as before. I missed him again, having fired a little over him. The fifth shot brought luck, and sunk him. I do not know where he was hit, as of course I could not get to him; but most likely it was in the spine, as so small a portion of his body was above water.

I passed nearly the whole day in practising at long ranges, but with no very satisfactory effect; several buffalos badly wounded had reached the jungle, and my shoulder was so sore from the recoil of the heavy rifle during several days' shooting with the large charge of powder, that I was obliged to reduce the charge to six drachms, and give up the long shots.

It was late in the afternoon, and the heat of the day had been intense. I was very hungry, not having breakfasted, and I made up my mind to return to the tent, which was now some eight miles distant. I was riding over the plain on my way home, when I saw a fine bull spring from a swampy hollow, and gallop off. Putting spurs to my horse, I was soon after him, carrying the four-ounce rifle; and upon seeing himself pursued, he took shelter in a low but dry hollow, which was a mass of lofty bulrush and coarse tangled grass, rising about ten feet high in an impervious mass. This had been a pool in the wet weather, but was now dried up, and was nothing but a bed of sedges and high rushes. I could see nothing of the bull, although I knew he was in it. The hollow was in the centre of a wide plain, so I knew that the buffalo could not have passed out without my seeing him, and my gun-bearers having come up, I made them pelt the rushes with dried clods of earth. It was of no use, he would not break cover; so I determined to ride in and hunt him up. The grass was so thick and entangled with the rushes, that my horse could with difficulty force his way through it; and when within the dense mass of vegetation, it towered high above my head, and was so thick,

CHARGE IN HIGH REEDS.

that I could not see a yard to my right or left. I beat about to no purpose for about twenty minutes, and I was on the point of giving it up when I suddenly saw the tall reeds bow down just before me. I heard the rush of an animal as he burst through, and I just saw the broad black nose, quickly followed by the head and horns, as the buffalo charged into me. The horse reared to his full height as the horns almost touched his chest, and I fired as well as I was able. In another instant I was rolling on the ground, with my horse upon me, in a cloud of smoke and confusion.

In a most unsportsmanlike manner (as persons may exclaim who were not there), I hid behind my horse, as he regained his legs. All was still—the snorting of the frightened horse was all that I could hear. I expected to have seen the infuriated buffalo among us. I peeped over the horse's back, and, to my delight and surprise, I saw the carcase of the bull lying within three feet of him. His head was pierced by the ball exactly between the horns, and death had been instantaneous. The horse having reared to his full height, had entangled his hind legs in the grass, and he had fallen backwards without being touched by the buffalo, although the horns were close into him.

I was rather pleased at being so well out of this scrape, and I made up my mind never again to follow buffalos into high grass. Turning towards the position of the tent, I rode homewards. The plain appeared deserted, and I rode for three or four miles along the shores of the lake, without seeing a head of game. At length, when within about three miles of the encampment, I saw a small herd of five buffalos and three half-grown calves standing upon a narrow point of muddy ground, which projected for some distance into the lake.

I immediately rode towards them, and upon approaching to within sixty yards, I found they consisted of three cows, two bulls, and three calves. I had advanced towards them upon the neck of land upon which they stood; there was, therefore, no retreat for them unless they took to the water. They perceived this themselves, but they preferred the bolder plan of charging through all opposition, and then reaching the main-land. After a few preliminary grunts and tosses of the head, one of the bulls charged straight at me at full gallop; he was not followed by his companions, who were still irresolute; and, when within forty yards, he sprung high in the air, and pitching upon his horns, he floundered upon his back as the rifle-ball passed through his neck and broke his spine. I immediately commenced reloading, but the ball was only half-way down the barrel, when the remaining bull, undismayed by the fate of his companion, rushed on at full speed. Snatching the long two-ounce rifle from a gun-bearer, I made a lucky shot. The ball must have passed through his heart, as he fell stone dead.

The three cows remained passive spectators of the death of their mates, although I was convinced by their expression that they would eventually show fight. I was soon reloaded, and not wishing to act simply on the defensive, and thus run the risk of a simultaneous onset, I fired at the throat of the most vicious of the party. The two-ounce ball produced no other effect than an immediate charge. She bounded towards me, and, although bleeding at the mouth, the distance was so short, that she would have been into me had I not stopped her with the four-ounce rifle, which brought her to the ground when within fifteen paces ; here she lay disabled but not dead, and again I reloaded as fast as possible.

The two remaining cows appeared to have taken a lesson from the fate of their comrades ; and showing no disposition to charge, I advanced towards them to within twenty yards. One of the cows now commenced tearing the muddy ground with her horns, and thus offered a certain shot, which I accordingly took, and dropped her dead with a ball in the nape of the neck. This was too much for the remaining buffalo; she turned to plunge into the lake, but the four-ounce through her shoulder brought her down before she could reach the water into which the three calves had sprung, and were swimming for the main shore. I hit the last calf in the head with a double-barrelled gun, and he immediately sank; and I missed another calf with the left-hand barrel; therefore two escaped. I sent a man into the water to find the dead calf, which he soon did, and hauled it to the shore; and having reloaded, I proceeded to examine the hits on the dead buffalos. It was fortunate that I had reloaded; for I had no sooner approached to within three or four yards of the cow that I had left dying, when she suddenly sprang to her feet, and would have charged, had I not killed her by a ball in the head from a light double-barrel that I was then carrying. These animals had shown as good sport as I had ever witnessed in buffalo-shooting, but the two heavy rifles were fearful odds against them, and they were added to the list of the slain. It was now late in the evening, and I had had a long day's work in a broiling sun. I had bagged ten buffalos, including the calf, and having cut a fillet from the latter, I took a gun, loaded with shot, from my horsekeeper, and gave up ball-shooting, having turned my attention to a large flock of teal, which I had disturbed in attacking the buffalos. This flock I had marked down in a small stream which flowed into the lake. A cautious approach upon my hands and knees, through the grass, brought me undiscovered to the banks of the stream, where, in a small bay, it emptied itself into the lake, and a flock of about eighty teal were swimming among the water-lilies within twenty yards of me. I fired one barrel on the water, and the other in the air, as they rose, killing five, and wounding a sixth, which escaped by continual diving. On my way home I killed a few snipe, till at length the cessation of daylight put an end to all shooting.

The moon was full, and shone over the lake with great brilliancy; the air was cool and refreshing, after the great heat of the day; and the chirp of the snipe, and whistling sound of the wildfowl on the lake, were the only noises that disturbed the wild scene around. The tent-fires were blazing brightly in the forest at about a mile distant; and giving my gun to the horsekeeper, I mounted, and rode towards the spot.

I was within half a mile of the tent, and had just turned round an angle made by the forest, when I suddenly saw the grey forms of several elephants, who had just emerged from the forest, and were feeding in the high grass within a hundred yards of me. I counted seven, six of which were close to the edge of the jungle, but the seventh was a large bull elephant, who had advanced by himself about sixty yards into the plain. I thought I could cut this fellow off, and, taking my big rifle, I dismounted and crept cautiously towards him. He winded me before I had gone many paces, gave a shrill trumpet of alarm, and started off for the jungle; the rest of the herd vanished like magic, while I ran after the bull elephant at my best speed. He was too quick for me, and I could not gain upon him, so, halting suddenly, I took a steady shot at his ear with the four-ounce at about seventy yards. Down he went to the shot, but I heard him roar as he lay upon the ground, and I knew he would be up again in a moment. In the same instant, as I dropped my empty rifle, a double-barrelled gun was pushed into my hand, and I ran up to him, just in time to catch him as he was half risen. Feeling sure of him, I ran up within two yards of his head, and fired into his forehead. To my amazement, he jumped quickly up, and with a loud trumpet, he rushed towards the jungle. I could just keep close alongside him, as the grass was short, and the ground level, and being determined to get him, I ran close to his shoulder, and, taking a steady shot behind the ear, I fired my remaining barrel. Judge of my surprise,—it only increased his speed, and in another moment he reached the jungle: he was gone. He seemed to bear a charmed life. I had taken two shots within a few feet of him that I would have staked my life upon. I looked at my gun. Ye Gods! I had been firing *snipe shot* at him. It was my rascally horsekeeper, who had actually handed me the shot-gun, which I had received as the double-barrelled ball-gun, that I knew was carried by a gun-bearer. How I did thrash him! If the elephant had charged instead of making off I should have been caught, to a certainty.

This day's shooting was the last day of good sport that I ever had at Minneria. It was in June, 1847. The next morning I moved my encampment, and started homewards. To my surprise I saw a rogue elephant drinking in the lake, within a quarter of a mile of me; but the Fates were against his capture. I stalked him as well as I could, but he winded me, and came on in full charge with his trunk up. The heavy rifle fortunately turned, but did not kill him, and he escaped in thorny jungle, through which I did not choose to follow.

On my way to the main road from Trincomalee to Kandy, I walked on through the jungle path, about a mile ahead of my followers, to look out for game. Upon arriving at the open country in the neighbourhood of Cowdellai, I got a shot at a deer at a killing distance. She was not twenty yards off, and was looking at me as if spell-bound. This provided me with venison for a couple of days. The rapid decomposition of all things in a tropical climate renders a continued supply of animal food very precarious, if the produce of the rifle is alone to be depended upon. Venison, killed on one day, would be uneatable on the day following, unless it were half-dressed shortly after it was killed: thus the size of the animal in no way contributes to the continuation of the supply of food, as the meat will not keep. Even snipe killed on one morning are putrid the next evening; the quantity of game required for the subsistence of one person is consequently very large.

After killing the deer I stalked a fine peacock, who gave me an hour's work before I could get near him. These birds are very wary and difficult to approach; but I at length got him into a large bush, surrounded by open ground. A stone thrown into this dislodged him, and he gave me a splendid flying-shot at about thirty yards. I bagged him with the two-ounce rifle, but the large ball damaged him terribly. There are few better birds than a Ceylon peafowl, if kept for two days, and then washed in vinegar: they combine the flavour of the turkey and the pheasant.

I was obliged to carry the bird myself, as my two gun-bearers were staggering under the weight of the deer, and the spare guns were carried by my tracker. We were proceeding slowly along, when the tracker, who was in advance, suddenly sprang back, and pointed to some object in the path. It was certainly enough to startle any man. An enormous serpent lay coiled in the path. His head was about the size of a very small cocoa-nut, divided lengthways, and this was raised about eighteen inches above the coil. His eyes were fixed upon us, and his forked tongue played in and out of his mouth with a continued hiss. Aiming at his head, I fired at him with a double-barrelled gun, within four paces, and blew his head to pieces. He appeared stone dead; but upon pulling him by the tail, to stretch him out at full length, he wreathed himself in convulsive coils, and lashing himself out in full length, he mowed down the high grass in all directions. This obliged me to stand clear, as his blows were terrific, and the thickest part of his body was as large as a man's thigh. I at length thought of an expedient for securing him. Cutting some sharp-pointed stakes, I waited till he was again quiet, when I suddenly pinned his tail to the ground with my hunting-knife, and thrusting the pointed stake into the hole, I drove it deeply into the ground with the butt of my rifle. The boa made some objection to this, and again he commenced his former muscular contortions. I waited till they were over, and having provided myself with some tough jungle rope (a species of creeper), I once more approached him, and pinning his throat to the ground with a stake, I tied the rope through the incision, and the united exertions of myself and three men hauled him out perfectly straight. I then drove a stake firmly through his throat, and pinned him out. He was fifteen feet in length; and it required our united strength to tear off his skin, which shone with a variety of passing colours. On losing his hide he tore away from the stakes; and although his head was shivered to atoms, and he had lost three feet of his length of neck by the ball having cut through this part, which separated in tearing off the skin, still he lashed out and wreathed in frightful convulsions, which continued until I left him, bearing as my trophy his scaly hide. These boas will kill deer, and by crushing them into a sort of sausage, they are enabled by degrees to swallow them. There are many of these vermin in Ceylon; but they are seldom seen, as they generally wander forth at night. There are marvellous stories of their size; and my men assured me that they had seen much larger than the snake now mentioned; — to me he appeared a horrible monster.

I do not know anything so disgusting as a

snake. There is an instinctive feeling that the arch enemy is personified when these wretches glide by you, and the blood chills with horror. I took the dried skin of this fellow to England; it measures twelve feet in its dry state, minus the piece that was broken from his neck, making him the length, before mentioned, of fifteen feet.

I have often been astonished that comparatively so few accidents happen in Ceylon from snake-bites; the immense number of these vermin, and the close nature of the country, making it a dangerous risk to the naked feet of the natives. I was once lying upon a sofa in a rest-house at Kandellai, when I saw a snake about four feet long glide in at the open door, and, as though accustomed to a particular spot for his lodging, he at once climbed upon another sofa and coiled himself under the pillow. My brother had only just risen from this sofa, and was sitting at the table watching the movements of his uninvited bedfellow. I soon poked him out with a stick, and cut off his head with a hunting-knife. This snake was of a very poisonous description, and was evidently accustomed to lodge behind the pillow, upon which the unwary sleeper might have received a fatal bite. Upon taking possession of an unfrequented rest-house, the cushions of the sofas and bedsteads should always be examined, as they are great attractions to snakes, scorpions, centipedes, and all manner of reptiles.

CHAP. VII.

CAPABILITIES OF CEYLON.—DEER AT ILLEPECADÉWÉ.—SAGACITY OF A PARIAH DOG.—TWO DEER AT ONE SHOT.—DEER STALKING.—HAMBANTOTTE COUNTRY.—KATTREGAM FESTIVAL.—SITRAWELLÉ.—RUINS OF ANCIENT MAHAGAM.—WIHARÉWELLÉ.—A NIGHT ATTACK UPON ELEPHANTS.—SHOOTING BY MOONLIGHT.—YALLÉ RIVER.—ANOTHER ROGUE.—A STROLL BEFORE BREAKFAST.—A CURIOUS SHOT.—A GOOD DAY'S SPORT.

THERE are few countries which present a more lovely appearance than Ceylon. There is a diversity in the scenery which refreshes the eye; and although the evergreen appearance might appear monotonous to some persons, still, were they residents, they would observe that the colour of the foliage is undergoing a constant change by the varying tints of the leaves in the different stages of their growth. These tints are far more lovely than the autumnal shades of England, and their brilliancy is enhanced by the idea that it is the bursting of the young leaf into life, the freshness of youth instead of the sere leaf of a past summer, which, after gilding for a few days the beauty of the woods, drops from the frozen branches and deserts them. Every shade of colour is seen in the

Ceylon forests, as the young leaves are constantly replacing those which have fallen without being missed. The deepest crimson, the brightest yellow, and green of every shade, combine to form a beautiful crest to the forest-covered surface of the island.

There is no doubt, however, that there is too much wood in Ceylon; it prevents the free circulation of air, and promotes dampness, malaria, and consequently fevers and dysentery, the latter disease being the scourge of the colony. The low country is accordingly decidedly unhealthy.

This vast mass of forest and jungle is a great impediment to the enjoyment of travelling. The heat in the narrow paths cut through dense jungles is extreme; and after a journey of seventy or eighty miles through this style of country the eye scans the wild plains and mountains with delight. Some districts, however, are perfectly devoid of trees, and form a succession of undulating downs of short grass. Other parts, again, although devoid of heavy timber, are covered with dense thorny jungles, especially the country adjoining the sea-coast, which is generally of a uniform character round the whole island, being interspersed with sandy plains producing a short grass.

Much has been said by some authors of the "capabilities" of Ceylon; but, however enticing the description of these capabilities may have been, the proof has been decidedly in opposition to the theory. Few countries exist with such an immense proportion of bad soil. There are no minerals except iron, no limestone except dolomite, no other rocks than quartz and gneiss. The natural pastures are poor; the timber of the forests is the only natural production of any value, with the exception of cinnamon. Sugar estates do not answer; and coffee requires an expensive system of cultivation by frequent manuring. In fact, the soil is wretched; so bad that the natives, by felling the forest and burning the timber upon the ground, can only produce one crop of some poor grain; the land is then exhausted, and upon its consequent desertion it gives birth to an impenetrable mass of low jungle, comprising every thorn that can be conceived. This deserted land, fallen again into the hand of nature, forms the jungle of Ceylon; and as native cultivation has thus continued for some thousand years, the immense tract of country now in this impenetrable state is easily accounted for. The forests vary in appearance; some are perfectly free from underwood, being composed of enormous trees, whose branches effectually exclude the rays of the sun; but they generally consist of large trees, which tower above a thick, and for the most part thorny, underwood, difficult to penetrate.

The features of Ceylon scenery may, therefore, be divided as follows:—

Natural forest, extending over the greater portion.

Thorny jungle, extending over a large portion.

Flat plains and thorny jungles, in the vicinity of the coast.

Open down country, extending over a small portion of the interior.

Open park country, extending over the greater portion of the Veddah district.

The mountains, forming the centre of the island.

The latter are mostly covered with forest, but they are beautifully varied by numberless open plains and hills of grass-land at an altitude of from three to nearly nine thousand feet.

If Ceylon were an open country, there would be no large game, as there would be no shelter from the sun. In the beautiful open down country throughout the Ouva district, there is no game larger than wild hogs, red-deer, mouse-deer, hares, and partridges. These animals shelter themselves in the low bushes, which generally consist of the wild guavas, and occupy the hollows between the undulations of the hills. The thorny jungles conceal a mass of game of all kinds; but in this retreat the animals are secure from attack. In the vicinity of the coast, among the "flat plains and thorny jungles," there is always excellent shooting at particular seasons. The spotted deer abound throughout Ceylon, especially in these parts, where they are often seen in herds of a hundred together. In many places they are far too numerous, as, from the want of inhabitants in these parts, there are no consumers, and these beautiful beasts would be shot to waste.

In the neighbourhood of Paliar, and Illepecadéwé on the north-west coast, I have shot them till I was satiated, and it ceased to be sport. We had nine fine deer hanging up in one day, and they were putrifying faster than the few inhabitants could preserve them by smoking and drying them in steaks. I could have shot them in any number, had I chosen to kill simply for the sake of murder; but I cannot conceive any person finding an enjoyment in slaying these splendid deer to rot upon the ground.

I was once shooting at Illepecadéwé, which is a lonely, miserable spot, when I met with a very sagacious and original sportsman in a most unexpected manner. I was shooting with a friend, and we had separated for a few hundred paces. I presently got a shot at a pea-fowl, and killed her with my rifle. The shot was no sooner fired, than I heard another shot in the jungle, in the direction taken by my friend. My rifle was still unloaded when a spotted doe bounded out of the jungle, followed by a white pariah dog in full chase. Who would have dreamt of meeting with a dog at this distance from a village (about four miles)? I whistled to the dog, and to my surprise he came to me, the deer having left him out of sight in a few seconds. He was a knowing-looking brute, and was evidently out hunting on his own account. Just at this moment my friend called to me, that he had wounded a buck, and that he had found the blood-track. I picked a blade of grass from the spot which was tinged with blood; and holding it to the dog's nose, he eagerly followed me to the track, upon which I dropped it. He went off in a moment; but, running mute, I was obliged to follow; and after a chase of a quarter of a mile I lost sight of him. In following up the foot-track of the wounded deer, I heard the distant barking of the dog, by which I knew that he had brought the buck to bay, and I was soon at the spot. The buck had taken up a position in a small glade, and was charging the dog furiously; but the pariah was too knowing to court the danger, and kept well out of the way. I shot the buck, and, tying a piece of jungle-rope to the dog's neck, gave him to a gun-bearer to lead, as I hoped he might be again useful in hunting up a wounded deer.

I had not proceeded more than half a mile, when we arrived at the edge of a small sluggish stream, covered in most places with rushes and water-lilies. We forded this about hip-deep, but the gun-bearer who had the dog could not prevail upon our mute companion to follow; he pulled violently back, and shrinked, and evinced every symptom of terror at the approach of water.

I was now at the opposite bank, and nothing would induce him to come near the river, so I told the gun-bearer to drag him across by force. This he accordingly did, and the dog swam with frantic exertions across the river, and managed to disengage his head from the rope. The moment that he arrived on terra firma, he rushed up a steep bank and looked attentively down into the water beneath.

We now gave him credit for his sagacity in refusing to cross the dangerous passage. The reeds bowed down to the right and left as a huge crocodile of about eighteen feet in length moved slowly from his shallow bed into a deep hole. The dog turned to the right-about, and went off as fast as his legs would carry him. No calling or whistling would induce him to return, and I never saw him again. How he knew that a crocodile was in the stream I cannot imagine. He must have had a narrow escape at some former time, which was a lesson that he seemed determined to profit by.

Shortly after the disappearance of the dog, I separated from my companion and took a different line of country. Large plains with thorny jungles and bushes of the long cockspur thorn interspersed, formed the character of the ground. This place literally swarmed with pea-fowl, partridges, and deer. I killed another peacock, and the shot disturbed a herd of about sixty deer, who bounded over the plain till out of sight. I tracked up this herd for nearly a mile, when I observed them behind a large bush; some were lying down, and some were standing. A buck and doe presently quitted the herd, and advancing a few paces from the bush, they halted, and evidently winded me. I was screening myself behind a small tree, and the open ground between me and the game precluded the possibility of a nearer approach. It was a random distance for a deer, but I took a rest against the stem of the tree and fired at the buck as he stood with his broadside exposed, being shoulder to shoulder with the doe. Away went the herd, flying over the plain; but, to my delight, there were two white bellies struggling upon the ground. I ran up to cut their throats*; the two-ounce ball had passed through the shoulders of both; and I stepped the distance to the tree from which I had fired, "two hundred and thirteen paces."

Shortly after this, I got another shot, which, by a chance, killed two deer. I was strolling through a narrow glade with open jungles upon either side, when I suddenly heard a quick double-shot, and I heard the rush of a large herd of deer coming through the jungle. I immediately lay flat upon the ground, and presently an immense herd of

* This is necessary, to allow the blood to escape, otherwise they would be unfit for food.

full a hundred deer passed across the glade at full gallop, within seventy yards of me. Jumping up, I fired at a doe, and, to my surprise, two deer fell to the shot, one of which was a fawn: the ball had passed through the shoulder of the mother, and had broken the fawn's neck upon the opposite side. I am astonished that this chance of killing two at one shot does not more often happen when the dense body of a herd of deer is exposed to a rifle-ball.

Deer-stalking is one of the most exciting sports in the world. I have often crept upon hands and knees for upwards of a quarter of a mile through mud and grass, to get a shot at a fine antlered buck. It frequently happens that after a long stalk in this manner, when some sheltering object is reached which you have determined upon for the shot, just as you raise your head above the grass in expectation of seeing the game, you find a blank. He has watched your progress by the nose, although the danger was hidden from his view, and your trouble is unrewarded.

In all wild shooting, in every country and climate, the "wind" is the first consideration. If you hunt down wind, you will never get a deer. You will have occasional glimpses of your game, who will be gazing intently at you at great distances long before you can see them, but you will never get a decent shot. The great excitement and pleasure of all sport consists in a thorough knowledge of the pursuit. When the dew is heavy upon the ground at break of day, you are strolling noiselessly along with the rifle, scanning the wide plains and searching the banks of the pools and streams for tracks of the spotted deer. Upon discovering the tracks their date is immediately known, the vicinity of the game is surmised, the tracks are followed up, and the herd is at length discovered. The wind is observed; dry leaves crumbled into powder and let fall from the hand detect the direction if the slightest air is stirring, and the approach is made accordingly. Every stone, every bush, or tree, or tuft of grass is noted as a cover for an advance, and the body being kept in a direct line with each of these objects, you approach upon hands and knees from each successive place of shelter till a proper distance is gained. The stalking is the most exciting sport in the world. I have frequently heard my own heart beat while creeping up to a deer. He is an animal of wonderful acuteness, and possessing the keenest scent; he is always on the alert, watching for danger from his stealthy foe the leopard, who is a perfect deer-stalker.

To kill spotted deer well, if they are tolerably wild, a person must be a really good rifle shot, otherwise he will wound many, but seldom bag one. They are wonderfully fast, and their bounding pace makes them extremely difficult to hit when running. Even when standing, they must be struck either through the head, neck, or shoulder, or they will rarely be killed on the spot; in any other part if wounded, they will escape as though untouched, and die a miserable death in solitude.

In narrating long shots that I have made, I recount them as bright moments in the hours of sport; they are the exceptions and not the rule. I consider a man a first-rate shot who can *always* bag his deer standing at eighty yards, or, running, at fifty. *Hitting* and *bagging* are widely different. If a man can always bag at the distance that I have named, he will constantly hit, and frequently bag, at extraordinary ranges, as there is no doubt of his shooting, and, when he misses, the ball has whizzed somewhere very close to the object; the chances are, therefore, in favour of the rifle.

The deer differ in character in various parts of Ceylon. In some places where they are rarely disturbed they can be approached to within thirty or forty paces, in which case a very moderate shot can easily kill them; but it is better sport when they are moderately wild. The greatest number of deer that I ever saw was in the south-eastern part of Ceylon, in the neighbourhood of Potané and Yalle. The whole of this country is almost uninhabited, and accordingly undisturbed. Yalle is the nearest town of importance, from which a good road, lined on either side with cocoa-nut and bread-fruit trees, extends as far as Tangalle, fifty miles. A few miles beyond this village the wild country begins, and Hambantotte is the next station, nearly ninety miles from Yalle. The country around Hambantotte is absolutely frightful,—wide extending plains of white sand and low scrubby bushes scattered here and there; salt lakes of great extent, and miserable plains of scanty herbage, surrounded by dense thorny jungles. Notwithstanding this, at some seasons the whole district is alive with game. January and February are the best months for elephants and buffalos, and August and September are the best seasons for deer, at which time the whole country is burnt up with drought, and the game is forced to the vicinity of Yallé river and the neighbouring pools. In the wet season this district is nearly flooded, and forms a succession of immense marshes, the malaria from which is extremely unhealthy. At this time the grass is high, and the elephants are very numerous.

When I was in this part of the country the drought was excessive; the jungle was parched, and the leaves dropped from the bushes under the influence of a burning sun. Not a cloud ever appeared upon the sky, but a dazzling haze of intense heat spread over the scorched plains. The smaller streams were completely dried up, and the large rivers were reduced to small streams in the midst of a bed of sand.

The whole of this country is a succession of flat sandy plains and low jungles contiguous to the sea-coast. The intense heat and the glare of the sun rendered the journey most fatiguing. I at length descried a long line of noble forest in the distance, and this I conjectured to be near the river, which turned out to be the case; and we were soon relieved from the burning sun by the shade of as splendid a forest as I have ever seen. A few hundred yards from the spot at which we had entered, Yallé river rolled along in a clear stream. In the wet season this is a rapid torrent of about a hundred and fifty yards in width, but at this time the bed of the river was dry, with the exception of a stream of about thirty paces broad, which ran directly beneath the bank we were descending.

An unexpected scene now presented itself. The wide bed of the river was shaded on either side by groves of immense trees, whose branches stretched far over the channel; and not only beneath their shade, but in every direction, tents formed of talipot-leaves were pitched, and about 1000 men, women, and children lay grouped together; some were bathing in the river, some were sitting round their fires cooking a scanty meal, others lay asleep upon the sand, but all appeared to be congregated together for one purpose; and so various were the castes and costumes, that every nation of the East seemed to have sent a representative. This was the season for the annual offerings to the Kattregam god, to whose temple these pilgrims were flocking, and they had made the dry bed of Yallé river their temporary halting-place. A few days after, no less than 18,000 pilgrims congregated at Kattregam.

I was at this time shooting with my friend, a Mr. H. Walters, then of the 15th regiment. We waded up the bed of the river for about a mile, and then pitched the tent under some fine trees in the open forest. Several wild buffalos were drinking in the river within a short distance of us; but thinking this a likely spot for elephants, we determined not to disturb the neighbourhood by firing a shot until we had first explored the country. After a walk of a couple of hours through fine open forest and small bushy plains, we came to the conclusion that there were very few elephants in the country, and we devoted ourselves to other game.

After a day or two spent in killing deer, a few wild buffalos and only one elephant, I felt convinced that we should never find the latter, in the dry state of the country, unless by watching at some tank at night. We therefore moved our encampment inland about twenty-five miles from Yallé. Here there is a large tank, which I concluded would be the resort of elephants.

A long day's journey through a burning sun brought us to Sitrawellé. This is a small village about six miles inland from the sea-coast village of Kesindé. Here the natives brought us plaintains and buffalo-milk, while we took shelter from the sun under a splendid tamarind-tree. Opposite to this was a "bo" tree*; this grew to an extraordinary size; the wide-spreading branches covered about half an acre of ground, and the trunk measured upwards of forty feet in circumference. The tamarind-tree was nearly the same size; and I never saw together two such magnificent specimens of vegetation. A few paces from this spot a lake of about four miles' circuit lay in the centre of a plain; this was surrounded by open forests and jungles, all of which looked like good covers for game. Skirting the opposite banks of the lake, we pitched the tent under some shady trees upon a fine level sward. By this time it was nearly dusk, and I had barely time to stroll out and kill a peacock for dinner before night set in.

The next morning, having been joined by my friend, a Mr. P. Braybrook, then government agent of this district, our party was increased to three, and seeing no traces of elephants in this neighbourhood we determined to proceed to a place called Wiharéwellé, about six miles further inland.

Our route now lay along a broad causeway of solid masonry. On either side of this road stone

* Very similar to the banian-tree.

pillars of about twelve feet in height stood in broken rows, and lay scattered in every direction through the jungle. Ruined dagobas and temples jutted their rugged summits above the tree-tops, and many lines of stone columns stood in parallel rows, the ancient supports of buildings of a similar character to those of Pollanarua and Anarajahpoora. We were among the ruins of ancient Mahagam. One of the ruined buildings had apparently rested upon seventy-two pillars. These were still erect, standing in six lines of twelve columns: every stone appeared to be about fourteen feet high by two feet square, and twenty-five feet apart. This building must therefore have formed an oblong of three hundred feet by one hundred and fifty. Many of the granite blocks were covered with rough carving; large flights of steps, now irregular from the inequality of the ground, were scattered here and there; and the general appearance of the ruins was similar to that of Pollanarua, but of smaller extent. The stone causeway which passed through the ruins was about two miles in length, being for the most part overgrown with low jungle and prickly cactus. I traversed the jungle for some distance until arrested by the impervious nature of the bushes; but wherever

I went the ground was strewed with squared stones and fallen brickwork overgrown with rank vegetation.

The records of Ceylon do not afford any satisfactory information concerning the original foundation of this city; the first time that we hear of it is in the year 286 B.C.; but we have no account of the era or cause of its desertion. Although Mahagam is the only vestige of an ancient city in this district there are many ruined buildings and isolated dagobas of great antiquity scattered throughout the country. I observed on a peak of one of the Kattregam hills large masses of fallen brickwork, the ruins of some former buildings, probably coeval with Mahagam. The whole of this district, now so wild and desolate, must in those days have been thickly populated and highly cultivated, although from the present appearance of the country it does not seem possible that it has ever altered its aspect since the creation.

Descending a steep bank shaded by large trees, we crossed the bed of the Manick Ganga (Jewel River). The sand was composed of a mixture of mica, quartz, sapphire, ruby, and jacinth, but the large proportion of ruby sand was so extraordinary that it seemed to rival Sinbad the Sailor's vale of gems. The whole of this was valueless, but the appearance of the sand was very inviting as the shallow stream in rippling over it magnified the tiny gems into stones of some magnitude. I passed an hour in vainly searching for a ruby worth collecting, but the largest did not exceed the size of mustard seed.

The natives use this sand for cutting elephants' teeth in the same manner that a stonemason uses sand to assist him in sawing through a stone. Elephants' teeth or grinders are so hard that they will produce sparks upon being struck with a hatchet.

About two miles from the opposite bank of the river, having journeyed through a narrow path bordered upon either side by thick jungle, we opened upon an extensive plain close to the village of Wiharéwellé. This plain was covered with wild indigo, and abounded with pea-fowl. Passing through the small village at the extremity of the plain, we pitched the tent upon the borders of the lake, about a quarter of a mile beyond it. This tank was about three miles in circumference, and, like that of Sitrawellé, was one of the ancient works of the Mahagam princes.

The village was almost deserted; none but the

old men and women and children remained, as the ablebodied men had gone to the Kattregam festival. We could, therefore, obtain no satisfactory information regarding elephants; but I was convinced from the appearance of the country, and from the high grass around the lake, that if any elephants were in the district some would be here. It was late in the evening, the coolies were heaping up the night-fires, and as darkness closed upon us the savoury steam of a peacock that was roasting on a stick betokened the welcome approach of dinner. We had hardly commenced when the roaring of elephants within a short distance of the tent gave us hope of sport on the following day.

At daybreak the next morning I strolled round the lake to look for tracks. A herd of about seven had been feeding during the night within half a mile of the tent. During my walk I saw innumerable pea-fowl, jungle-fowl, hares, and ducks, in addition to several herds of deer; but not wishing to disturb the country, I did not fire, but returned to the tent and sent out trackers.

In the afternoon the natives returned with intelligence of a small pool two miles from the opposite shore of the lake, situated in dense jungle; here they had seen fresh elephant-tracks, and they proposed that we should watch the pool that evening at the usual drinking hour of the game. As this was the only pool of water for miles round with the exception of the lake, I thought the plan likely to succeed, and we, therefore, started without loss of time.

On arrival at the pool we took a short survey of our quarters. A small round sheet of water of perhaps eighty yards in diameter lay in the midst of a dense jungle. Several large trees were growing close to the edge, and around these lay numerous rocks of about four feet high, forming a capital place for concealment. Covering the tops of the rocks with boughs to conceal our heads, we lay quietly behind them in expectation of the approaching game.

The sun sunk, and the moon rose in great beauty, throwing a silvery light upon the surface of the water chequered by the dark shadows of the surrounding trees. Suddenly the hoarse bark of an elk sounded within a short distance, and I could distinguish two or three dark forms on the opposite bank. The shrill and continual barking of spotted deer now approaching nearer and nearer, the rustling in the jungle and the splashing in the water, announced continual arrivals of game to the lonely drinking place. Notwithstanding the immense quantity of animals that were congregated together, we could not distinguish them plainly on account of the dark background of jungle. Elk, deer, buffalos, and hogs were all bathing and drinking in immense numbers, but there were no elephants.

For some hours we watched the accumulation of game; there was not a breath of air, although the scud was flying fast above us, occasionally throwing a veil over the moon, and casting a sudden obscurity on the dim scene before us. Our gun-bearers were crouched around us; their dark skins matching with the ground on which they squatted, they looked like so many stumps of trees. It was nearly ten o'clock, and my eyes ached with watching; several times I found myself nodding, as sleep took me by surprise, so, leaving a man to look out, we sat quietly down and discussed a cold fowl that we had brought with us.

We had just finished a pint bottle of cherry brandy when I felt a gentle touch upon my shoulder, and our look-out man whispered in my ear the magic word "alia" (elephant), at the same time pointing in the direction of the tank. The guns were all wrapped up in a blanket to keep them from the dew, so telling W. to uncover them and to distribute them to the respective gun-bearers without noise, I crept out and stole unperceived along the margin of the tank to discover the number and position of the elephants. So deceitful was the moonlight, being interrupted by the dark shadows of the jungle, that I was within ten paces of the nearest elephant before I distinguished her. I counted three elephants, one large and two others about six feet high. Being satisfied with my information, and having ascertained that no others were in the jungle, I returned to my companions: they were all ready, and we crept forward. We were within ten paces of the large elephant when a branch of hooked thorn caught W. by the clothes; the noise that he made in extricating himself immediately attracted the attention of the elephant, and she turned quickly round, receiving at the same moment an ineffectual shot from W. B. at the same time fired without effect at one of the small elephants. The mother, hearing a roar from the small elephant that B. had wounded, immediately rushed up to it, and they stood side by side in the water about fifteen yards from the bank. The large elephant now cocked her ears and turned her head from side to side with great quickness to discover an enemy. I ran close to the water's edge, and the mother perceiving me immediately came forward. I could hardly distinguish the sights of my rifle, and I was, therefore, obliged to wait till she was within four or five paces before I fired. She gave me a good shot, and dropped dead. The young one was rushing about and roaring in a tremendous manner, having been again fired at and wounded by B. and W. By this time I had got a spare gun, and, wading into the tank, I soon came to such close quarters that I could not miss, and one shot killed him. The other small elephant escaped unseen in the confusion caused by the firing.

The following evening we again watched the pool, and once more a mother and her young one came to drink. W. and B. extinguished the young one while I killed the mother.

This watching by moonlight is a kind of sport that I do not admire; it is a sort of midnight murder; and many a poor brute who comes to the silent pool to cool his parched tongue finds only a cup of bitterness, and retires again to his jungle haunts to die a lingering death from some unskilful wound. The best shot must frequently miss by moonlight; there is a silvery glare which renders all objects indistinct and the shot very doubtful; thus two animals out of three fired at will generally escape wounded.

I was tired of watching by night, and I again returned to the neighbourhood of Yallé. After a long ride through a burning sun, I went down to the river to bathe. The water was not more than three feet deep, and was so clear that every pebble was plainly distinguishable at the bottom.

I had waded hip-deep into the river when my servant, who was on the bank, suddenly cried out, "Sar! Sar! come back, Sar! Mora! Mora!" and he pointed to some object a little higher up the stream. It was now within ten or twelve yards of me, and I fancied that it was a piece of drift timber, but I lost no time in reaching the shore. Slowly the object sailed along with the stream, but as it neared me, to my astonishment a large black fin protruded from the water, and the mystery was at once cleared up. It was a large *shark* about nine feet long.

In some places the water was so shallow that his tail and a portion of his back was now and then above the surface. He was in search of grey mullet, with which fish the river abounded; and at this season sharks were very numerous, as they followed the shoals for some distance up the river. My servant had been in a great state of alarm, as he thought his master would have been devoured in a few seconds; but the natives of the village quietly told me not to be afraid, but to bathe in peace, "*as sharks would not eat men at this season.*" I was not disposed to put his epicurean scruples to the test: as some persons may kill a pheasant before the 1st of October, so he might have made a grab at me a little before the season, which would have been equally disagreeable to my feelings. The novelty of a white skin in that clear river might have proved too strong a temptation for a shark to withstand.

I never saw game in such masses as had now collected in this neighbourhood. The heat was intense, and the noble forest in the vicinity of Yallé river offered an asylum to all animals beneath its shade, where good water and fine grass upon the river's bank supplied their wants. In this forest there was little or no underwood; the trees grew to an immense size, and stood far apart, so that a clear range might be obtained for a hundred yards. It was, therefore, a perfect spot for deer-stalking; the tops of the trees formed an impervious skreen to the sun's rays; and I passed several days in wandering with my rifle through these shady solitudes, killing an immense quantity of game. The deer were in such masses that I restricted myself to bucks, and I at length became completely satiated. There was too much game; during a whole day's walk I was certainly not *five minutes* without seeing either deer, elk, buffalos, or hogs. The noise of the rifle did not appear to scare them from the forest; they would simply retreat for a time to some other portion of it, and fresh herds were met with in following up one which had been disturbed. Still there were no elephants. Although I had upwards of fifty coolies and servants, they could not dry the venison sufficiently fast to prevent the deer from stinking as they were killed, and I resolved to leave the country.

I gave orders for everything to be packed up in readiness for a start, after an early breakfast on the following morning. The servants were engaged in arranging for the departure, when a native brought intelligence of a rogue elephant within four miles of the tent. It was late in the afternoon, but I had not seen an elephant for so long, that I was determined to make his acquaintance. My friend B. accompanied me, and we immediately started on horseback.

Our route lay across very extensive plains, interspersed with low thorny bushes and wide salt lakes. Innumerable wild hogs invited us to a chase. There could not be a better spot for boar-spearing, as the ground is level and clear for riding. There were numerous herds of deer and buffalos, but we did not fire a shot, as we had determined upon an interview with the rogue. We traversed about four miles of this style of country, and were crossing a small plain, when our guide suddenly stopped and pointed to the elephant, who was about a quarter of a mile distant. He was standing on a little glade of about fifty yards across; this was surrounded upon all sides but one with dense thorny jungle, and he therefore stood in a small bay of open ground. It was a difficult position for an attack. The wind blew directly from us to him, therefore an advance in that direction was out of the question; on the other hand, if we made a circuit so as to get the wind, we should have to penetrate through the thorny jungle to arrive at him, and we should then have the five o'clock sun directly in our eyes. However, there was no alternative, and, after a little consultation, the latter plan was resolved upon.

Dismounting, we ordered the horsekeepers to conceal the horses and themselves behind a thick bush, lest the elephant should observe them, and with this precaution we advanced, making a circuit of nearly a mile to obtain the wind. On arrival at the belt of thick jungle which divided us from the small glade upon which he stood, I perceived, as I had expected, that the sun was full in our eyes. This was a disadvantage which I felt convinced would lose us the elephant, unless some extraordinary chance intervened; however, we entered the thick jungle before us, and cautiously pushed our way through it. This belt was not more than fifty yards in width, and we soon broke upon the small glade.

The elephant was standing with his back towards us, at about forty paces distant, close to the thick jungle by his side, and, taking my four-ounce rifle, I walked quietly but quickly towards him. Without a moment's warning he flung his trunk straight up, and, turning sharp round, he at once charged into us. The sun shone full in my eyes, so that I could do nothing but fire somewhere at his head. He fell, but immediately recovered himself, and before the smoke had cleared away he was in full retreat through the thorny jungle, the heavy ball having taken all the pluck out of him. This was just as I had expected; pursuit in such a jungle was impossible, and I was perfectly contented with having turned him.

The next morning, having made all arrangements for starting homewards, after breakfast I took my rifle and one gun-bearer with a double-barrelled gun to enjoy one last stroll in the forest. It was just break of day when I entered the forest. My first course was towards the river which flowed through it, as I expected to find the game near the water, an hour before sunrise being their time for drinking. I had not proceeded far before immense herds of deer offered tempting shots; but I was out simply in search of large antlers, and none appearing of sufficient size, I would not fire. Buffalos continually presented themselves: I was tired of shooting these brutes, but I killed two who looked rather vicious; and I amused myself with remarking the immense quantity of game, and imagining the number of heads that I could bag had I chosen to indulge in indiscriminate slaughter. At length I noticed a splendid buck lying on the sandy bed of the river, beneath a large tree; his antlers were beautiful, and I stalked him to within sixty yards and shot him. I had not been reloaded ten minutes, and was walking quietly through the forest, when I saw a fine antlered buck standing within thirty yards of me, in a small patch of underwood. His head was turned towards me, and his nostrils were distended in alarm as he prepared to bound off. I had just time to cock my rifle as he dashed off at full speed; but it was a murderous distance, and he fell dead. His antlers matched exactly with those I had last shot.

I turned towards the direction of the tent, and, descending to the bed of the river, I followed the course of the stream upon the margin of dry sand. I had proceeded about half a mile, when I noticed at about a hundred and fifty paces some object moving about the trunk of a large fallen tree which lay across the bed of the river. This stem was about five feet in diameter, and I presently distinguished the antlers and then the head of a large buck, as they appeared above it: he had been drinking in the stream on the opposite side, and he now raised his head, sniffing the fresh breeze. It was a tempting shot, and taking a very steady aim, I fired. For a moment he was down, but recovering himself he bounded up the bank, and was soon in full speed through the forest with only one antler upon his head. I picked up the fellow-antler, which the rifle-ball had cut off within an inch of his skull. This was a narrow escape.

I did not reload my rifle, as I was not far from the tent, and I was tired of shooting. Giving my rifle to the gun-bearer, I took the double-barrelled gun which he carried, and walked quickly towards breakfast. Suddenly I heard a crash in a small nook of thick bushes, like the rush of an elephant, and the next instant a buck came dashing past in full speed; his long antlers lay upon his back as he flew through the tangled saplings with a force that seemed to defy resistance. He was the largest spotted buck that I ever saw, and, being within thirty paces, I took a flying shot with the right-hand barrel. He faltered for a moment, and I immediately fired the remaining barrel. Still he continued his course, but at a reduced speed, and dead lame. Loading the rifle I soon got upon the blood-track, and I determined to hunt him down.

There were many saplings in this part of the forest, and I noticed that many of them in the deer's track were besmeared with blood about two feet and a half from the ground. The tracks in the sandy soil were uneven — one of the fore-feet showed a deep impression, while the other was very faint, showing that he was wounded in the leg, as his whole weight was thrown upon one foot. Slowly and cautiously I stalked along the track, occasionally lying down to look under the bushes. For about an hour I continued this slow and silent chase; the tracks became fainter, and the bleeding appeared to have almost ceased; so few and far between were the red drops upon the ground that I was constantly obliged to leave the gun-bearer upon the last trace while I made a cast to discover the next track. I was at length in despair of finding him, and I was attentively scrutinising the ground for a trace of blood, which would distinguish his track from those of other deer with which the ground was covered, when I suddenly heard a rush in the underwood, and away bounded the buck at about fifty yards' distance, apparently as fresh as ever. The next instant he was gasping on the ground, the rifle-ball having passed exactly through his heart. I never could have believed that a spotted buck would have attained so large a size; he was as large as a doe elk, and his antlers were the finest that I have ever seen of that species. It required eight men with two cross poles to bring him home.

I reached the tent to breakfast at eight o'clock, having bagged three fine bucks and two buffalos that morning; and being, for the time, satiated with sport, I quitted Ceylon.

CHAP. VIII.

BEAT-HOUNDS FOR ELK-HUNTING. — SMUT. — KILLBUCK. — THE HORTON PLAINS. — A SECOND SOYER. — THE FIND. — THE BUCK AT BAY. — THE BAY. — THE DEATH. — RETURN OF LOST DOGS. — COMPARATIVE SPEED OF DEER. — VEDDAH RIPPED BY A BOAR. — A MÊLÉE. — BUCK AT BLACK POOL. — OLD SMUT'S RUSE. — MARGOSSE OIL.

THE foregoing description of sporting incidents closed my first visit to Ceylon. I had arrived in the island to make a tour of the country and to enjoy its sports; this I had accomplished by a residence of twelve months, the whole of which had been occupied in wandering from place to place. I now returned to England, but the Fates had traced *another* road for me, and after a short stay in the old country, I again started for Ceylon, and became a resident at Newera Ellia.

Making use of the experience that I had gained in wild sports, I came out well armed, according to my own ideas of weapons for the chase. I had ordered four double-barrelled rifles of No. 10. bore,* to be made to my own pattern; my hunting

* By Beattie, Regent Street.

knives and boar-spear heads I had made to my own design by Paget of Piccadilly, who turned out the perfection of steel; and I arrived in Ceylon with a pack of fine foxhounds and a favourite greyhound of wonderful speed and strength, "Bran," who, though full of years, is still alive.

The usual drawbacks and discomforts attendant upon a new settlement having been overcome, Newera Ellia forms a delightful place of residence. I soon discovered that a pack of thorough-bred foxhounds were not adapted to a country so enclosed by forest: some of the hounds were lost, others I parted with, but they are all long since dead, and their progeny, the offspring of crosses with pointers, bloodhounds, and half-bred foxhounds, have turned out the right stamp for elk hunting.

It is a difficult thing to form a pack for this sport which shall be perfect in all respects. Sometimes a splendid hound in character may be more like a butcher's dog than a hound in appearance, but the pack cannot afford to part with him if he is really good.

The casualties from leopards, boars, elk, and lost dogs, are so great that the pack is with difficulty kept up by breeding. It must be remembered, that the place of a lost dog cannot be easily supplied in Ceylon. Newera Ellia is one of the rare climates in Ceylon which is suited to the constitution of a dog. In the low and hot climates they lead a short and miserable life, which is soon ended by a liver complaint; thus, if a supply for the pack cannot be kept up by breeding, hounds must be procured from England at a great expense and risk.

The pack now in the kennel is as near perfection as can be attained for elk-hunting, comprising ten couple, most of whom are nearly thorough-bred foxhounds, with a few couple of immense seizers, a cross between bloodhound and greyhound, and a couple of large wire-haired lurchers, like the Scotch deer-hound.

In describing the sport, I must be permitted to call up the spirits of a few heros, who are now dead, and place them in the vacant places which they formerly occupied in the pack.

The first who answers to the magic call is "Smut," hero of at least four hundred deaths of elk and boar. He appears—the same well remembered form of strength, the sullen growl which greeted even his master, the numerous scars and seams upon his body: behold old "Smut!" His sire was a Manilla bloodhound, which accounted for the extreme ferocity of the son. His courage was indomitable. He was a large dog, but not high, considering his great length, but his limbs were immense in proportion. His height at the shoulders was 26½ inches; his girth of brisket 34 inches. In his younger days he always opened upon a scent, and the rocky mountains and deep valleys have often echoed back his deep notes, which have now, like himself, passed away. As he grew older he became cunning, and he ran entirely mute, knowing well that the more noise the elk heard behind him the faster he would run. I have frequently known him to be out by himself all night, and return the next morning blown out with food which he had procured for himself by pulling down a doe single-handed. When he was a young dog, and gave tongue upon a scent, a challenge was offered, but never accepted, that the dog should find, hunt, and pull down two buck elk, single-handed, within a fortnight, assisted only by his master, with no other weapon than a hunting knife: there is no doubt whatever that he would have performed it easily. He then belonged to Lieut. Pardoe, of the 15th regiment.

He had several pitched battles with leopards, from which he has returned frightfully torn, but with his yellow hair bristled up, his head and stern erect; and his deep growl, with which he gave a dubious reception to both man and beast, was on those occasions doubly threatening.

I never knew a dog that combined superlative valour with discretion in the degree exhibited by "Smut." I have seen many dogs who would rush heedlessly upon a boar's tusks to certain destruction; but Smut would never seize until the proper time arrived, and when the opportunity offered he never lost it. This rendered him of great value in these wild sports, where the dog and his master are mutually depending upon each other. There was nothing to fear if Smut was there: whether boar or buck you might advance fearlessly to him with the knife with the confidence that the dog would pin the animal the instant that it turned to attack you; and when he once obtained his hold he was seldom shaken off until in his old age when he lost his teeth. Even then he was always one of the first to seize. Although comparatively useless, the spirit was ever willing; and this courage, poor fellow, at length caused his death.

The next dog who claims a tribute to his memory is "Killbuck." He was an Australian greyhound of the most extraordinary courage. He stood at the shoulder 28 inches high; girth of brisket, 31 inches.

Instead of the surly and ferocious disposition of "Smut," he was the most gentle and affectionate creature. It was a splendid sight to witness the bounding spring of Killbuck as he pinned an elk at bay that no other dog could touch. He had a peculiar knack of seizing that I never saw equalled: no matter where or in what position an elk might be, he was sure to have him. When once started from the slips it was certain death to the animal he coursed, and even when out of view, and the elk had taken to the jungle, I have seen the dog, with his nose to the ground, following upon the scent at full speed like a foxhound. I never heard him bark at game when at bay. With a bulldog courage he would recklessly fly straight at the animal's head, unheeding the wounds received in the struggle. This unguided courage at length caused his death when in the very prime of his life. Poor Killbuck! his was a short but glorious career, and his name will never be forgotten.

Next in rotation in the chronicles of seizers appears "Lena," who is still alive, an Australian bitch of great size, courage, and beauty, wire-haired, like a Scotch deer-hound.

"Bran," a perfect model of a greyhound.

"Lucifer," combining the beauty, speed, and courage of his parents "Bran" and "Lena," in a superlative degree.

There are many others that I could call from the pack and introduce as first-rate hounds, but as no jealousy will be occasioned by their omission, I shall be contented with those already named.

Were I to recount the twentieth part of the scenes that I have witnessed in this sport, it would fill a volume, and become very tedious. A few instances related will at once explain the whole character of the sport, and introduce a stranger to the wild hunts of the Ceylon mountains.

I have already described Newera Ellia, with its alternate plains and forests, its rapid streams and cataracts, its mountains, valleys, and precipices; but a portion of this country, called the Horton Plains, will need a further description.

Some years ago, I hunted with a brother Nimrod, Lieut. De Montenach, of the 15th regiment, in this country; and in two months we killed forty-three elk.

The Horton Plains are about twenty miles from Newera Ellia. After a walk of sixteen miles through alternate plains and forests, the steep ascent of Totapella mountain is commenced by a rugged path through jungle the whole way. So steep is the track that a horse ascends with difficulty, and riding is of course impossible. After a mile and a quarter of almost perpendicular scrambling, the summit of the pass is reached, commanding a splendid view of the surrounding country, and Newera Ellia can be seen far beneath in the distance. Two miles further on, after a walk through undulating forest, the Horton Plains burst suddenly upon the view as you emerge from the jungle path. These plains are nearly 800 feet higher than Newera Ellia, or 7000 feet above the sea. The whole aspect of the country appears at once to have assumed a new character; there is a feeling of being on the top of everything, and instead of a valley among surrounding hills, which is the feature of Newera Ellia and the adjacent plains, a beautiful expanse of flat table-land stretches before the eye, bounded by a few insignificant hill-tops. There is a peculiar freedom in the Horton Plains, an absence from everywhere, a wildness in the thought that there is no tame animal within many miles, not a village, nor hut, nor human being. It makes a man feel in reality one of the "lords of the creation," when he first stands upon this elevated plain, and, breathing the pure thin air, he takes a survey of his hunting-ground: no boundaries but mountain-tops and the horizon; no fences but the trunks of decayed trees fallen from old age; no game laws but strong legs, good wind, and the hunting-knife; no paths but those trodden by the elk and elephant. Every nook and corner of this wild country is as familiar to me as my own garden. There is not a valley that has not seen a burst in full cry; not a plain that has not seen the greyhounds in full speed after an elk; and not a deep pool in the river that has not echoed with a bay that has made the rocks ring again.

To give a person an interest in the sport, the country must be described minutely. The plain already mentioned as the flat table-land first seen on arrival, is about five miles in length and two in breadth in the widest part. This is tolerably level, with a few gentle undulations, and is surrounded, on all sides but one, with low, forest-covered slopes. The low portions of the plains are swamps, from which springs a large river, the source of the Mahawelli Ganga.

From the plain now described about fifteen others diverge, each springing from the parent plain, and increasing in extent as they proceed; these are connected more or less by narrow valleys and deep ravines. Through the greater portion of these plains the river winds its wild course. In the first a mere brook, it rapidly increases as it traverses the lower portions of every valley, until it attains a width of twenty or thirty yards within a mile of the spot where it is first discernible as a stream. Every plain in succession being lower than the first, the course of the river is extremely irregular; now a maze of tortuous windings, then a broad, still stream, bounded by grassy undulations; now rushing wildly through a hundred channels formed by obtruding rocks, then in a still, deep pool, gathering itself together for a mad leap over a yawning precipice, and roaring at a hundred feet beneath, it settles in the lower plain in a pool of unknown depth, and once more it murmurs through another valley.

In the large pools formed by the sudden turns in the river, the elk generally takes his last determined stand, and he sometimes keeps dogs and men at bay for a couple of hours. These pools are generally about sixty yards across, very deep in some parts, with a large shallow sandbank in the centre, formed by the eddy of the river.

We built a hunting bivouac in a snug corner of the plains, which gloried in the name of "Elk Lodge." This famous hermitage was a substantial building, and afforded excellent accommodation: a verandah in the front, twenty-eight feet by eight; a dining-room twenty feet by twelve, with a fire-place eight feet wide; and two bed-rooms of twenty feet by eight. Deer hides were pegged down to form a carpet upon the floors, and the walls were neatly covered with talipot-leaves. The outhouses consisted of the kennel, stables for three horses, kitchen, and sheds for twenty coolies and servants.

The fire-place was a rough piece of art, upon which we prided ourselves extremely. A party of eight persons could have sat before it with comfort. Many a roaring fire has blazed up that rude chimney; and dinner being over, the little round table before the hearth has steamed forth a fragrant attraction, when the nightly bowl of mulled port has taken its accustomed stand. I have spent many happy hours in this said spot; the evenings were of a decidedly social character. The day's hunting over, it was a delightful hour at about seven P. M., — dinner just concluded, the chairs brought before the fire, cigars, and the said mulled port. Eight o'clock was the hour for bed, and five in the morning was the hour to rise, at which time a cup of hot tea and a slice of toast and anchovy paste was always ready before the start. The great man of our establishment was the cook. This knight of the gridiron was a famous fellow, and could perform wonders; of stoical countenance, he was never seen to smile. His whole thoughts were concentrated in the mysteries of gravies, and the magic transformation of one animal into another by the art of cookery: in this he excelled to a marvellous degree. The farce of ordering dinner was always absurd. It was something in this style. "Cook!" (*Cook answers*) "Coming sar!" (*enter cook*).—"Now, cook, you make a good dinner; do you hear?" *Cook:* "Yes, sar: master tell, I make."—"Well, mulligatawny soup." "Yes, sar."—"Calves' head, with tongue, and brain-sauce." "Yes, sar."—"Gravy omelette." "Yes, sar."—"Mutton chops." "Yes, sar."—"Fowl cotelets." "Yes, sar."—"Beefsteaks." "Yes, sar."—"Marrow-bones." "Yes, sar."—"Rissoles." "Yes, sar." All these various dishes he literally imitated uncommonly well, the different portions of an elk being their only foundation.

The kennel bench was comfortably littered, and the pack took possession of their new abode with the usual amount of growling and quarrelling for places; the angry grumbling continuing throughout the night between the three champions of the kennel, Smut, Bran, and Killbuck. After a night much disturbed by this constant quarrelling, we unkennelled the hounds just as the first grey streak of dawn spread above Totapella peak.

The mist was hanging heavily on the lower parts of the plain like a thick snowbank, although the sky was beautifully clear above, in which a few pale stars still glimmered. Long lines of fog were slowly drifting along the bottoms of the valleys, dispelled by a light breeze; and day fast advancing bid fair for sport; a heavy dew lay upon the grass; and we stood for some moments in uncertainty as to the first point of our extensive hunting-grounds that we should beat. There were fresh tracks of elk close to our "lodge," who had been surveying our new settlement during the night. Crossing the river by wading waist deep, we skirted along the banks, winding through a narrow valley with grassy hills capped with forest upon either side. Our object in doing this was to seek for tracks where the elk had come down to drink during the night, as we knew that the tracks would then lead to the jungle upon either side the river. We had strolled quietly along for about half a mile when the loud bark of an elk was suddenly heard in the jungle upon the opposite hills. In a moment the hounds dashed across the river towards the well-known sound, and entered the jungle at full speed. Judging the direction which the elk would most probably take when found, I ran along the bank of the river, down stream, for a quarter of a mile, towards a jungle through which the river flowed previous to its descent into the lower plains, and I waited upon a steep, grassy hill, about a hundred feet above the river's bed. From this spot I had a fine view of the ground. Immediately before me rose the hill from which the elk had barked; beneath my feet the river stretched into a wide pool on its entrance to the jungle. This jungle clothed the precipitous cliffs of a deep ravine, down which the river fell in two cataracts, which were concealed from view by the forest. I waited in breathless expectation of "the find." A few minutes passed, when the sudden burst of the pack in full cry came sweeping down upon the light breeze; loudly the cheering sound swelled as they topped the hill, and again it died away as they crossed some deep ravine. In a few minutes the cry became very distant, as the elk was evidently making straight up the hills: once or twice I feared he would cross them, and make away for a different part of the country. The cry of the pack was so indistinct that my ear could barely catch it, when suddenly a gust of wind from that direction brought down a chorus of voices that there was no mistaking: louder and louder the cry became; the elk had turned, and was coming down the hill-side at a slapping pace. The jungle crashed as he came rushing through the yielding branches. Out he came, breaking cover in fine style, and away he dashed over the open country. He was a noble buck, and had got a long start: not a single hound had yet appeared, but I heard them coming through the jungle in full cry. Down the side of the hill he came straight to the pool beneath my feet. Yoick to him! Hark forward to him! and I gave a view holloa till my lungs had well nigh cracked. I had lost sight of him as he had taken to water in the pool within the jungle.

One more holloa! and out came the gallant old fellow Smut from the jungle, on the exact line that the elk had taken. On he came bounding along the rough side of the hill like a lion, followed by only two dogs, Dan, a pointer (since killed by a leopard), and Cato, a young dog who had never yet seen an elk. The remainder of the pack had taken after a doe that had crossed the scent, and they were now running in a different direction. I now imagined that the elk had gone down the ravine to the lower plains by some run that might exist along the edge of the cliff, and accordingly started off along a deer path through the jungle, to arrive at the lower plains by the shortest road that I could make.

Hardly had I run a hundred yards, when I heard the ringing of the bay and the deep voice of Smut, mingled with the roar of the water-fall, to which I had been running parallel. Instantly changing my course, I was in a few moments on the bank of the river just above the fall. There stood the buck at bay in a large pool about three feet deep, where the dogs could only advance by swimming. Upon my jumping into the pool he broke his bay, and, dashing through the dogs, appeared to leap over the verge of the cataract, but in reality he took to a deer path which skirted the steep side of the wooded precipice. So steep was the inclination that I could only follow on his track by clinging to the stems of the trees. The roar of the waterfall, now only a few feet on my right hand, completely overpowered the voices of the dogs wherever they might be, and I carefully commenced a perilous descent by the side of the fall, knowing that both dogs and elk must be somewhere before me. So stunning was the roar of the water that a cannon might have been fired without my hearing it. I was now one-third of the way down the fall, which was about fifty feet deep. A large flat rock projected from the side of the cliff, forming a platform of about six feet square, over one corner of which the water struck, and again bounded downwards. This platform could only be reached by a narrow ledge of rock, beneath which, at a depth of thirty feet, the water boiled at the foot of the fall. Upon this platform stood the buck, having gained his secure but frightful position by passing along the narrow ledge of rock. Should either dog or man attempt to advance, one charge from the buck would send them to perdition, as they would fall into the abyss below. This the dogs were fully aware of, and they accordingly kept up a continual bay from the edge of the cliff, while I attempted to dislodge him by throwing stones and sticks upon him from above. Finding this uncomfortable, he made a sudden dash forward, and, striking the dogs over, away he went down the steep sides of the ravine, followed once more by the dogs and myself.

By clinging from tree to tree and lowering myself by the tangled creepers, I was soon at the foot of the first fall, which plunged into a deep pool on a flat plateau of rock bounded on either side by a wall-like precipice.

This plateau was about eighty feet in length, through which the water flowed in two rapid but narrow streams from the foot of the first fall towards a second cataract at the extreme end. This second fall leaped from the centre of the ravine into the lower plain.

When I arrived on this fine level surface of rock, a splendid sight presented itself. In the centre of one of the rapid streams the buck stood at bay, belly-deep, with the torrent rushing in foam between his legs. His mane was bristled up, his nostrils were distended, and his antlers were lowered to receive the dog who should first attack him. I happened to have a spear on that occasion, so that I felt he could not escape, and I gave the baying dogs a loud cheer on. Poor Cato! it was his first elk, and he little knew the danger of a buck at bay in such a strong position. Answering with youthful ardour to my holloa, the young dog sprang boldly at the elk's face, but, caught upon the ready antlers, he was instantly dashed senseless upon the rocks. Now for old Smut, the hero of countless battles, who, though pluck to the back-bone, tempers his valour with discretion.

Yoick to him, Smut! and I jumped into the water. The buck made a rush forward, but at that moment a mass of yellow hair dangled before his eyes as the true old dog hung upon his cheek. Now came the tug of war—only one seizer! The spring had been so great, and the position of the buck was so secure, that the dog had missed the ear, and only held by the cheek. The elk, in an instant, saw his advantage, and quickly thrusting his sharp brow antlers into the dog's chest, he reared to his full height and attempted to pin the apparently fated Smut against a rock. That had been the last of Smut's days of prowess had I not fortunately had a spear. I could just reach the elk's shoulder in time to save the dog. After a short but violent struggle, the buck yielded up his *spirit.* He was a noble fellow, and pluck to the last.

Having secured his horns to a bush, lest he should be washed away by the torrent, I examined the dogs. Smut was wounded in two places, but not severely, and Cato had just recovered his senses, but was so bruised as to move with great difficulty. In addition to this, he had a deep wound from the buck's horn, under the shoulder.

The great number of elks at the Horton Plains, and the open character of the country, make the hunting a far more enjoyable sport than it is in Newera Ellia, where the plains are of much smaller extent, and the jungles are frightfully thick. During a trip of two months at the Horton Plains, we killed forty-three elks, exclusive of about ten, which the pack ran into and killed by themselves, bringing home the account of their performances in distended stomachs. These occurrences freqently happen when the elk takes away through an impervious country, through which a man cannot possibly follow. In such cases, the pack is either beaten off, or they pull the elk down and devour it.

This was exemplified some time ago, when the three best dogs were nearly lost. A doe elk broke cover from a small jungle at the Horton Plains, and, instead of taking across the patinas (plains), she doubled back to an immense pathless jungle, closely followed by three greyhounds, Killbuck, Bran, and Lena. The first dog, who ran beautifully by nose, led the way, and their direction was of course unknown, as the dogs were all mute. Night came, and they had not returned. The next day passed away, but without a sign of the missing dogs. I sent natives to search the distant jungles and ravines in all directions. Three days passed away, and I gave up all hope of them. We were sitting at dinner one night, the fire was blazing cheerfully within, but the rain was pouring without, the wind was howling in fitful gusts, and neither moon nor stars relieved the pitchy darkness of the night, when the conversation naturally turned to the poor lost dogs. What a night for the poor brutes to be exposed to, roaming about the wet jungles without a chance of return!

A sudden knock at the door arrested our attention;—it opened. Two natives stood there dripping with wet and shivering with cold. One had in his hand an elk's head, much gnawed; the other man, to my delight, led the three lost dogs. They had run their elk down; and were found by the side of a rocky river several miles distant,—the two dogs asleep in a cave, and the bitch was gnawing the remains of the half-consumed animal. The two men who had found them were soon squatted before a comfortable fire, with a good feed of curry and rice, and their skins full of brandy.

Although the elks are so numerous at the Horton Plains, the sport at length becomes monotonous from the very large proportion of the does. The usual ratio in which they were killed was one buck to eight does. I cannot at all account for this small proportion of bucks in this particular spot. At Newera Ellia they are as two to three, as compared with the does. The following extract of deaths, taken from my game-book during three months of the year, will give a tolerably accurate idea of the number killed.

1852. March 24.	Doe - -	Killed in the Elk Plains.
30.	Two Does	Killed in Newera Ellia Plain.
April 3.	Doe - -	Killed at the foot of Hack Galla.
5.	Buck - -	Killed at the foot of Pedro.
8.	Doe - -	Killed at the top of the Pass.
13.	Buck - -	Killed at the foot of the Pass.

1852. April	16.	Buck - -	Killed in the river at the Pass.
	19.	Doe - -	Killed on the patinas on Badulla road.
	21.	Buck -	Killed in the river at the base of Pedro.
	23.	Buck - -	Killed in Matturatta Plain.
	25.	Doe - -	Killed in the Elk Plains.
	25.	Sow - -	Killed in ditto ditto.
	27.	Boar - -	Killed at the Limestone Quarry.
May	3.	Sow - -	Killed in Elk Plains.
	6.	Two Does	Killed in the Barrack Plain.
	10.	Two Does	One killed in the Barrack Plain, and the other at the bottom of the Pass.
	12.	Buck - -	Killed in Newera Ellia Plain.
	19.	Buck - -	Killed in the Newera Ellia River.
	22.	Doe - -	Killed at the Pioneer Lines—Laboukellé.
	31.	Two Does	Killed in the Barrack Plain.
June	5.	Buck - -	Killed at the foot of Pedro.
	8.	Buck - -	Killed in the Barrack Plain.
	11.	Two Bucks	Killed on Kicklamané Patina.
	24.	Two Does	Killed on Newera Ellia Plain.
	28.	Boar - -	Killed on Elk Plains.
	29.	Doe - -	Killed at "Rest and be thankful" bottom.

Total — 28 Elk, 11 Bucks, 17 Does, and 4 Hogs.

This is a tolerable show of game when it is considered that the sport continues from year to year: there are no seasons at which time the game is spared, but the hunting depends simply on the weather. Three times a week the pack turns out in the dry season, and upon every fine day during the wet months. It must appear a frightful extravagance to English ideas, to feed the hounds upon venison, but as it costs nothing it is a cheaper food than beef, and no other flesh is procurable in sufficient quantity. Venison is in its prime when the elk's horns are in velvet. At this season, when the new antlers have almost attained their full growth, they are particularly tender, and the buck moves slowly and cautiously through the jungle, lest he should injure them against the branches, taking no further exercise than is necessary in the search of food He therefore grows very fat, and is then in fine condition.

The speed of an elk, although great, cannot be compared to that of the spotted deer. I have seen the latter almost distance the best greyhounds for the first two hundred yards, but with this class of dogs the elk has no chance upon fair open ground. Coursing the elk, therefore, is a short-lived sport, as the greyhounds run into him immediately, and a tremendous struggle then ensues, which must be terminated as soon as possible by the knife, otherwise the dogs would most probably be wounded. I once saw Killbuck perform a wonderful feat in seizing. A buck elk broke cover in the Elk Plains, and I slipped a brace of greyhounds after him, Killbuck and Bran. The buck had a start of about two hundred yards, but the speed of the greyhounds told rapidly upon him, and after a course of a quarter of a mile they were at his haunches, Killbuck leading. The next instant he sprang in full fly, and got his hold by the ear. So sudden was the shock that the buck turned a complete sommersault, but, recovering himself immediately, he regained his feet and started off at a gallop down hill towards a stream, the dog still hanging on. In turning over in his fall the ear had twisted round, and Killbuck, never having left his hold, was therefore on his back, in which position he was dragged at great speed over the rugged ground. Notwithstanding the difficulty of his position, he would not give up his hold. In the mean time Bran kept seizing the other ear, but continually lost his hold as the ear gave way. Killbuck's weight kept the buck's head on a level with his knees; and after a run of some hundred yards, during the whole of which the dog had been dragged upon his back without once losing his hold, the elk's pace was reduced to a walk. With both greyhounds now hanging on his ears, the buck reached the river, and he and the dogs rolled down the steep bank into the deep water. I came up just at this moment and killed the elk, but both dogs were frightfully wounded, and for some time I despaired of their recovery.

This was an extraordinary feat in seizing; but Killbuck was matchless in this respect, and accordingly of great value, as he was sure to retain his hold when he once got it. This is an invaluable qualification in a dog, especially with boars, as any uncertainty in the dog's hold renders the advance of the man doubly dangerous. I have frequently seen hogs free themselves from a dog's hold at the very moment that I have put the knife into them: this with a large boar is likely to cause an accident.

I once saw a Veddah who nearly lost his life by one of these animals. He was hunting "guanas" (a species of large lizard which is eaten by all the natives), with several small dogs, and they suddenly found a large boar, who immediately stood to bay. The Veddah advanced to the attack with his bow and arrows; but he had no sooner wounded the beast than he was suddenly charged with great fury. In an instant the boar was into him, and the next moment the Veddah was lying on the ground with his bowels out. Fortunately a companion was with him, who replaced his entrails and bandaged him up. I saw the man some years after; he was perfectly well, but he had a frightful swelling in the front of the belly, traversed by a wide blue scar of about eight inches in length.

A boar is at all times a desperate antagonist, where the hunting knife and dogs are the only available weapons. The largest that I ever killed weighed four hundredweight. I was out hunting accompanied by my youngest brother. We had walked through several jungles without success, but on entering a thick jungle in the Elk Plains, we immediately noticed the fresh ploughings of an immense boar. In a few minutes we heard the pack at bay without a run, and, shortly after, a slow running bay — there was no mistake as to our game. He disdained to run, and, after walking before the pack for about three minutes, he stood to a determined bay. The jungle was frightfully thick, and we hastily tore our way through the tangled underwood towards the spot. We had two stanch dogs by our side, Lucifer and Lena, and when within twenty paces of the bay we gave them a holloa on. Away they dashed to the invisible place of conflict, and we almost

SKETCHED BY [illegible]   M & N HANHART IMP[T]   J. BRANDARD LITH

immediately heard the fierce grunting and roaring of the boar. We knew that they had him, and scrambled through the jungle as fast as we could towards the field of battle. There was a fight! the underwood was levelled, and the boar rushed to and fro with Smut, Bran, Lena, and Lucifer, all upon him. Yoick to him! and some of the most daring of the maddened pack went in. The next instant we were upon him mingled with a confused mass of hounds, and throwing our whole weight upon the boar, we gave him repeated thrusts, apparently to little purpose. Round came his head and gleaming tusks to the attack of his fresh enemies, but old Smut held him by the nose, and, although the bright tusks were immediately buried in his throat, the stanch old dog kept his hold. Away went the boar covered by a mass of dogs, and bearing the greater part of our weight in addition, as we hung on to the hunting knives buried in his shoulders. For about fifty paces he tore through the thick jungle, crashing it like a cobweb. At length he again halted; the dogs, the boar, and ourselves were mingled in a heap of confusion. All covered with blood and dirt, our own cheers added to the wild bay of the infuriated hounds, and the savage roaring of the boar. Still he fought and gashed the dogs right and left. He stood about thirty-eight inches high, and the largest dogs seemed like puppies beside him; still not a dog relaxed his hold, and he was covered with wounds. I made a lucky thrust for the nape of his neck. I felt the point of the knife touch the bone; the spine was divided, and he fell dead.

Smut had two severe gashes in the throat, Lena was cut under the ear, and Bran's mouth was opened completely up to his ear in a horrible wound. The dogs were completely exhausted, and lay panting around their victim. We cut off the boar's head, and, slinging it upon a pole, we each shouldered an end and carried it to the kennel. The power of this animal must have been immense. My brother's weight and mine, together being upwards of twenty-four stone, in addition to that of half-a-dozen heavy dogs, did not appear to trouble him, and had we not been close to the spot when he came to bay, so that the knives came to the instant succour of the dogs, he would have most probably killed or wounded half the pack.

In this wild and rough kind of sport the best dogs are constantly most seriously wounded, and after a fight of this kind needles and thread and bandages are in frequent requisition. It is wonderful to see the rapid recovery of dogs from wounds which at first sight appear incurable. An instance occurred a short time ago, when I certainly gave up one of the best dogs for lost. We had found a buck, who after a sharp run came to bay in a deep part of the river known by the name of Black Pool. My youngest brother (who is always my companion in hunting) and I were at some distance, but feeling certain of the locality of the bay, we started off at full speed towards the supposed spot. A run of a mile, partly through jungle leading into a deep wooded ravine, brought us to the river, which flowed through the hollow, and upon approaching the water we distinctly heard the pack at bay at some distance down the stream. Before we could get up, the buck dashed down the river, and turning sharp up the bank he took up the hill through a dense jungle. Every hound was at fault, except two, who were close at his heels, and being very fast they never lost sight of him. These two dogs were Merriman and Tiptoe; and having followed the whole pack to their track, we soon heard them in full cry on the top of the high hills which overlook the river; they were coming down the hill-side at full speed towards the Black Pool. Hiding behind the trees lest we should head the buck, who we now heard crashing towards us through the jungle, we suddenly caught a glimpse of his dun hide as he bounded past us and splashed into the river. A few seconds after, and Tiptoe, the leading hound, came rushing on his track, but to our horror *he was dragging his entrails after him.* The excitement of the chase recognised no pain, and the plucky animal actually plunged into the river, and in spite of his mangled state he swam across and disappeared in the jungle on the opposite side upon the track which the elk had taken. The pack now closed up, and swimming the river they opened upon a hot scent on the opposite bank, and running parallel to the stream they drove the buck out of the jungle, and he came to bay in a rocky part of the river where the velocity of the torrent swept every dog past him and rendered his position secure. The whole pack was there with the exception of Tiptoe; we looked for him among the baying hounds in vain. For about twenty minutes the buck kept his impregnable position, when in a foolish moment he forsook it, and dashing along the torrent he took to deep water. The whole pack was after him; once Merriman got a hold, but was immediately beaten off. Valiant, who was behaving nobly, and made repeated attempts to seize, was struck beneath the water as often as he advanced. The old veteran Smut was well to the point, and his deep voice was heard loud above the din of the bay; but he could do nothing. The buck had a firm footing, and was standing shoulder-deep; rearing to his full height, and, springing at the dogs as they swam towards him, he struck them beneath the water with his fore-feet. The bay lasted for half an hour; at the expiration of this time a sudden thought appeared to strike old Smut: instead of continuing the attack he swam direct for the shore, leaving the buck still occupied with the baying pack. The elk was standing about fourteen feet from the bank, which was covered with jungle. Presently we saw the cunning old hero Smut creeping like a leopard along the edge of the bank till opposite the elk; he slowly retreated for a few paces, and the next moment he was seen flying through the air, having made a tremendous spring at the elk's ear. A cloud of spray for an instant concealed the effect. Both dog and buck were for a few moments beneath the water; when they re-appeared, the old dog was hanging on his ear. Merriman at once had him by the other ear; and one after another the seizers had him. In vain he tried to drown them off by diving; as his head again rose above the surface the dogs were at their places: his struggles were useless, and the knife finished him.

We now searched the jungle for Tiptoe's body, expecting to find him dead where we had last seen him enter the jungle. Upon reaching the spot we found him lying down with his bowels in a heap by his side; the quantity would have filled a hat. The hole in his side was made by a blow from the buck's hoof, and not being more than two inches in length strangulation had taken place, and I could not return the bowels. The dog was still alive, though very faint. Fortunately we had a small-bladed knife, with which I carefully enlarged the aperture, and, having cleaned the bowels from the dirt and dead leaves which had adhered to them, I succeeded in returning them, although I expected the dog's death every instant. Taking off my neck-tie, I made a pad, with which I secured the aperture, and bound him tightly round with a handkerchief. Making a sling with a couple of jackets upon a pole, we placed the dog carefully within it and carried him home. By dressing the wound every day with margosse oil, and keeping the pad and bandage in the place, to my astonishment the dog recovered, and he is now as well as ever he was, with the exception of the loss of one eye, which was knocked out by the horn of an elk on another occasion.

The margosse oil that I have mentioned is a most valuable balsam for wounds, having a peculiar smell, which prevents the attacks of flies, who would otherwise blow the wound and occasion a nest of maggots in a few hours. This oil is very healing, and soon creates a healthy appearance in a bad cut. It is manufactured from the fruit of a plant in Ceylon, but I have never met with it in the possession of an English medical man. The smell of this oil is very offensive, even worse than assafœtida, which it in some degree resembles. There are many medicinal plants in Ceylon of great value, which, although made use of by the natives, are either neglected or unknown to the profession in our own country. One of the wild fruits of the jungle, the wood-apple or wild quince, is very generally used by the natives in attack of diarrhœa and dysentery in the early stages of the disease; this has been used for some years by English medical men in this island, but with no very satisfactory effect.

CHAP. IX.

A MORNING'S DEER COURSING.—KONDAWATAWENY.—ROGUE AT KONDAWATAWENY.—A CLOSE SHAVE.—PREPARATIONS FOR CATCHING AN ELEPHANT.—CATCHING AN ELEPHANT.—TAMING HIM.—FLYING SHOT AT A BUCK.—CAVE AT DIMBOOLDÉNÉ.—AWKWARD GROUND.—A CHARMED LIFE.

It was in July 1848, that I pitched my tent in the portion of Ceylon known as the "Park," for the purpose of deer coursing. I had only three greyhounds, Killbuck, Bran, and Lena, and these had been carried in a palanquin from Newera Ellia, a distance of one hundred miles. The grass had all been burnt about two months previously, and the whole country was perfectly fresh and green, the young shoots not being more than half a foot high. The deer were numerous but wild, which made the sport the more enjoyable. I cannot describe the country better than by comparing it to a rich English park, well watered by numerous streams and large rivers, but ornamented by many beautiful rocky mountains, which are not to be met with in England. If this part of the country had the advantage of the Newera Ellia climate it would be a Paradise, but the intense heat destroys much of the pleasure in both shooting and coursing, especially in the latter sport, as the greyhounds must be home by 8 A. M., or they would soon die from the effects of the sun.

It was in the cool hour of sunrise, when the deer lay thickly upon the grass, and the foliage glistened with the first beams of morning, that we stalked over the extensive plains with Killbuck and Lena in the slips in search of deer. Several herds winded us at a distance of half a mile, and immediately bounded away, rendering pursuit impossible; and we determined not to slip the dogs unless they had a fair start, as one run in this climate was quite work enough for a morning. After several disappointments in stalking, we at length discovered a noble buck standing alone by the edge of a narrow belt of jungle; the instant that he observed us, he stepped proudly into the cover. This being open forest, my brother took the greyhounds in at the spot where the deer had entered, while I ran round to the opposite side of the cover, and took my position upon an extensive lawn of fine grass about half a mile in width.

I had not remained a minute at my post before

I heard a crash in the jungle, as though an elephant were charging through, and in another instant a splendid buck burst upon the plain at full speed, and away he flew over the level lawn with the brace of greyhounds laying out about fifty paces behind him. Here was a fair trial of speed over a perfect bowling green, and away they flew, the buck exerting his utmost stride, and the greyhounds stetching out till their briskets touched the ground; Killbuck leading with tremendous bounds, and Lena about a length behind him.

By degrees the beautiful spring of the greyhounds appeared to tell, and the distance between them and the buck gradually decreased, although both deer and dogs flew along with undiminished speed. The plain was nearly crossed, and the opposite jungle lay within two hundred yards of them. To gain this the buck redoubled his exertions: the greyhounds knew as well as he did, that it was his chance of escape, and with equal efforts they pressed upon him. Not fifty paces now separated the buck from the jungle, and with prodigious bounds he sped along; he neared it, he won it; the yielding branches crashed before him, but the dogs were at his haunches as the jungle closed over them and concealed the chase.

I was soon up; and upon entering the jungle I could neither hear nor see anything of them, but, by following up the track, I found them about fifty yards from the entrance to the jungle. The buck was standing on the sandy bed of a dry stream, endeavouring in vain to free himself, while the greyhounds pinned his nose to the ground, each hanging upon his ears. The knife finished him immediately. There never was a more exciting course; it had been nobly run by both the dogs and well contested by the buck, who was a splendid fellow and in fine condition.

On my way to the tent, I wounded a doe at full speed, which Lena followed singly and pulled down, thus securing our coolies a good supply of venison. The flesh of the spotted deer is more like mutton than English venison, and is excellent eating; it would be still better if the climate would allow of its being kept for a few days.

There is no sport in Ceylon, in my opinion, that is equal to deer-coursing, but the great difficulty attending it is the lack of good greyhounds. The spotted buck (or axis) is an animal of immense power and courage; and although most greyhounds would course him, very few would have sufficient courage and strength to hold him, unless slipped two brace at a time, which would immediately spoil the sport. A brace of greyhounds to one buck is fair play, and a good strong horse will generally keep them in view. In two weeks' coursing in the Park we killed seventeen deer with three greyhounds; at the expiration of which time the dogs were so foot-sore and wounded by the hard burnt stubble of the old grass, that they were obliged to be sent home.

When the greyhounds had left, I turned my attention to elephants. There were very few at this season in the Park, and I therefore left this part of the country, which was dried up, and proceeded to Kondawataweny, in the direction of Batticaloa. Kondawataweny is a small village, inhabited by Moormen, situated on the edge of a large lake or tank. Upon arrival, I found that the neighbourhood was alive with game of all kinds, and the Moormen were excellent hands at elephants. There was accordingly no difficulty in procuring good gun-bearers and trackers, and at 4 P. M. of the day of our arrival we started to make a circuit of the tank in quest of elephants. At about 5 P. M. we observed several tank rogues scattered in various directions around the tank; one of these fellows, whose close acquaintance I made with the telescope, I prophesied would show some fight before we owned his tail. This elephant was standing some distance in the water feeding and bathing. There were two elephants close to the water's edge between him and us, and we determined to have a shot at them *en passant*, and then try to bag the big fellow.

Although we stalked very cautiously along the edge of the jungle which surrounded the lake, divided from it by a strip of plain of about two hundred yards in width, the elephants winded us and retreated over the patina* at full speed towards the jungle. Endeavouring to cut them off before they could reach the thick cover, we ran at our best pace along the edge of the jungle, so as to meet them at right-angles. One reached the jungle before us, but a lucky shot at a distance of sixty paces floored the other, who lay struggling on the ground, and was soon extinguished. Having reloaded, we went in quest of the large rogue, who was bathing in the tank. This gentleman had decamped, having taken offence at the firing.

Close to the edge of the tank grew a patch of thick thorny jungle of about two acres, completely isolated and separated from the main jungle by

* Grassy plains.

about eighty paces' length of fine turf. The Moormen knew the habits of this rogue, who was well known in the neighbourhood, and they at once said that he had concealed himself in the small patch of jungle. Upon examining the tracks from the tank we found they were correct.

The question was, how to dislodge him; the jungle was so dense that it was impossible to enter, and driving was the only chance.

There was a small bush within a few paces of the main jungle, exactly opposite that in which the elephant was concealed, and we determined to hide hehind this while a few Moormen should endeavour to drive him from his retreat, in which case he would be certain to make for the main forest, and would most probably pass near the bush behind which we lay in wait for him. Giving the Moormen a gun, we took to our hiding-place. The men went round to the tank side of the patch of jungle, and immediately commenced shouting and firing, securing themselves from an attack by climbing into the highest trees. A short interval elapsed, and not a sound of the elephant could be heard. The firing and shouting ceased, and all was as still as death. Some of the Moormen returned from the jungle, and declared that the elephant was not there; but this was all nonsense; the fact was they did not like the idea of driving him out. Knowing the character of these "rogues," I felt convinced that he was one of the worst description, and that he was quietly waiting his time until some one should advance within his reach. Having given the Moormen a supply of powder, I again despatched them to drive the jungle. Once more the firing and shouting commenced, and continued until their supply of powder was exhausted: no effects had been produced; it was getting late, and the rogue appeared determined not to move. A dead silence ensued, which was presently disturbed by the snapping of a bough; in another moment the jungle crashed, and forth stepped the object of our pursuit. He was a magnificent elephant, one of the most vicious in appearance that I have ever seen; he understood the whole affair as well as we did; and flourishing his trunk, he paced quickly backwards and forwards for a few turns before the jungle he had just quitted, and, suddenly making his resolution, he charged straight at the bush behind which we had imagined ourselves concealed. He was about eighty yards off when he commenced his onset; and seeing that we were discovered, I left the hiding-place and stepped to the front of the bush to meet him with the four-ounce rifle. On he came at a great pace, carrying his head very high, and making me the sole object of his attack. I made certain of the shot, although his head was in a difficult position, and I accordingly waited for him till he was within fifteen paces. At this distance I took a steady shot and fired. A cloud of smoke, from the heavy charge of powder, obscured everything, but I felt so certain that he was down, that I looked under the smoke to see where he lay. Ye Gods! he was just over me in full charge! I had not even checked him by the shot, and he was within three feet of me, going at a tremendous pace. Throwing my heavy rifle into the bush, I doubled quickly to one side, hoping that he would pass me, and take to the main jungle, to which I ran parallel as fast as my legs could carry me. Instead of taking to the jungle, he turned short and quickly after me, and a fair race commenced. I had about three feet start of him, and I saw with delight that the ground was as level and smooth as a lawn; there was no fear of tripping up, and away I went at the fastest pace that I ever ran either before or since, taking a look behind me to see how the chase went on. I saw the bullet-mark in his forehead, which was covered with blood; his trunk was stretched to its full length to catch me, and was now within two feet of my back: he was gaining on me, although I was running at a tremendous pace. I could not screw an inch more speed out of my legs, and I kept on, with the brute gaining upon me at every stride. He was within a foot of me, and I had not heard a shot fired, and not a soul had come to the rescue. The sudden thought struck me that my brother could not possibly overtake the elephant at the pace at which we were going, and I suddenly doubled short to my left into the open plain, and back towards the guns. The rogue overshot me. I met my brother close to his tail, which position he had with difficulty maintained; but he could not get a shot, and the elephant turned into the jungle and disappeared just as I escaped him by a sharp turn. This was a close shave; had not the ground been perfectly level, I must have been caught to a certainty, and even as it was he would have had me in another stride, had I not turned from my straight course. It was nearly dark, and we returned to the tent, killing several peacocks and ducks on our way, with which the country swarmed.

We passed a miserable night, not being able to

sleep on account of the musquitos, which were in swarms. I was delighted to see the first beam of morning, when our little winged enemies left us, and a "chatty" bath was most enjoyable after the restless tossings of a sleepless night. The Moormen were out at dawn to look for elephants, the guns were cleaned, and I looked forward to the return of the trackers with peculiar interest, as we had determined to "*catch an elephant.*" The Moormen were full of excitement and preparation. These men were well practised in this sport, and they were soon busied in examining and coiling their hide ropes for the purpose.

At about mid-day the trackers returned, having found a herd about five miles from the village. We were all ready, and we set off without a moment's delay, our party consisting of my brother, myself, four gun-bearers, and about thirty Moormen, each of whom carried a coil of finely twisted rope made of thongs of raw deer's hide: these ropes were each twenty yards in length, and about an inch in diameter.

Having skirted the borders of the tank for about three miles, we turned into the forest, and continued our route through alternate open and thick forests, until we at length reached a rough open

SKETCHED BY S. W. BAKER. M & N. HANHART IMP. J. BRANDARD LITH.

STALKING A HERD.

country interspersed with low jungles. Here we met the watchers, who reported the herd to be a few hundred paces from us, in some patches of thick jungle. Taking the wind, we carefully approached their position. The ground was very rough, being a complete city of ant-hills, about two feet high; these were overgrown with grass, giving the open country an appearance of a vast churchyard of turf graves. Among these tumps grew numerous small clusters of bushes, above which we shortly discovered the flapping ears of the elephants; they were slowly feeding towards the more open ground. It was a lovely afternoon, the sky was covered with a thin grey cloud, and the sun had little or no power. Hiding behind a bush, we watched the herd for some time, until they had all quitted the bushes, and were well out in the open. There were two elephants facing us, and the herd, which consisted of seven, were tolerably close together, with the exception of one, who was about thirty yards apart from the main body; this fellow we determined to catch. We therefore arranged that our gun-bearers and four rope-carriers should accompany us, while the remaining portion of our party should lie in reserve to come to our assistance when required, as so large a body of men could not possibly stalk the herd without being discovered. Falling upon our hands and knees, we crept between the grassy ant-hills towards the two leading elephants, who were facing us. The wind was pretty brisk, and the ant-hills effectually concealed us till we were within seven paces of our game. The two leaders then both dropped dead to the front shot, and the fun began. The guns were so well handed up that we knocked over the six elephants before they had given us a run of twenty yards, and we all closed up and ran under the tail of the retreating elephant that we devoted to the ropes. He was going at about seven miles an hour; we therefore had no difficulty in keeping up with him, as we could run between the ant-hills much faster than he could. The ropes were in readiness, and with great dexterity one of the Moormen slipped a noose over one of his hind feet as he raised it from the ground, and drawing it tight, he dropped his coil. We all halted and allowed the unconscious elephant to run out his length of line; this he soon did, and the rope trailed after him like a long snake, we all following at about the centre of the length of rope or twenty paces behind him. He was making for the jungle, which was not far distant, and we were running him like a pack of hounds, but keeping a gun in readiness lest he should turn and charge. He at length reached the wooded bank of a dry river, and thick rattan jungle bordered the opposite side; he thought he was safe, and he plunged down the crumbling bank. We were a little too quick for him, by taking a double turn round a tree with the slack end of the rope just as he descended the bank; the effect of this was to bring him to a sudden stand-still, and the stretching of the hide rope threw him upon his knees. He recovered himself immediately, and used extraordinary efforts to break the rope: tightening the rope to its utmost length, he suddenly lifted up his tied leg and threw his whole weight forward. Any but a hide rope of that diameter must have given way, but this stretched like a harp-string, and, at every effort to break it, the yielding elasticity of the hide threw him upon his head, and the sudden contraction after the fall jerked his leg back to its full length.

After many vain but tremendous efforts to free himself, he turned his rage upon his pursuers, and charged every one right and left; but he was safely tied, and we took some little pleasure in teasing him. He had no more chance than a fly in a spider's web. As he charged in one direction several nooses were thrown round his hind-legs; then his trunk was caught in a slip-knot, then his fore-legs, then his neck, and the ends of all these ropes being brought together and hauled tight, he was effectually hobbled.

This had taken some time to effect (about half an hour), and we now commenced a species of harness to enable us to drive him to the village.

The first thing was to secure his trunk by tying it to one of his fore-legs; this leg was then fastened with a slack rope to one of his hind-legs, which prevented him from taking a longer stride than about two feet; his neck was then tied to his other fore-leg, and two ropes were made fast to both his fore and hind-legs; the ends of these ropes being manned by thirty men.

Having completed these arrangements, he was released from the ties which hobbled him, and we commenced the arduous task of driving him towards the village, a distance of five miles. The only method of getting him along was to keep two men to tease him in front, by shouting and waving cloths before his face; he immediately charged these fellows, who, of course, ran in the right direction for the village; and by this repeated manœuvre we reached the borders of the tank by nightfall. We were still at least two miles from the village, and we were therefore obliged to tie him to a tree for the night. The next morning we succeeded in driving him to the village. He was a fine elephant, but not full-grown, and for this reason he had been selected from the herd for capture, as they are more valuable at this particular period of their growth, being more easily rendered docile than when older. He was about sixteen years of age; and by starving for two days and subsequent gentle treatment, the natives mounted and rode him on the third day of his capture, taking the precaution, however, of first securing his trunk. This elephant was then worth fifteen pounds to be sold to the Arabs for the Indian market.

After a stay of a few days in this neighbourhood, during which we had good sport in elephant-shooting, we returned to the Park country. The first evening of our return we heard elephants roaring in the jungle, within a short distance of the tent. At daybreak the next morning we were on their tracks, and after a walk of five miles, we found them in thick thorny jungle, and only killed three. We had a long day's work, and we were returning home in the afternoon, when we suddenly observed a herd of deer grazing in the beautiful park. The headman of this part of the country is a first-rate sportsman, and has always accompanied me in shooting through this district. This man, whose name is Banda, is the only Cingalese that I have ever seen who looks like a man of good birth in his nation. Strikingly handsome and beautifully proportioned, with the agility of a deer, he is in all respects the *beau ideal* of a native hunter. His skill in tracking is superb, and his thorough knowledge of the habits of all Ceylon animals, especially of elephants, renders him a valuable ally to a sportsman. He and I commenced a careful stalk, and after a long circuit I succeeded in getting within seventy paces of the herd of deer. The ground was undulating, and they were standing on the top of a low ridge of hills. I dropped a buck with my two-ounce rifle, and the herd immediately disappeared behind the top of the hill. Taking one of my double-barrelled rifles, which Banda gave me, I ran to the top of the hill as fast as I could, just in time to see the herd going at a flying speed along a small valley at a long distance. Another buck was separated from the herd by about forty paces, and putting up the second sight of my rifle, I took a shot at him; to my delight he plunged heavily upon the turf. I fired my remaining barrel at the herd, but I must have missed, as none fell. I immediately stepped the distance to the dead buck, one hundred and eighty-seven paces. I had fired a little too high, and had missed his body, but the ball had struck him in the neck and broke his spine. A successful flying shot at this distance has a very pretty effect, and Banda was delighted.

There were very few elephants at this season at the Park, and the numberless "ticks," which swarmed in the grass, spoiled all the pleasure of shooting. These little wretches, which are not larger than a small grain of gunpowder, find their way to every part of the body, and the irritation of their bites is indescribable. Scratching is only adding fuel to fire; there is no certain prevention or relief from their attacks; the best thing that I know is cocoa-nut oil rubbed daily over the whole body, but the remedy is almost as unpleasant as the bite. Ceylon is, at all times, a frightful place for vermin: in the dry weather we have ticks; in the wet weather musquitos, and, what are still more disgusting, "leeches," which swarm in the grass and upon the leaves of the jungle. These creatures insinuate themselves through all the openings in a person's dress, — up the trowsers, under the waistcoat, down the neck, up the wrists, and in fact everywhere drawing blood with insatiable voracity, and leaving an unpleasant irritation for some days after.

All these annoyances form great drawbacks to the enjoyment of the low-country sports; although they are afterwards forgotten, and the bright moments of the sport are all that are looked back to, they are great discomforts at the time. When the day is over, and the man, fatigued by intense heat and a hard day's work, feels himself refreshed by a bath and a change of clothes, the incurable itching of a thousand tick-bites destroys all his pleasure, he finds himself streaming with blood from leech-bites, and for the time he feels disgusted with the country. First-rate sport can alone compensate for all these annoyances.

There is a portion of the Park country known as Dimbooldéné. In this part there is a cave formed by a large overhanging rock, which is a much cooler residence than the tent. Here we accordingly bivouacked, the cave being sufficiently large to contain the horses in addition to ourselves and servants. After a delightfully cool night free from musquitos we made a day of it, but we walked from sunrise till five P. M. without seeing a sign of an elephant. At length, from the top of a high hill on the very confines of the Park country, we looked across a deep valley, and with the assistance of the telescope we plainly distinguished a large single elephant feeding on the grassy side of an opposite mountain. To cross the deep valley that separated us and to ascend the mountain would have taken several hours, and at this time of the day it was, therefore, impracticable; we were thus compelled to turn our backs upon the game and return towards our rocky home. Tired more from our want of success than from the day's work, we strolled leisurely along, and we were talking of the best plan to be adopted for the next day's work when I suddenly observed a herd of eight elephants going up the side of a small hill at their best pace within two hundred yards of us. They had just quitted a small jungle at the bottom of a ravine, and they had been alarmed by our approach.

Off we started in pursuit, down the rugged side

of the hill we were descending, and up the opposite hill, upon the elephants' tracks, as hard as we could run. Just as we reached the top of the hill the elephants were entering a small jungle on the other side. My brother got a shot and killed the last of the herd; in another moment they had disappeared. It had been a sharp burst up the steep hill, and we stopped to breathe, but we were almost immediately in pursuit again as we saw the herd emerge from the jungle at the base of the hill and plough their way through a vast field of high lemon-grass.

Upon arriving on their tracks they had fairly distanced us. The grass, which was as thick as a hedge, was trodden into lanes by the elephants, and upon either side it stood like a wall ten or twelve feet high. Upon these tracks we ran along for some time until it became dusk. We halted and were consulting as to the prudence of continuing the chase at this late hour when we suddenly heard the cracking of the branches in a small jungle in a hollow close to our left, and upon taking a position upon some rising ground we distinctly saw several elephants standing in the high grass about a hundred paces before us close to the edge of the jungle in which the remaining portion of the herd were concealed. Two of the elephants were looking at us, and as there was no time to lose we walked straight up to them. They stood quietly watching us till we were within twenty yards, when they came a few paces forward; one immediately falling dead to my shot, while the other was turned by a shot from my brother; the rest retreated to the jungle over the most difficult ground for both man and beast. Immense rocks lay scattered in heaps over the surface of the ground, forming chasms by the intervening crevices of five and six feet in depth; from these crevices the long lemon-grass grew in dense tufts, completely hiding the numerous pitfalls, and making the retreat of the elephants and our pursuit equally difficult. I was close to the tail of a large elephant, who was picking his way carefully over the treacherous surface, and I was waiting for an opportunity for a shot should he turn his head, when I suddenly pitched head first into one of these rocky holes. Here I scrambled for some seconds before I could extricate myself, as I was carrying my heavy four-once rifle; and at length, upon recovering my footing, I found that all the elephants had gained the jungle, except the one that I had been following. He was about twenty yards from me, and was just entering the jungle, but I got a splendid shot at him behind the ear and rolled him over.

It was very nearly dark, and we could not of course follow the herd any further, we therefore reloaded and turned towards the direction of the cave, which was plainly shown by a distant blaze of light from the night fires, which were already lit. We were walking slowly along parallel to the jungle, into which the elephants had retreated, when my man Wallace, who is a capital gun-bearer, holloed out "Here comes an elephant," and in the dim twilight I could see an elephant bowling along at a great pace towards us, but close to the jungle. He was forty yards from me, but my brother fired at him and without effect. I took a quick shot with a double-barrelled rifle, and he dropped immediately. Hearing him roar as he lay in the high lemon-grass by the edge of the jungle, I ran down the gentle slope to the spot, followed by my trusty gun-bearer Wallace, as I knew the elephant was only stunned and would soon recover. Upon arriving within a few feet of the spot, pushing my way with difficulty through the tangled lemon-grass I could not see where he lay, as daylight had now vanished. I was vainly looking about when I suddenly heard a rush in the grass close to me, and I saw the head and cocked ears of the elephant within six feet as he came at me. I had just time to fire my remaining barrel, and down he dropped to the shot. I jumped back a few paces to assure myself of the result, as the smoke hanging in the high grass, added to the darkness, completely blinded me. Wallace pushed the spare rifle into my hand, and to my astonishment I saw the head and cocked ears again coming at me. It was so dark that I could not take an aim, but I floored him once more by a front shot, and again I jumped back through the tangled grass just in time to avoid him, as he, for the third time, recovered himself and charged. He was not five paces from me, and I took a steady shot at him with my last barrel, and I immediately bolted as hard as I could run. This shot once more floored him, but he must have borne a charmed life, as he again recovered his legs, and to my great satisfaction he turned into the jungle and retreated. This all happened in a few seconds; had it been daylight I could, of course, have killed him, but, as it happened, I could not even distinguish the sights at the end of my rifle. In a few minutes afterwards it was pitch dark, and we could only steer for the cave by the light of the fire, which was nearly two miles distant.

The next day we found a herd of eight elephants in very favourable ground, and succeeded in killing seven; but this was the last herd in the Park, and after a few days spent in beating up the country without success, I returned to Newera Ellia, the bag being twenty-two elephants during a trip of three weeks, in addition to deer, hogs, buffalo, and small game, which had afforded excellent sport.

CHAP. X.

ANOTHER TRIP TO THE PARK. — A HARD DAY'S WORK. — DISCOVER A HERD.—DEATH OF THE HERD.—A FURIOUS CHARGE. — CAUGHT AT LAST. — THE CONSEQUENCES. — A THOROUGH ROGUE. — ANOTHER HERD IN HIGH LEMON-GRASS. — BEARS. —A FIGHT BETWEEN A MOORMAN AND A BEAR.—A MUSICAL HERD.—HERD ESCAPE.—A PLUCKY BUCK.—DEATH OF KILL-BUCK. — GOOD SPORT WITH A HERD. — END OF THE TRIP.

ABOUT twelve months elapsed without my pulling a trigger. I had contented myself with elk-hunting in Newera Ellia and the vicinity, but in November, 1850, the greyhounds were again in their palanquin, and, accompanied by my brother V., I was once more in the saddle on my steady-going old horse Jack, *en route* for the Park.

It was 5 P. M., on a cool and lovely evening, that we halted and unsaddled in this beautiful country. Our tents and coolies were far behind, our horse-keepers were our only attendants, and we fixed upon a spot as the most eligible site for the tents. A large open park lay before us interspersed with trees and clumps of forest. A clear stream flowed from some low rocky hills upon our right, and several detached masses of rock lay scattered irregularly here and there, like the ruins of an old castle. Large trees grew from the crevices of these rocks, and beneath their shade we turned our horses loose to graze upon a soft sweet grass with which this part of the park is covered. We had the greyhounds with us and a single rifle, but no other guns, as the servants were far behind. Having given directions to the horsekeepers to point out the spot for the tents on the arrival of the people, we took a stroll with the greyhounds to get a deer, as we depended upon this chance for our dinner.

Just as we were starting, we noticed two large elephants feeding on the rocky hills within a quarter of a mile of us; but having no guns up with the exception of one rifle, we were obliged to postpone the attack, and, cautioning the horsekeepers to observe silence lest the game should be alarmed, we left the elephants to their meal, while we struck off in another direction with the greyhounds. We found a herd of deer within half a mile of our starting place; they had just come out from the forest for the night's feeding; and when I first saw them, they were barking to each other in a small glade within sixty paces of the jungle. Dinner depending upon success, I stalked them with the greatest caution. Taking Killbuck and Lena in the slips, I crept from tree to tree without the slightest noise; I had the wind, and if any dogs could kill a deer in the difficult position in which the herd stood, these two dogs I knew would do it. I got within sixty yards of the herd before they observed me, and as they dashed off towards the jungle, I slipped the straining greyhounds. A loud cheer to the dogs confused the herd, and they scattered to the right and left as they gained the forest, the dogs being close up with them, and Killbuck almost at a buck's throat as he reached the jungle. Following as well as I could through the dusky jungle, I shortly heard the cry of a deer, and on arriving at the spot I found Killbuck and Lena with a buck on the ground. No deer had a chance with this wonderful dog Killbuck. When he was once slipped, there was no hope for the game pursued; no matter what the character of the country might be, it was certain death to the deer. We gralloched the buck, and having fed the dogs with the offal, we carried him on a pole to the place where we had left the horses. On arrival we deposited our heavy burden; and to our satisfaction we found all our people had arrived.

The tents were pitched, and the night fires were already blazing as daylight had nearly ceased.

In the course of an hour we were comfortably seated at our table with venison steaks and chops smoking before us, thanks to the dogs who were now soundly sleeping at our feet. During the progress of dinner, I planned the work for the day following. We were now eight miles from Niel-galla (Blue Rock), the village at which Banda resided, and I ordered a man to start off at daybreak to tell him that I was in his country, and to bring old Medima and several other good men (that I knew) to the tent without delay. I proposed that we should, in the mean time, start at daylight on the tracks of the two elephants that we had seen upon the hills, taking Wallace and a few of the best coolies as gun-bearers. Wallace is a Cochin man, who prides himself upon a mixture of Portuguese blood. He speaks six different languages fluently, and is without exception the best interpreter and the most plucky gun-bearer that I have ever seen. He has accompanied me through so many scenes with unvarying firmness, that I never have the slightest anxiety about my spare guns if he is there, as he keeps the little troop of gun-bearers in their places in a most methodical manner.

At break of day on the following morning, we were upon the tracks of the two elephants, but a slight shower during the night had so destroyed them, that we found it was impossible to follow them up. We therefore determined to examine the country thoroughly for fresh tracks, and we accordingly passed over many miles of ground, but to little purpose, as none were to be seen.

We at length discovered fresh tracks of a herd in thick thorny jungle, which was too dense to enter, but marking their position, we determined to send out watchers on the following day to track them into better country. Having killed a deer, we started him off with some coolies that we had taken with us on this chance, and we continued our route till 3 P.M. We had lost our way, and, not having any guide, we had no notion of the position of the tents: the heat of the day had been intense, and not having breakfasted, we were rather anxious about the direction. Strolling through this beautiful expanse of park country, we directed our course for a large rocky mountain, at a few miles distance, at the base of which I knew lay the route from the tent to Nielgalla. To our great satisfaction we found the path at about 4 P.M., and we walked briskly along at the foot of the mountain in the direction of our encampment, which was about four miles distant.

We had just arrived at an angle of the mountain, which, in passing, we were now leaving to our left, when we suddenly halted; our attention having been arrested by the loud roaring of elephants in a jungle at the foot of the mountain, within a quarter of a mile of us. The roaring continued at intervals, reverberating among the rocks like distant thunder, till it at length died away to stillness.

We soon arrived in the vicinity of the sound, and shortly discovered tracks upon a hard sandy soil, covered with rocks and overgrown with a low but tolerably open jungle, at the base of the mountain. Following the tracks, we began to ascend steep flights of natural steps formed by the successive layers of rock which girded the foot of the mountain: these were covered with jungle, interspersed with large detached masses of rock, which in some places formed alleys through which the herd had passed. The surface of the ground being nothing but hard rock, tracking was very difficult, and it took me a considerable time to follow them up, by the pieces of twigs and crunched leaves which the elephants had dropped while feeding. I at length tracked them to a small pool formed by the rain-water in the hollow of the rock; here they had evidently been drinking only a few minutes previous, as the tracks of their feet upon the margin of the pool were still wet. I now went on in advance of the party with great caution, as I knew that we were not many paces from the herd. Passing through several passages among the rocks, I came suddenly upon a level plateau of ground covered with dense lemon-grass about twelve feet high, which was so thick and tangled that a man could with difficulty force his way through it. This level space was about two acres in extent, and was surrounded by jungle upon all sides but one; on this side, to our right as we entered, the mountain rose in rocky steps, from the crevices of which the lemon-grass grew in tall tufts.

The instant that I arrived in this spot I perceived the flap of an elephant's ear in the high grass, about thirty paces from me, and upon careful inspection I distinguished two elephants standing close together. By the rustling of the grass in different places I could see that the herd was scattered, but I could not make out the elephants individually, as the grass was above their heads.

I paused for some minutes to consider the best

plan of attack; but the gun-bearers, who were behind me, being in a great state of excitement, began to whisper to each other, and in arranging their positions behind their respective masters, they knocked several of the guns together. In the same moment the two leading elephants discovered us, and throwing their trunks up perpendicularly, they blew the shrill trumpet of alarm without attempting to retreat. Several trumpets answered the call immediately from different positions in the high grass, from which trunks were thrown up and huge heads just appeared in many places, as they endeavoured to discover the danger which the leaders had announced.

The growl of an elephant is exactly like the rumbling of thunder, and from their deep lungs the two leaders, who had discovered us, kept up an uninterrupted peal, thus calling the herd together. Nevertheless, they did not attempt to retreat, but stood gazing attentively at us with their ears cocked, looking extremely vicious. In the meantime, we stood perfectly motionless, lest we should scare them before the whole herd had closed up. In about a minute, a dense mass of elephants had collected round the two leaders, who were all gazing at us; and thinking this a favourable moment, I gave the word, and we pushed towards them through the high grass. A portion of the herd immediately wheeled round and retreated as we advanced, but five elephants, including the two who had first discovered us, formed in a compact line abreast, and thrashing the long grass to the right and left with their trunks, with ears cocked, and tails up, they came straight at us. We pushed on to meet them, but they still came on in a perfect line, till within ten paces of us.

A cloud of smoke hung over the high grass as the rifles cracked in rapid succession, and the *five elephants lay dead* in the same order as they had advanced. The spare guns had been beautifully handed. And running between the carcasses, we got into the lane that the remaining portion of the herd had made by crushing the high grass in their retreat. We were up with them in a few moments: down went one, then another; up he got again, almost immediately recovering from V.'s shot; down he went again as I floored him with my last barrel.

I was now unloaded, as I had only two of my double-barrelled No. 10. rifles out that day, but the chase was so exciting that I could not help following empty-handed, in the hope that some gun-bearer might put one of V.'s spare guns in my hand. A large elephant and her young one, who was about three feet and a half high, were retreating up the rugged side of the mountain, and the mother, instead of protecting the little-one, was soon a hundred paces ahead of him, and safely located in a thick jungle which covered that portion of the mountain. Being empty-handed, I soon scrambled up and caught the little fellow by the tail; but he was so strong that I could not hold him, although I exerted all my strength, and he dragged me slowly towards the jungle to which his mother had retreated. V. now came up; and he being loaded, I told him to keep a look out for the mother's return, while I secured my captive, by seizing him by the trunk with one hand, and by the tail with the other; in this manner I could just master him by throwing my whole weight down the hill; and he began to roar like a full-grown elephant. The mother was for a wonder faithless to her charge, and did not return to the little one's assistance. While I was engaged in securing him, the gun-bearers came up, and at this moment I observed, at the foot of the hill, another elephant not quite full-grown, who was retreating through the high grass towards the jungle. There were no guns charged except one of my No. 10. rifles, which some one had reloaded; taking this, I left the little "Poonchy" with V. and the gun-bearers, and running down the side of the hill, I came up with the elephant just as he was entering the jungle, and getting the ear-shot, I killed him.

We had now bagged nine elephants, and only one had escaped from the herd; this was the female who had forsaken her young one.

Wallace now came up and cut off the tails of those that I had killed. I had one barrel still loaded, and I was pushing my way through the tangled grass towards the spot where the five elephants lay together, when I suddenly heard Wallace shriek out, "Look out, sir! Look out! — an elephant's coming!"

I turned round in a moment; and close past Wallace, from the very spot where the last dead elephant lay, came the very essence and incarnation of a "rogue" elephant in full charge. His trunk was thrown high in the air, his ears were cocked, his tail stood high above his back as stiff as a poker, and screaming exactly like the whistle of a railway engine, he rushed upon me through the high grass with a velocity that was perfectly wonderful. His eyes flashed as he came on, and he had singled me out as his victim.

I have often been in dangerous positions, but I never felt so totally devoid of hope as I did in this instance. The tangled grass rendered retreat impossible. I had only one barrel loaded, and that was useless, as the upraised trunk protected his forehead. I felt myself doomed; the few thoughts that rush through men's minds in such hopeless positions flew through mine, and I resolved to wait for him till he was close upon me before I fired, hoping that he might lower his trunk and expose his forehead.

He rushed along at the pace of a horse in full speed; in a few moments, as the grass flew to the right and left before him, he was close upon me, but still his trunk was raised and I would not fire. One second more, and at this headlong pace he was within three feet of me; down slashed his trunk with the rapidity of a whip-thong, and with a shrill scream of fury he was upon me.

I fired at that instant; but in a twinkling of an eye I was flying through the air like a ball from a bat. At the moment of firing I had jumped to the left, but he struck me with his

J. BRANDARD, LITH.

CAUGHT AT LAST.

tush in full charge upon my right thigh, and hurled me eight or ten paces from him. That very moment he stopped, and, turning round, he beat the grass about with his trunk, and commenced a strict search for me. I heard him advancing close to the spot where I lay as still as death, knowing that my last chance lay in concealment. I heard the grass rustling close to the spot where I lay; closer and closer he approached, and he at length beat the grass with his trunk several times exactly above me. I held my breath, momentarily expecting to feel his ponderous foot upon me. Although I had not felt the sensation of fear while I had stood opposed to him, I felt like what I never wish to feel again while he was deliberately hunting me up. Fortunately I had reserved my fire until the rifle had almost touched him, for the powder and smoke had nearly blinded him and had spoiled his acute power of scent. To my joy I heard the rustling of the grass grow fainter; again, I heard it at a still greater distance; at length it was gone!

At that time I thought that half my bones were broken, as I was numbed from head to foot by the force of the blow. His charge can only be compared to a blow from a railway engine going at twenty miles an hour.

Not expecting to be able to move, I crept to my hands and knees. To my delight there were no bones broken, and with a feeling of thankfulness I stood erect. I with difficulty reached a stream of water near the spot, in which I bathed my leg, but in a few minutes it swelled to the size of a man's waist. In this spot every one had congregated and were loading their guns, but the rogue had escaped.

My cap and rifle were now hunted for, and they were at length found near the spot where I had been caught. The elephant had trodden on the stock of the rifle, and it bears the marks of his foot to this day.

In a few minutes I was unable to move. We therefore sent to the tent for the horses, and arrived at 6 P.M., having had a hard day's work from 5 A.M. without food.

On arrival at the tent, we found Banda and the trackers.

There could not be a better exemplification of a rogue than in this case. A short distance apart from the herd he had concealed himself in the jungle, from which position he had witnessed the destruction of his mates. He had not stirred a foot until he saw us totally unprepared, when he instantly seized the opportunity and dashed out upon me. If I had attempted to run from him I should have been killed, as he would have struck me in the back; my only chance was in the course which I pursued,—to wait quietly until he was just over me, and then to jump on one side: he thus struck me on the thickest part of the thigh instead of striking me in the stomach, which he must have done had I remained in my first position; this would have killed me on the spot.

I passed an uncomfortable night, my leg being very painful and covered with wet bandages of vinegar and water. The bruise came out from my ankle to my hip; the skin was broken where the tush had struck me; and the blood had started under the skin over a surface of nearly a foot, making the bruise a bright purple, and giving the whole affair a most unpleasant appearance. The next morning I could not move my leg, which felt like a sack of sand, and was perfectly numbed; however, I kept on a succession of cold lotions, and after breakfast I was assisted upon my horse, and we moved the encampment to Nielgalla.

On the following day I could just manage to hobble along, my leg being at least double its usual size, and threatening to spoil my sport for the whole trip.

We were seated at breakfast when a native came in, bringing intelligence of a herd of elephants about four miles distant. I was not in a state for shooting, but I resolved to mount my steady old horse Jack, and take my chance of revenge for my mishap. The guns were accordingly loaded, and we started.

We had ridden through the Park for about three miles, and had just turned round the corner of a patch of jungle, when we came suddenly upon a large rogue elephant, who was standing in the open, facing us at about seventy yards. The moment that he saw the horses, he turned sharp round and retreated to a long belt of fine open forest which was close behind him. There was no resisting the invitation upon such favourable ground, and immediately dismounting, we followed him. I now found that my leg was nearly useless, and I could only move at a snail's pace, and even then with great pain. Upon reaching the forest, we found that the rogue had decamped, not wishing to meet us in such advantageous ground.

We followed his tracks for a few hundred yards through the forest, till we suddenly emerged upon a large tract of high lemon-grass. Into this our cunning foe had retreated, and with my decreased powers of locomotion I did not wish to pursue him further. I was at length persuaded by Banda to make a trial, and we accordingly left the track and pushed our way through the high grass to some rising ground, from which we could look over the surface of waving vegetation, and find out the exact position of the elephant. While forcing our way through the dense mass I momentarily expected to hear the rush of the rogue charging down upon us, and I was glad to find myself at length safe in the position we had steered for.

Upon scanning the surface of the grass, I distinguished the elephant immediately; he was standing close to the edge of the jungle in the high grass, facing us, at about a hundred and fifty yards distant. He was a picture of intense excitement and attention, and was evidently waiting for us. In the position that we now occupied, we unavoidably gave him the wind, and he of course almost immediately discovered us. Giving two or three shrill trumpets, he paced quickly to and fro before the jungle, as though he were guarding the entrance. To enter the high grass to attack him would have been folly, as he was fully prepared, and when once in the tangled mass, we could not have seen him until he was upon us; we therefore amused ourselves for about ten minutes by shooting at him. During this time he continued pacing backwards and forwards, screaming almost without intermission; and having suddenly made up his mind to stand this bullying no longer, he threw his trunk up in the air and charged straight at us. The dust flew like smoke from the dry grass as he rushed through it; but we were well prepared to receive him. Not wishing him to come to close quarters with my useless leg, I gave him a shot with my two-ounce rifle, at about a hundred and twenty paces. It did not even check him, but it had the effect of making him lower his trunk, and he came on at undiminished speed. Taking the four-ounce rifle from Wallace, I heard the crack of the ball as it entered his head at about a hundred yards. He was down! A general shout of exclamation rose from Banda and all the gun-bearers. I reloaded the four-ounce immediately, and the ball was just rammed home when we heard the supposed dead elephant roaring on the ground. In another moment he regained his legs and stood with his broadside exposed to us, stunned with the heavy ball in his head. Taking a steady shot at his shoulder, I gave him a second dose of the four-ounce: he reeled to and fro, and staggered into the jungle. I dared not follow him in my crippled state, and we returned to the horses; but the next day he was found dead by the natives.

I much feared that the shot fired might have disturbed the herd of elephants, as they were reported to be not far distant; this, however, proved not to be the case, as we met the watchers about a mile further on, who reported the herd to be perfectly undisturbed, but located in the everlasting lemon-grass. At this time, the greater portion of the Park was a mass of this abominable grass, and there was no chance of getting the elephants in any other position, this serving them at the same time for both food and shelter. How they can eat it is a puzzle,—it is as sharp as a knife, and as coarse as a file, with a flavour of the most pungent lemon-peel.

We shortly arrived at the spot in which the herd was concealed; it was a gentle slope covered with dense lemon-grass, terminated by a jungle. We could just distinguish the tops of the elephants' heads in several places, and, having dismounted, we carefully entered the grass, and crept towards the nearest elephants. The herd was much scattered, but there were five elephants close to each other, and we made towards these, Banda leading the way. My only chance of making a bag lay in the first onset, I therefore cautioned Wallace to have the spare guns handed with extra diligence, and we crept up to our game. There were two elephants facing us, but we stalked them so carefully through the high grass that we got within four paces of them before they discovered us; they cocked their ears for an instant and both rolled over at the same moment to the front shot. Away dashed the herd, trumpeting and screaming as they rushed through the high grass. For a few moments my game leg grew quite lively, as it was all down-hill work, and I caught up an elephant and killed him with the left-hand barrel. Getting a spare gun, I was lucky enough to get between two elephants who were running abreast towards the jungle, and I bagged them by a right and left shot. Off went the herd at a slapping pace through the jungle, V. pitching it into them, but unfortunately to very little purpose, as they had closed up and formed a barrier of sterns, and we could not get a good shot. For about a quarter of a mile I managed to hobble along, carried away by the excitement of the chase, through jungles, hollows, and small glades, till my leg, which had lost all feeling, suddenly gave way, and I lay sprawling on my face, incapable of going a step further. I had killed four elephants: six had been killed altogether. It was very bad luck, as the herd consisted of eleven; but the ground was very unfavourable, and my leg gave way when it was most required.

A few days after this, the tents were pitched on the banks of the broad river of Pattapalaar, about eight miles beyond Neigalla. Elephants were very scarce, and the only chance of getting them was to work hard. We were on horseback at break of day, and having forded the river, we rode silently through plain and forest in search of tracks. We refused every shot at deer, lest we should disturb the country and scare away the elephants.

We had ridden for some distance upon an elephant path, through a tolerably open forest at the foot of a range of rocky mountains, when Banda, who was some paces in advance, suddenly sprang back again, crying, "Wallaha! Wallaha!" (Bears! Bears!) We were off our horses in a moment, but I fell sprawling upon my back, my leg being so powerless and numbed that I could not feel when I touched the ground. I recovered myself just in time to see a bear waddling along through the jungle, and I pushed after him in pursuit at my best pace. V. had disappeared in the jungle in pursuit of another bear, and I presently heard two or three shots. In the meantime my game had slackened speed to a careless kind of swaggering walk; and the underwood being rather thick, I was determined to get close to him before I fired, as I knew that I could not follow him far, and my success would therefore depend upon the first shot. I overtook him in a few moments, and I was following within a foot of his tail, waiting for a chance for a clear shot between his shoulders, as the thick underwood parted above his back, when he suddenly sprung round, and with a fierce roar he leaped upon the muzzle of the gun. I fired both barrels into him as he threw his whole weight against it, and I rolled him over in a confused cloud of smoke and crackling bushes. In a moment he was on his legs again, but going off through the thick underwood at a pace that in my helpless state soon left me far behind. His state must have been far from enviable, as he left portions of his entrails all along his track. V. had killed his bear; he weighed about two hundred pounds, and measured fourteen inches round the arm, without his hide.

The Ceylon bear is a most savage animal, constantly attacking men without the slightest provocation. I have seen many natives frightfully disfigured by the attacks of bears, which they dread more than any other animal. Nothing would induce my trackers to follow up the wounded bear. I followed him as far as I could, but my useless limb soon gave way, and I was obliged to give him up. I once saw a Moorman, who was a fine powerful fellow, and an excellent elephant tracker, who had a narrow escape from a bear. He was cutting bamboos with a catty or kind of bill-hook, when one of these animals descended from a tree just above him and immediately attacked him. The man instinctively threw his left arm forward to receive the bear, who seized it in his mouth and bit the thumb completely off, lacerating the arm and wrist at the same time in a frightful manner. With one blow of the bill-hook the Moorman cleft the bear's skull to the teeth, at the same time gashing his own arm to the bone by the force of the blow;

and he never afterwards recovered the proper use of the limb.

The Ceylon bear feeds upon almost anything that offers ; he eats honey, ants, fruit, roots, and flesh whenever he can procure it: his muscular power is enormous, and he exerts both teeth and claws in his attack. They are very numerous in Ceylon, although they are seldom met with in any number, owing to their nocturnal habits, which attract them to their caves at break of day.

After strolling over the country for some miles, we came upon fresh elephant tracks in high grass, which we immediately followed up. In the course of half an hour, after tracking them for about two miles through open country, we entered a fine forest, in which the herd had retired; but our hopes of meeting them in this favourable ground were suddenly damped by arriving at a dense chénar jungle in the very heart of the forest. This chénar extended for some acres, and rose like a hedge, forming a sudden wall of thorns, which effectually checked our advance. The elephants had retired to this secure retreat, and having winded us they kept up an uninterrupted roaring. I never heard such a musical herd;—the deep and thunder-like growls, combined with the shrill trumpet and loud roars, as they all joined in concert, had a particularly grand effect, and a novice in elephant-shooting would have felt his heart beat in double time.

There was a rogue consorting with this herd, and it was necessary to be particularly cautious in the attack. It was impossible to enter such thick jungle, and we waited for some hours in the forest, close to the edge of the chénar, trying every dodge in vain to induce the herd to quit their stronghold. They were continually on the *qui vive*. Sometimes a tremendous rush would be heard in the thick jungle as the herd would charge towards us; but they invariably stopped just upon the borders, and would not venture into the open forest. On one occasion, I thought we had them: they rushed to the edge of the thick jungle, and suddenly filed off to the left, and halted in a line within a few feet of the forest. We were within six paces of them, concealed behind the trunks of several large trees, from which we could discover the dim forms of six elephants through the skreen of thorns, which had a similar effect to that produced by looking through a gauze veil. For some moments they stood in an attitude of intense attention, and I momentarily expected them to break cover, as we were perfectly still and motionless in our concealed position. Suddenly they winded us, and whisked round to the thick jungle, disappearing like magic.

We now tried the effect of bullying, and we sent men to different parts of the jungle to shout and fire guns; this stirred up the wrath of the rogue, and he suddenly burst from the thick jungle, and rushed into the open forest right among us. We were both standing behind the trees; and the gun-bearers, with the exception of Wallace, had thrown the guns down and had bolted up the trees when they heard the rush of the elephant through the jungle; thus, upon his arrival in the open forest, he could see no one, and he stood gazing about him with his ears cocked and tail on end, not knowing exactly what to do, but ready to charge the first person that showed himself. He was an immense elephant, being one of the largest that I have ever seen, and he had as fine an expression of vice in his appearance as any rogue could wish for. Suddenly he turned his trunk towards us, but he was puzzled as to the exact position of any one, as so many men were scattered among the trees. I was within twenty yards of him, and he turned his head towards the spot, and was just on the move forward, when I anticipated his intentions, by running up to him and knocking him over by a shot in the forehead, which killed him. Unfortunately the herd at the same moment broke cover on the opposite side of the jungle, and escaped without a shot being fired at them. It was nearly dusk, and we were five miles from the tent; we were therefore obliged to give them up.

The next morning, at daybreak, I rode out with the greyhounds, Killbuck, Bran, and Lena, to kill a deer. The lemon-grass was so high at this season that the dogs had no chance, and I was therefore compelled to pick out some spot which was free from this grass, and employ beaters to drive the jungles, instead of stalking the deer in the usual manner. I tracked a herd of deer into a large detached piece of cover, and, sending the beaters round to the opposite side, I posted myself with the greyhounds in the slips behind a clump of trees upon a small plain of low soft grass.

The noise of the beaters approached nearer and nearer, and presently two splendid bucks with beautiful antlers rushed from the jungle about two hundred yards from me, and scudded over the plain. I slipped the greyhounds and away they went in full fly, bounding over the soft turf in beautiful style.

Mounting old Jack, who was standing at my elbow, and giving him the spur, I rode after them. It was a splendid course ; the two bucks separated, Bran and Lena taking after one, and Killbuck following the other in his usual dashing manner. Away they went with wonderful speed, the bucks constantly doubling to throw the dogs out; but Killbuck never overshot his game, and as the buck doubled, he was round after him in fine style. I now followed him, leaving Bran and Lena to do their best, and at a killing pace we crossed the plain — through a narrow belt of trees, down a stony hollow, over another plain, through a small jungle, on entering which Killbuck was within a few yards of the buck's haunches.

Now old Jack is as fond of the sport as I am, and he kept up the chase in good style; but just as we were flying through some high lemon-grass, a fallen tree, which was concealed beneath, tripped up the horse's fore-legs, and in an instant he was on his nose, turning a complete sommersault. I was pitched some yards, and upon instinctively mounting again, the sparks were dancing in my eyes for some seconds before I recovered myself, as we again continued the chase with unabated speed.

We pressed along up some rising ground, having lost sight of the game; and as we reached the top of the hill, I looked around and saw the buck at bay about a hundred paces from me, upon fine level ground, fighting face to face with the dog, who sprang boldly at his head. That buck was a noble fellow; he rushed at the dog, and they met like knights in a tournament: but it was murderous work; he received the reckless dog upon his sharp antlers and bored him to the ground. In another instant Killbuck had recovered himself, and he again came in full fly at the buck's face with wonderful courage; again the buck rushed forward to meet him, and once more the pointed antlers pinned the dog, and the buck following up his charge rolled him over and over for some yards.

By this time I had galloped up, and I was within a few feet of the buck when he suddenly sprung round with the evident intention of charging the horse. In the same moment Killbuck seized the opportunity, and the buck plunged violently upon the ground, with the stanch dog hanging upon his throat. I jumped off my horse, and the buck fell dead by a thrust with the knife behind the shoulder.

I now examined the dog; he was wounded in several places, but as he bled but little, I hoped that his apparent exhaustion arose more from the fatigue of the fight than from any severe injury.

At this time Bran and Lena came up; they had lost their deer in some high lemon-grass, but they also were both wounded by the buck's horns. I now put Killbuck and Lena together in the slips, and with the buck, carried upon cross poles by six men, I rode towards the tent. I had not proceeded far when the man who was leading the greyhounds behind my horse suddenly cried out, and on turning round I saw Killbuck lying on the ground. I was at his side in a moment, and I released his neck from the slips. It was too late; his languid head fell heavily upon the earth; he gave me one parting look, and after a few faint gasps he was gone.

I could hardly believe he was dead. Taking off my cap I ran to a little stream and brought some water, which I threw in his face; but his teeth were set, his eyes were glazed, and the best and truest dog that was ever born was dead. Poor Killbuck! he had died like a hero, and though

I grieved over him I could not have wished him a more glorious death.

I was obliged to open him to discover the real injury. I had little thought that the knife which had so often come to his assistance was destined to so sad a task. His lungs were pierced through by the deer's horns in two places, and he had died of sudden suffocation by internal hemorrhage. A large hollow tree grew close to the spot in which I buried him. The stag's antlers now hang in the hall, a melancholy but glorious memento of poor Killbuck.

In a few days my leg had so much improved that I could again use it without much inconvenience; I therefore determined to pay the cave a visit, as I felt convinced that elephants would be more numerous in that neighbourhood. We started in the cool of the afternoon, as the distance was not more than eight miles from our encampment. We had proceeded about half way, and our horses were picking their way with difficulty over some rocky hills, when we came upon fresh tracks of a herd of elephants. It was too late to go after them that evening, we therefore pitched the tent upon the spot, resolving to track them up at daybreak on the following morning.

We were accordingly out before sunrise, and came upon the tracks within a mile of the tent. We at length discovered the herd upon the summit of a steep rocky hill. There were no trees in this part, and we carefully ascended the hill, stepping from rock to rock, and occasionally concealing ourselves in the high grass, till we at length stood at the very feet of the elephants, two of whom were standing upon a large platform of rock, about seven feet above us. They were so high above us that I was obliged to aim about four inches down the trunk, so that the ball should reach the brain in an upward direction; this shot proved successful, and killed him. V., who had not taken this precaution, missed; and the whole herd of eight elephants started off in full retreat.

The rocks were so steep that it occupied some time in climbing over the top of the hill, upon reaching which, we saw the elephants going off at great speed, with a start of about two hundred paces. The ground was perfectly open, covered by small loose rocks free from grass, and the chase commenced in good earnest. With the elephants in view the whole time, and going at a great pace, a mile was run without the possibility of firing a shot. By this time we had arrived at an undulating country covered with small rocks and grass about four feet high, which made the pace dreadfully fatiguing; still we dared not slacken the speed for an instant lest the elephants should distance us. This was the time for rifles to tell, although their weight (15 lbs.) was rather trying in so long and fast a run. I was within eighty paces of the herd, and I could not decrease the distance by a single yard. I halted and took a shot at the ear of a large elephant in the middle of the herd. The shot so stunned him that, instead of going on straight, he kept turning round and round as though running after his tail; this threw the herd into confusion, and some ran to the right and others to the left, across some steep hollows. Running up to my wounded elephant, I extinguished him with my remaining barrel; and getting a spare rifle from Wallace, who was the only gun-bearer who had kept up, I floored another elephant, who was ascending the opposite side of a hollow about forty yards off: this fellow took two shots, and accordingly I was left unloaded. V. had made good play with the rifles as the herd was crossing the hollow, and he had killed three, making six bagged in all. The remaining two elephants reached a thick jungle and escaped.

We returned to the tent, and after a bath we sat down with a glorious appetite to breakfast, having bagged six elephants before seven o'clock A.M.

In the afternoon we went to the cave and sent out trackers. We were very hard up for provisions in this place: there were no deer in the neighbourhood, and we lived upon squirrels and parrots, both of which are excellent eating, but not very substantial fare.

The whole of this part of the country was one dark mass of high lemon-grass, which, not having been burnt, was a tangled mixture of yellow stalks and sharp blades, which completely destroyed the pleasure of shooting.

In this unfavourable ground we found a herd of ten elephants, and after waiting for some time in the hope of their feeding into a better country, we lost all patience, and resolved to go in at them and do the best we could. It was late in the afternoon, and the herd, who were well aware of our position, had all closed up in a dense body, and with their trunks thrown up, they were trumpeting and screaming as though to challenge us to the attack.

Pushing our way through the high grass, we got within six paces of the elephants before they attempted to turn, and the heavy battery opened upon them in fine style. Levelling the grass in their path, they rushed through it in a headlong retreat, V. keeping on one flank while I took the other; and a race commenced, which continued for about half a mile at full speed, the greater part of this distance being up hill. None of these elephants proved restive; and on arriving at thick jungle two only entered out of the ten that had composed the herd; the remaining eight lay here and there along the line of the hunt.

Out of four herds and three rogues fired at, we had bagged thirty-one elephants in a few days' shooting. My mishap on the first day had much destroyed the pleasure of the sport, as the exercise was too much for my wounded leg, which did not recover from the feeling of numbness for some months.

CHAP. XI.

EXCITEMENT OF ELEPHANT SHOOTING. — AN UNEXPECTED VISITOR. — A LONG RUN WITH A BUCK. — HARD WORK REWARDED. — A GLORIOUS BAY. — END OF A HARD DAY'S WORK. — BEE HUNTERS. — DISASTERS OF ELK HUNTING. — BRAN WOUNDED. — "OLD SMUT'S" BUCK. — BOAR AT HACKGALLA. — DEATH OF "OLD SMUT." — SCENERY FROM THE PÉREWELLÉ MOUNTAINS. — DIABOLICAL DEATH OF "MERRIMAN." — SCENE OF THE MURDER.

In describing so many incidents in elephant-shooting, it is difficult to convey a just idea of the true grandeur of the sport: it reads too easy. A certain number are killed out of a herd after an animated chase, and the description of the hunt details the amount of slaughter, but cannot possibly explain the peculiar excitement which attends elephant-shooting beyond all other sports. The size of the animal is so disproportionate to that of the hunter, that the effect of a large herd of these monsters flying before a single man would be almost ridiculous, could the chase be witnessed by some casual observer who was proof against the excitement of the sport. The effect of a really good elephant shot in the pursuit of a herd over open country is very fine. With such weapons as the double-barrelled No. 10. rifles, a shot is seldom wasted; and during the chase, an elephant drops from the herd at every puff of smoke. It is a curious sight, and one of the grandest in the world, to see a fine rogue-elephant knocked over in full charge. His onset appears so irresistible, and the majesty of his form so overwhelming, that I have frequently almost mistrusted the power of man over such a beast; but one shot well placed, with a heavy charge of powder behind the ball, reduces him in one instant to a mere heap of flesh.

One of the most disgusting sights is a dead elephant, four or five days after the fatal shot. In a tropical climate, where decomposition proceeds with such wonderful rapidity, the effect of the sun upon such a mass can be readily understood. The gas generated in the inside distends the carcase to an enormous size, until it at length bursts and becomes in a few hours afterwards one living heap of maggots. Three weeks after an elephant is killed nothing remains but his bones and a small heap of dried cases, from which the flies have emerged when the time arrived for them to change from the form of maggots. The sight of the largest of the animal creation being thus reduced from life to nothingness within so short a space of time is an instance of the perishable tenure of mortality which cannot fail to strike the most unthinking. The majesty, the power, and the sagacity of the enormous beast are scattered in the myriads of flies which have fed upon him.

It is a delightful change after a sporting trip of a few weeks in the hot climates to return again to the cool and even temperature of Newera Ellia. The tent is a pleasant dwelling when no other can be obtained, but the comfort of a good house is never so much appreciated as on the return from the jungle.

One great pleasure in the hunting at Newera Ellia is the ease with which it is obtained. In fact, the sport lies at the very door. This may be said to be literally true and not a *façon de parler*, as I once killed an elk that jumped through a window. It was a singular incident. The hounds found three elk at the same time on the mountain at the back of the hotel at Newera Ellia. The pack divided: several hounds were lost for two days, having taken their elk to an impossible country, and the rest of the pack concentrated upon a doe, with the exception of old Smut, who had another elk all to himself. This elk, which was a large doe, he brought down from the top of the mountain to the back of the hotel, just as we had killed the other, which the pack had brought to the same place. A great number of persons were standing in the hotel yard to view the sport, when old Smut and his game appeared, rushing in full fly through the crowd. The elk was so bothered and headed that she went through the back door of the hotel at full gallop, and Smut, with his characteristic sagacity, immediately bolted round to the front of the house, naturally concluding that if she went in at the back door she must come out at the front. He was perfectly right; the old dog stood on the lawn before the hotel, watching the house with great eagerness. In the meantime, the elk was galloping from room to room in the hotel, chased by a crowd of people, until she at length took refuge in a lady's bed-room, from which there was no exit as the window was closed. The crash of glass may be imagined, as an animal as large as a pony leaped through it; but old Smut was ready for her, and after a chase of a few yards he pulled her down. This is the only instance that I have ever known of an elk entering a building, although it is a common occurrence with hunted deer in England.

An elk found on the top of Pedro talla Galla, which rises from the plain of Newera Ellia, will generally run straight down the mountain, and, unless headed, he will generally come to bay in the river close to the hotel, which is situated at the foot of the mountain. This, however, is not a rule without an exception, as the elk on some occasions takes a totally different direction, and gives a hard day's work.

It was on the 27th of July, 1852, that I had a run of this kind. It was six A. M. when my youngest brother and I started from the foot of Pedro to ascend the mountain. The path is three miles long, through jungle the whole way, to the summit. There were fresh tracks of elk near the top of the mountain, the dew lay heavily upon the leaves, and the scent was evidently strong, as Merriman and Ploughboy, the two leading hounds, dashed off upon it, followed by the whole pack. In a few minutes we heard them in full cry about a quarter of a mile from us, going straight down the hill. Giving them a good holloa, we started off down the path at a round pace, and in less than a quarter of an hour we were at the foot of the mountain on the plain. Here we found a number of people who had headed the elk (a fine buck) just as he was breaking cover, and he had turned back, taking off to some other line of country at a great pace, as we could not hear even a whimper. This was enough to make a saint swear, and, blessing heartily the fellows who had headed him, we turned back and retraced our steps up the mountain to listen for the cry of the pack among the numerous ravines which furrow the sides.

It was of no use, — we could hear nothing but the mocking chirp of birds and the roaring of the mountain torrents. Not a sign of elk or dogs. The greyhounds were away with the pack, and knowing that the dogs would never leave him till dark, we determined not to give them up. No less than three times in the course of the day did we re-ascend the mountain to listen for them in vain. We went up to the top of the Newera Ellia Pass, in the hope of hearing them in that direction, but with the same want of success. Miles of ground were gone over to no purpose. Scaling the steep sides of the mountains at the back of the barracks, we listened among the deep hollows on the other side, but again we were disappointed; the sound of the torrents was all that we could hear.

Descending again to the plain, we procured some breakfast at a friend's house, and we started for the Matturatta plains. These plains are about three or four miles from the barracks; and I had a faint hope that the buck might have crossed over the mountain, and descended into this part of the country to a river which flows through the patinas. We now mounted our horses, having been on foot all the morning. It was three o'clock P.M., and, with little hope of finding the dogs, we rode along the path towards the Maturatta plains.

We had just entered the forest, when we met a young hound returning along the path with a wound from a buck's horn in the shoulder. There was now no doubt of the direction, and we galloped along the path towards the plains as hard as we could go. About half way to the plains, to my joy I saw an immense buck's track in the path going in the same direction; the toes were spread wide apart, showing the pace at which he had been going; and there were dogs' tracks following him, all as fresh as could be. This was a gladdening sight after a hard day's work, and we gave a random cheer to encourage any dogs that might be within hearing, rattling our horses over the ground at their best speed.

At last the plains were reached. We pulled up our panting steeds, and strained every nerve to hear the cry of the hounds. The snorting of the horses prevented our hearing any distant sound, and I gave a holloa and listened for some answering voice from a dog. Instead of a sound, Bran and Lucifer suddenly appeared. This was conclusive evidence that the pack was somewhere in this direction, and we rode out into the plain and again listened. Hark to old Smut! there was his deep voice echoing from the opposite hills. Yoick to him, Bran! forward to him, Lucifer! and away the greyhounds dashed towards the spot from which the sound proceeded. The plain forms a wide valley with a river winding through the centre, and we galloped over the patinas after the greyhounds in full speed. There was no mistaking the bay. I could now distinguish Merriman's fine voice in addition to that of old Smut, and a general chorus of other tongues joined in, till the woods rung again. The horses knew the sport and away they went, but suddenly over went old Jack belly-deep in a bog, and sent me flying over his head. There is nothing like companionship in an accident, and Momus accordingly pitched upon his nose in the same bog, my brother describing a fine spread eagle as he sprawled in the soft ground. We were close to the bay; the horses extricated themselves directly, and again mounting we rode hard to the spot.

The buck was at bay in the river, and the exhausted dogs were yelling at him from the bank. The instant that we arrived and cheered them on, old Smut came from the pack towards us with an expression of perfect delight; he gave himself two or three rolls on the grass, and then went to the fight like a lion. The buck, however, suddenly astonished the whole pack by jumping out of the river, and, charging right through them, he started over the plain towards the jungle, with the whole pack after him. He had refreshed himself by standing for so long in the cold stream, while the dogs, on the contrary, were nearly worn out. He reached the jungle with the whole pack at his heels; but after doubling backwards and forwards in the forest for about five minutes, we heard the crash in the bushes, as he once more rushed towards the plain, and he broke cover in fine style, with the three greyhounds, Bran, Lucifer, and Lena, at his haunches. In another instant he was seized, but he fell with such a shock, that it threw the greyhounds from their hold, and recovering himself with wonderful quickness, he went down the slope towards the river at a tremendous pace. The greyhounds overtook him just as he gained the steep banks of the river, and they all rolled over in a confused crowd into the deep water.

The next moment the buck was seen swimming proudly down the river, with the whole pack following him down the stream in full cry. Presently he gained his footing, and disdaining further flight, he turned bravely upon the hounds.

He was a splendid fellow; his nostrils were distended, his mane was bristled up, and his eyes flashed, as rearing to his full height he plunged forward and struck the leading dogs under water. Not a dog could touch him; one by one they were beaten down and half drowned beneath the water. Old Smut was to the front as usual; down the old dog was beaten, but he re-appeared behind the elk's shoulder, and the next moment he was hanging on his ear. The poor old dog had lost so many of his teeth in these encounters that he could not keep his hold, and the buck gave a tremendous spring forward, shaking off the old dog and charging through the pack, sinking nearly half of them for a few moments beneath the water. He had too much pluck to fly further, and, after wading shoulder-deep against the stream for a few yards, he turned majestically round, and, facing the baying pack, he seemed determined to do or die. I never saw a finer animal; there was a proud look of defiance in his aspect which gave him a most noble appearance; but at that time he had little pity bestowed upon him.

There he stood ready to meet the first dog. Old Smut had been thrown to the rear as the buck turned, and Lena came beautifully to the front, leading the whole pack. There was a shallow sandbank in the river where the bitch could get a footing, and she dashed across it to the attack. The buck met her in her advance by a sudden charge, which knocked her over and over, but at the same instant Valiant, who is a fine powerful dog, made a clever spring forward and pinned the buck by the ear. There was no shaking him off, and he was immediately backed up by Ploughboy, who caught the other ear most cleverly. There the two dogs hung like earrings as the buck, rearing up, swung them to and fro, but could not break their hold. In another moment the greyhounds were upon him—the whole pack covered him; his beautiful form was seen alternately rearing from the water with the dogs hanging upon him in all directions, then struggling in a confused mass nearly beneath the surface of the stream. He was a brave fellow, and had fought nobly, but there was no hope for him, and we put an end to the fight with the hunting-knife.

It was past four o'clock P.M., and he had been found at seven A.M., but the conclusion fully repaid us for the day's work. The actual distance run by the buck was not above eight miles, but we had gone about twenty during the day, the greater portion of which was over most fatiguing ground.

On an open country an elk would never be caught without greyhounds until he had run fifteen or twenty miles. The dense jungles fatigue him as he ploughs his way through them, and thus forms a path for the dogs behind him. How he can move in some of these jungles is an enigma; a horse would break his legs, and, in fact, could not stir in places through which an elk passes in full gallop.

The principal underwood in the mountain districts of Ceylon is the "nillho." This is a perfectly straight stem, from twelve to twenty feet in length, and about an inch and a half in diameter, having no branches except a few small arms at the top, which are covered with large leaves. This plant, in proportion to its size, grows as close as corn in a field, and forms a dense jungle most difficult to penetrate. When the jungles are in this state, the elk is at a disadvantage, as the immense exertion required to break his way through this mass soon fatigues him, and forces him to come to bay.

Every seven years this "nillho" blossoms. The jungles are then neither more nor less than vast bouquets of bright purple and white flowers; the perfume is delicious, and swarms of bees migrate from other countries to make their harvest of honey. The quantity collected is extraordinary. The bee-hunters start from the low country, and spend weeks in the jungle in collecting the honey and wax. When looking over an immense tract of forest from some elevated point, the thin blue lines of smoke may be seen rising in many directions, marking the sites of the bee-hunters' fires. Their method of taking the honey is simple enough. The bees' nests hang from the boughs of the trees, and a man ascends with a torch of green leaves, which creates a dense smoke. He approaches the nest, and smokes off the swarm, which, on quitting the exterior of the comb, exposes a beautiful circular mass of honey and wax, generally about eighteen inches in diameter and six inches thick. The bee-hunter being provided with vessels formed from the rind of the gourd, attached to ropes, now cuts up the comb and fills his chatties, lowering them down to his companions below.

When the blossom of the nillho fades, the seed forms; this is a sweet little kernel, with the flavour of a nut. The bees now leave the country, and the jungles suddenly swarm, as though by magic, with pigeons, jungle-fowl, and rats. At length the seed is shed, and the nillho dies.

The jungles then have a curious appearance. The underwood being dead, the forest-trees rise from a mass of dry sticks like thin hop-poles. The roots of these plants very soon decay, and a few weeks of high wind howling through the forest levels the whole mass, leaving the trees standing free from underwood. The appearance of the ground can now be imagined—a perfect chaos of dead sticks and poles, piled one on the other, in every direction, to a depth of between two and three feet. It can only be compared to a mass of hurdles being laid in a heap. The young nillho grows rapidly through this, concealing the mass of dead sticks beneath, and forms a tangled barrier which checks both dogs and man. With tough gaiters to guard the shins, we break through by main force and weight, and the dogs scramble sometimes over, sometimes under the surface. At this period the elk are in great numbers, as they feed with great avidity upon the succulent young nillho. The dogs are now at a disadvantage. While they are scrambling with difficulty through this mass of half-rotten sticks, the elk bounds over it with ease, leaving no path behind him, as he clears it by leaps, and does not exhaust himself by bursting through it. He now constantly escapes, and leaves the pack miles behind; the best hounds follow him, but with such a start he leads them into the unknown depths of the jungles, over high mountains, and across deep ravines, from which the lost dogs frequently never return.

There can be no question that it is a bad country for hunting at all times, as the mass of forest is so disproportionate to the patinas; but, on the other hand, were the forests of smaller size there would be less game. Elk-hunting is, on the whole, fine sport. There are many disappointments constantly occurring, but these must happen in all sports. The only important drawback to the pleasure of elk-hunting is the constant loss of the dogs. The best are always sure to go. What with deaths by boars, leopards, elk, and stray hounds, the pack is with difficulty maintained. Puppies are constantly lost in the commencement of their training by straying too far into the jungle, and sometimes by reckless valour. I lost a fine young greyhound, Lancer, own brother to Lucifer, in this way. It was his first day with the pack.

We found a buck who came to bay in a deep rocky torrent, where the dogs had no chance with him, and he amused himself by striking them under water at his pleasure. He at length took his stand among some large rocks between which the torrent rushed with great rapidity previous to its descent over a fall of sixty feet. In this impregnable position young Lancer chose to distinguish himself, and with a beautiful spring he flew straight at the buck's head; but the elk met him with a tremendous blow with the fore-feet, which broke his back, and the unfortunate Lancer was killed in his first essay, and swept over the waterfall. This buck was at bay for two hours before he was killed.

A veteran seizer is generally seamed with innumerable scars. Poor old Bran, who, being a thorough-bred greyhound, is too fine in the skin for such rough hunting, has been sewn up in so many places that he is a complete specimen of needlework. If any dog is hurt in a fight with elk or boar, it is sure to be old Bran. He has now a scar from a wound that was seven inches in length, which he received from a buck whose horns are hanging over my door.

I had started with the pack at daybreak, and I was riding down the Badulla road, about a mile from the kennel, when the whole pack suddenly took up a scent off the road, and dashed into the jungle in full cry. The road was enclosed by forest on either side. The pack had evidently divided upon two elk, as they were running in different directions.

Starting off down the pass I soon reached the steep patinas, and I heard the pack coming down through the jungle which crowns the hills on the left of the road. There was a crash in the underwood, and the next moment a fine buck broke cover and went away along the hill-side. Merriman and Tiptoe were the two leading dogs, and they were not fifty yards behind him. Old Smut came tearing along after them, and I gave Bran a holloa and slipped him immediately. It was a beautiful sight to see Bran fly along the patina: across the swampy bottom, taking the broad stream in one bound, and skimming up the hill, he was on the buck's path in a few minutes, pulling up to him at every stride. He passed the few dogs that were in chase like lightning, and in a few more bounds he was at the buck's side. With a dexterous blow, however, the buck struck him with his fore-foot, and sent him rolling down the hill with a frightful gash in his side. The buck immediately descended the hill-side, and came to bay in a deep pool in the river. Regardless of his wound old Bran followed him; Smut and the other dogs joined, and there was a fine bay, the buck fighting like a hero. The dogs could not touch him, as he was particularly active with his antlers.

I jumped into the water and gave them a cheer, on which the buck answered immediately by charging at me. I met him with the point of my hunting knife in the nose, which stopped him, and in the same moment old Smut was hanging on his ear, having pinned him the instant that I had occupied his attention. Bran had the other ear just as I had given the fatal thrust. In a few seconds the struggle was over. Bran's wound was four inches wide and seven inches long.

My brother had a pretty run with the doe with the other half of the pack, and we returned home by eight A.M., having killed two elk.

Daybreak is the proper time to be upon the ground for elk-hunting. At this hour they have only just retired to the jungle after their night's wandering on the patinas, and the hounds take up a fresh scent, and save the huntsman the trouble of entering the jungle. At a later hour the elk have retired so far into the jungle that much time is lost in finding them, and they are not so likely to break cover as when they are just on the edge of the forest. I had overslept myself one morning when I ought to have been particularly early, as we intended to hunt at the Matturatta plains, a distance of six miles. The scent was bad, and the sun was excessively hot; the dogs were tired and languid. It was two o'clock P.M. and we had not found, and we were returning through the forest homewards, having made up our minds for a blank day.

Suddenly I thought I heard a deep voice at a great distance; it might have been fancy, but I listened again. I counted the dogs, and old Smut was missing. There was no mistaking his voice when at bay, and I now heard him distinctly in the distance. Running towards the sound, through fine open forest, we soon arrived on the Maturatta plains. The whole pack now heard the old dog distinctly, and they rushed to the sound across the patinas. There was Smut sure enough, with a fine buck at bay in the river, which he had found and brought to bay single-handed.

The instant that the pack joined him the buck broke his bay, and, leaping up the bank, he gave a beautiful run over the patinas, with the whole pack after him, and Bran a hundred paces in advance of the other dogs, pulling up to him with murderous intent. Just as I thought that Bran would have him, a sudden kick threw the dog over, but he quickly recovered himself, and again came to the front, and this time he seized the buck by the ear, but this giving way, lost his hold and again was kicked over. This had checked the elk's speed for some seconds, and the other dogs were fast closing up, seeing which the buck immediately altered his course for the river, and took to water in a deep pool. Down came old Smut after him, and in a few moments there was a beautiful chorus, as the whole pack had him at bay.

The river went through a deep gorge, and I was obliged to sit down and slide for about thirty yards, checking a too rapid descent by holding on to the rank grass. On arriving at the river, I could at first see nothing for the high grass and bushes which grew upon the bank, but the din of the bay was just below me. Sliding through the tangled underwood, I dropped into deep water, and found myself swimming about with the buck and dogs around me. Smut and Bran had him by the ears, and a thrust with the knife finished him.

However great the excitement may be during the actual hunting, there is a degree of monotony in the recital of so many scenes of the same character that may be fatiguing; I shall therefore close the description of these mountain sports with the death of the old hero Smut, and the loss of the best hound, Merriman, both of whom have left a blank in the pack not easily replaced.

On the 16th October 1852, I started with a very short pack. Lucifer was left in the kennel lame; Lena was at home with her pups; and several other dogs were sick. Smut and Bran were the only two seizers out that day, and, being short-handed, I determined to hunt in the more green country at the foot of Hackgalla mountain.

My brother and I had entered the jungle with the dogs, and before we had proceeded a hundred yards we heard a fierce bay, every dog having joined. The bay was not a quarter of a mile distant, and we were puzzled as to the character of the game; whatever it was, it had stood to bay without a run. Returning to the patina, in which position we could distinctly assure ourselves of the direction, we heard the bay broken, and a slow run commenced. The next instant Bran came hobbling out of the jungle covered with blood, which streamed from a frightful gash in his hind quarters. There was no more doubt remaining as to the game at bay; it was an enormous boar.

Bran was completely *hors de combat;* and Smut, having lost nearly all his teeth, was of no use single-handed with such an enemy. We had no seizers to depend upon, and the boar again stood to bay in a thick jungle.

I happened to have a rifle with me that morning, as I had noticed fresh elephant tracks in the neighbourhood a few days previous, and, hoping to be able to shoot the boar, we entered the jungle and approached the scene of the bay.

When within twenty paces of the spot, I heard his fierce grunting as he charged right and left into the baying pack. In vain I cheered them on. I heard no signs of his being seized, but the fierce barking of old Smut mingled with the savage grunts of the boar, and the occasional cry of a wounded dog, explained the hopeless nature of the contest. Again I cheered them on, and suddenly Smut came up to me from the fight, which was now not ten paces distant, but perfectly concealed in thick bamboo underwood. The old dog was covered with blood, his back was bristled up, and his deep growl betokened his hopeless rage. Poor old dog! he had his deathwound. He seemed cut nearly in half; a wound fourteen inches in length from the lower part of the belly passed up his flank, completely severing the muscle of the hind leg, and extending up to the spine. His hind leg had the appearance of being nearly off, and he dragged it after him in its powerless state, and, with a fierce bark, he rushed upon three legs once more to the fight. Advancing to within six feet of the boar I could not even see him, both he and the dogs were so perfectly concealed by the thick underwood. Suddenly the boar charged. I jumped upon a small rock and hoped for a shot, but, although he came within three feet of the rifle, I could neither see him nor could he see me. Had it not been for the fear of killing the dogs, I would have fired where the bushes were moving; but as it was, I could do nothing. A rifle was useless in such jungle. At length the boar broke his bay, but again resumed it in a similar secure position. There was no possibility of assisting the dogs, and he was cutting up the pack in detail. If Lucifer and Lena had been there we could have killed him, but without seizers we were helpless in such jungle.

This lasted for an hour, at the expiration of which we managed to call the dogs off. Old Smut had stuck to him to the last, in despite of his disabled state. The old dog, perfectly exhausted, crawled out of the jungle: he had received several additional wounds, including a severe gash in his throat. He fell from exhaustion, and we made a litter with two poles and a horsecloth to carry him home. Bran, Merriman, and Ploughboy, were all severely wounded. We were thoroughly beaten. It was the first time that we had ever been beaten off, and I trust it may be the last. We returned home with our vanquished and bleeding pack — Smut borne in his litter by four men — and we arrived at the kennel a melancholy procession. The pack was disabled for weeks, as the two leading hounds, Merriman and Ploughboy, were severely injured.

Poor old Smut lingered for a few days and died. Thus closed his glorious career of sport, and he left a fame behind him which will never be forgotten. His son, who is now twelve months old, is the facsimile of his sire, and often recalls the recollection of the old dog. I hope he may turn out as good.*

Misfortunes never come alone. A few weeks after Smut's death, Lizzie, an excellent bitch, was killed by a leopard, who wounded Merriman in the throat, but he being a powerful dog beat him off and escaped. Merriman had not long recovered from his wound when he came to a lamentable and most diabolical end.

On the 24th December 1852, we found a buck in the jungles by the Badulla road. The dead nillho so retarded the pack, that the elk got a long start of the dogs, and stealing down a stream he broke cover, crossed the Badulla road, ascended the opposite hills, and took to the jungle before a single hound appeared upon the patina. At length

* Killed four months afterwards by a buck elk.

Merriman came bounding along upon his track, full a hundred yards in advance of the pack. In a few minutes every dog had disappeared in the opposite jungle on the elk's path.

This was a part of the country where we invariably lost the dogs, as they took away across a vast jungle country towards a large and rapid river situated among stupendous precipices. I had often endeavoured to find the dogs in this part, but to no purpose; this day, however, I was determined to follow them if possible. I made a circuit of twenty miles down into the low countries, and again ascending through precipitous jungles, I returned home in the evening, having only recovered two dogs, which I found on the other side of the range of mountains over which the buck had passed. No pen can describe the beauty of the scenery in this part of the country, but it is the most frightful locality for hunting that can be imagined. The high lands suddenly cease; a splendid panoramic view of the low country extends for thirty miles before the eye; but to descend to this, precipices of immense depth must be passed; and from a deep gorge in the mountain the large river, after a succession of falls, leaps in one vast plunge of three hundred feet into the abyss below. This is a stupendous cataract, about a mile below the foot of which is the village of Pérewellé. I passed close to this village, and, having ascended the steep sides of the mountain, I spent hours in searching for the pack, but the roaring of the river and the din of the waterfalls would have drowned the cry of a hundred hounds. Once, and only once, when half-way up the side of the mountain, I thought I heard the deep bay of a hound in the river below, then I heard the shout of a native; but the sound was not repeated, and I thought it might proceed from the villagers driving their buffalos. I passed on my arduous path, little thinking of the tragic fate which at that moment attended poor Merriman.

The next day all the dogs found their way home to the kennel with the exception of Merriman. I was rather anxious at his absence, as he knew the whole country so thoroughly that he should have been one of the first dogs to return. I was convinced that the buck had been at bay in the large river, as I had seen his tracks in several places on the banks with dog tracks in company; this, added to the fact of the two stray dogs being found in the vicinity, convinced me that they had brought the elk to bay in the river, in which I imagined he had beaten the dogs off. Two or three days passed away without Merriman's return, and, knowing him to be the leading hound of the pack, I made up my mind that he had been washed down a waterfall and killed.

About a week after this had happened, a native came up from the low country with the intelligence that the dogs had brought the buck to bay in the river close to the village of Pérewellé, and that the natives had killed the elk and driven the dogs away. The remaining portion of this man's story filled me with rage and horror. Merriman would not leave the body of the elk: the natives thought that the dog might be discovered in their village, which would lead to the detection of the theft of the elk; they, therefore, tied this beautiful hound to a tree, *knocked his brains out with a hatchet*, and threw his body into the river. This dog was a favourite with every one who knew the pack. The very instant that I heard the intelligence I took a good stick, and, in company with my brother, three friends, and my informant, we started to revenge Merriman. Pérewellé is twelve miles from my house across country: it was six P.M. when we started, and we arrived at a village within two miles of this nest of villains at half-past eight.

Here we got further information, and a man who volunteered to point out three men who were the principal actors in murdering the dog. We slept at this village, and, rising at four o'clock on the following morning, we marched towards Pérewellé to surprise the village and capture the offenders.

It was bright moonlight, and we arrived at the village just at break of day. The house was pointed out in which the villains lived, and we immediately surrounded it, and upon entering we seized the offenders. Upon searching the house we found a quantity of dried venison, a spear, and an axe covered with blood, with which they had destroyed the unfortunate dog.

A glorious satisfaction is the law of might! At every blow I thought of the dog's death, and we thrashed them till we dared not go much further. The whole village, which comprises nearly a hundred persons, took to flight, according to their usual cowardly nature. The captured wretches declared their innocence, and they lay down pretending to be at the point of death. Taking a fine gutta percha whip I flogged them till they revived again; and we forced them to lead the way and point out the very spot of the elk's death.

They would not confess the dog's murder, although it was proved against them.

It was a frightful spot — about two hundred paces below the foot of the great fall. The river, swollen by the late rain, boiled, and strove with the opposing rocks, lashing itself into foam, and roaring down countless cataracts, which, though well worthy of the name, sunk into insignificance before the mighty fall which fed them. High above our heads reared the rocky precipice of a thousand feet in height, the grassy mountains capped with forest, and I could distinguish the very spot from which I had heard the shouts of men on the day of Merriman's death. Had I only known what was taking place below I might perhaps have been in time to save the dog.

We found the blood and remains of the offal of the buck, but we, of course, saw no remains of the dog, as the power of the torrent must soon have dashed him to atoms against the rocks.

Thus ended poor Merriman: a better hound could not have lived, and his murderers should have been hanged. Unfortunately, Ceylon laws are often administered by persons who have never received a legal education, and these wretches escaped without further punishment than the thrashing they had received. Of this, however, they had a full dose, which was a sweet sauce to their venison which they little anticipated.

The few descriptions that I have given of elk-hunting should introduce a stranger thoroughly to the sport. No one, however, can enjoy it with as much interest as the owner of the hounds; he knows the character of every dog in the pack—every voice is familiar to his ear; he cheers them to the attack; he caresses them for their courage; they depend upon him for assistance in the struggle, and they mutually succour each other. This renders the dog a more cherished companion than he is considered in England, where his qualities are not of so important a nature; and it makes the loss of a good hound more deeply felt by his master.

Having thus described the general character of Ceylon sports in all branches, I shall conclude by a detailed journal of one trip of a few weeks in the low country, which will at once explain the whole minutiæ of the shooting in the island. This journal is taken from a small diary which has frequently accompanied me on these excursions, containing little memoranda which, by many, might be considered tedious. The daily account of the various incidents of a trip will, at all events, give a faithful picture of the jungle sports.

CHAP. XII.

A JUNGLE TRIP.

On the 16th November, 1851, I started from Kandy, accompanied by my brother, Lieutenant V. Baker, then of the Ceylon Rifle Regiment. Having sent on our horses from Newera Ellia some days previous, as far as Matillé, sixteen miles from Kandy, we drove there early in the morning, and breakfasted with F. Layard, Esq., who was then assistant government agent. It had rained without ceasing during twenty-four hours, and, hoping that the weather might change, we waited at Matillé till two o'clock P. M. The rain still poured in torrents, and, giving up all ideas of fine weather, we started.

The horses were brought round, and old Jack knew as well as I did that he was starting for a trip, as the tether rope was wound round his neck, and the horsecloth was under his saddle. The old horse was sleek and in fine condition for a journey, and, without further loss of time, we started for Dambool, a distance of thirty-one miles. Not wishing to be benighted, we cantered the whole way, and completed the distance in three hours and a half, as we arrived at Dambool at half-past five P. M.

I had started off Wallace and all the coolies from Newera Ellia about a week beforehand; and, having instructed him to leave a small box with a change of clothes at the Dambool rest-house, I now felt the benefit of the arrangement. The horsekeepers could not possibly arrive that night. We therefore cleaned and fed our own horses, and littered them down with a good bed of paddy straw; and, that being completed, we turned our attention to curry and rice.

The next morning, at break of day, we fed the horses. Old Jack was as fresh as a daisy. The morning was delightfully cloudy, but free from rain; and we cantered on to Innamalow, five miles from Dambool. Here we procured a guide to Minneria; and, turning off from the main road into a narrow jungle-path, we rode for twenty miles through dense jungle. Passing the rock of Sigiri, which was formerly used as a fort by the ancient inhabitants of the country, we gradually entered better jungle, and at length we emerged upon the beautiful plains of Minneria. I had ordered Wallace to pitch the encampment in the exact spot which I had frequently occupied some years ago. I therefore knew the place of rendezvous, and directed my course accordingly.

What a change had taken place! a continuous rought had reduced the lake from its original size of twenty-two miles in circumference, to a mere pool of about four miles in circuit; this was all that remained of the noble sheet of water around which I had formerly enjoyed so much sport.

From the rich bed of the dry lake sprung a fine silky grass of about two feet in height, forming a level plain of velvet green far as the eye could reach. The turf was firm and elastic; the four o'clock sun had laid aside the fiercest of his rays, and threw a gentle glow over the scene, which reminded me of an English midsummer evening.

There is so little ground in Ceylon upon which a horse can gallop without the risks of holes, bogs, and rocks, that we could not resist a canter upon such fine turf; and although the horses had made a long journey already, they seemed to enjoy a more rapid pace when they felt the inviting sward beneath their feet. Although every inch of this country had been familiar to me, I felt some difficulty in finding the way to the appointed spot, the scene was so changed by the disappearance of the water.

There were fresh elephant tracks in many parts of the plain, and I was just anticipating good sport for the next day, when we suddenly heard an elephant trumpet in the open forest which we were skirting. The next instant I saw eight elephants among the large trees which bordered the forest. For the moment I thought it was a herd, but I almost immediately noticed the constrained and unnatural positions in which they were standing. They were all tied to different trees by the legs, and upon approaching the spot we found an encampment of Arabs and Moormen who had been noosing elephants for sale. We at once saw that the country was disturbed, as these people had been employed in catching elephants for some weeks.

After a ride of seven or eight miles along the plain, I discovered a thin blue line of smoke rising from the edge of a distant forest, and shortly after I could distinguish forms moving on the plain in the same direction. Cantering towards the spot, we found our coolies and encampment. The tents were pitched under some noble trees, which effectually excluded every ray of sun. It was the exact spot upon which I had been accustomed to encamp some years ago. The servants had received orders when they started from Kandy to have dinner prepared at five o'clock on the 17th November; it was accordingly ready on our arrival.

Minneria was the appointed rendezvous from which this trip was to commence. Our party was to consist of the Honourable Stuart Wortley; E. Palliser, Esq.; Lieutenant V. Baker; S. W. Baker. My brother had unfortunately only fourteen days' leave from his regiment, and he and I had accordingly hurried on a day in advance of our party, they having still some preparations to complete in Kandy, and not being quite so well horsed for a quick journey.

Nothing could be more comfortable than our arrangements. Our followers and establishment consisted of four personal servants, an excellent cook, four horsekeepers, fifty coolies, and Wallace; in all, sixty people. The coolies were all picked men, who gave not the slightest trouble during the whole trip. We had two tents, one of which contained four beds and a general dressing-table;

the other, which was my umbrella-shaped tent, was arranged as the dining-room, with table and chairs. With complete dinner and breakfast services for four persons, and abundance of table linen, we had everything that could be wished for. Although I can rough it if necessary, I do not pretend to prefer discomfort from choice. A little method, and a trifling extra cost, will make the jungle trip anything but uncomfortable. There was nothing wanting in our supplies. We had sherry, Madeira, brandy and curaçoa, biscuits, tea, sugar, coffee, hams, tongues, sauces, pickles, mustard, sardines *en huile*, tins of soups, and preserved meats and vegetables, currant jelly for venison, macaroni, vermicelli, flour, and a variety of other things that add to the comfort of the jungle, including last, but not least, a double supply of soap and candles. No one knows the misery should either of these fail — dirt and darkness is the necessary consequence.

There was a large stock of talipots * to form tents for the people and coverings for the horses in case of rain; in fact, there never was a trip more happily planned or more comfortably arranged, and

* Large leaves from the Talipot tree.

there was certainly never such a battery assembled in Ceylon as we now mustered. Such guns deserve to be chronicled: —

Wortley	1 single barrel rifle		3-ounce.
„	1 double do. rifle	-	No. 12.
„	2 double do. guns	-	No. 12.
Palliser	1 single do. rifle	-	No. 8. (my old 2-ounce).
„	1 double do. rifle	-	No. 12.
„	2 double do. guns	-	No. 12.
V. Baker	3 double do. do.	-	No. 14.
„	1 double do. do.	-	No. 12.
„	1 single do. rifle	-	No. 14.
S. W. Baker	1 single do. rifle	-	4-ounce.
„	3 double do. rifles	-	No. 10.
„	1 double do. gun	-	No. 16.
	18 guns		

These guns were all by the first makers, and we took possession of our hunting country with the confidence of a good bag, provided that game was abundant.

But how changed was this country since I had visited it in former years, not only in appearance but in the quantity of game!

On these plains, where in times past I had so often counted immense herds of wild buffalos, not one was now to be seen. The deer were scared, and in small herds, not exceeding seven or ten, proving how they had been thinned out by shooting. In fact Minneria had become within the last four years a focus for most sportsmen, and the consequence was that the country was spoiled; not by the individual shooting of visitors, but by the stupid practice of giving the natives large quantities of powder and ball as a present at the conclusion of a trip. They of course, being thus supplied with ammunition, shoot the deer and buffalos without intermission, and drive them from the country by incessant harassing.

I saw immediately that we could not expect much sport in this disturbed part of the country, and we determined to waste no more time in this sport than would be necessary in procuring the elephant trackers from Doolana. We planned our campaign that evening at dinner.

Nov. 18.—At day-break I started Wallace off to Doolana to bring my old acquaintance the Rhatamahatmeya and the Moormen trackers. I felt confident that I could prevail upon him to accompany us to the limits of his district; this was all-important to our chance of sport, as without him we could procure no assistance from the natives.

After breakfast we mounted our horses and rode to Cowdellé, eight miles, as I expected to find elephants in this open but secluded part of the country. There were very fresh tracks of a herd, and as we expected Wortley and Palliser on the following day we would not disturb the country, but returned to Minneria, and passed the afternoon in shooting snipe and crocodiles. The latter were in incredible numbers, as the whole population of this usually extensive lake were now condensed in the comparatively small extent of water before us. The fish of course were equally numerous, and we had an unlimited supply of "Lola" of three to four pounds weight at a penny each. Our gang of coolies feasted upon them in immense quantities, and kept a native fully employed in catching them. Our cook exerted his powers in producing some *piquante* dishes with these fish. Stewed with melted butter (ghee), with anchovy sauce, Madeira, sliced onion, and green chilies; this was a dish worthy of "Soyer," but they were excellent in all shapes, even if plain boiled or fried.

Nov. 19.—At about four P.M. I scanned the plain with my telescope, in expectation of the arrival of our companions, whom I discovered in the distance, and as they approached within hearing, we greeted them with a shout of welcome to show the direction of our encampment. We were a merry party that evening at dinner, and we determined to visit Cowdellé, and track up the herd that we had discovered, directly that the Moormen trackers should arrive from Doolana.

The worst of this country was the swarm of musquitos which fed upon us at night; it was impossible to sleep with the least degree of comfort, and we always hailed the arrival of morning with delight.

Nov. 20. — At dawn this morning, before daylight could be called complete, Palliser had happened to look out from the tent, and to his surprise he saw a rogue elephant just retreating to the jungle, at about two hundred yards distance. We loaded the guns and went after him in as short a time as possible, but he was too quick for us, and he had retreated to thick jungle before we were out. Wortley and I then strolled along the edge of the jungle, hoping to find him again in some of the numerous nooks which the plain formed by running up the forest. We had walked quietly along for about half a mile, when we crossed an abrupt rocky promontory, which stretched from the jungle into the lake like a ruined pier. On the other side the lake formed a small bay, shaded by the forest which was separated from the water's edge by a gentle slope of turf, about fifty yards in width. This bay was a sheltered spot, and as we crossed the rocky promontory, the noise that we made over the loose stones, in turning the corner, disturbed a herd of six deer, five of whom dashed into the jungle; the sixth stopped for a moment at the edge of the forest to take a parting look at us. He was the buck of the herd, and carried a noble pair of antlers; he was about a hundred and twenty yards from us, and I took a quick shot at him with one of the No. 10 rifles. The brushwood closed over him as he bounded into the jungle, but an ominous crack sounded back from the ball, which made me think he was hit. At this moment Palliser and V. Baker came running up, thinking that we had found the elephant.

The buck was standing upon some snow-white quartz rocks when I fired, and upon an examination of the spot, frothy patches of blood showed that he was struck through the lungs. Men are bloodthirsty animals; for nothing can exceed the pleasure, after making a long shot, of finding the blood track on the spot when the animal is gone. We soon tracked him up, and found him lying dead in the jungle within twenty yards of the spot.

This buck was the first head of game we had bagged, with the exception of a young elk that I had shot on horseback during the ride from Dambool. We had plenty of snipe, and what with fish, wildfowl, and venison, our breakfast began to assume an inviting character. After breakfast we shot a few couple of snipe upon the plain, and in the evening we formed two parties, Palliser and V. Baker, and Wortley and myself, and taking different directions, we scoured the country, agreeing to meet at the tent at dusk.

W. and I saw nothing beyond the fresh tracks of game which evidently came out only at night. We wandered about till evening, and then returned towards the tent. On the way there I tried a long shot at a heron with a rifle; he was standing at about a hundred and fifty yards from us, and by a lucky shot I killed him.

On arrival at the tent we found P. and V. B., who had returned. They had been more fortunate in their line of country, having found two rogue elephants; one in thick jungle, which V. B. fired at and missed, and shortly after this shot, they found another rogue on the plain not far from the tent. The sun was nearly setting, and shone well in the elephant's eyes; thus they were able to creep pretty close to him without being observed, and P. killed him by a good shot with a rifle, at about twenty-five yards. In my opinion, this was the same elephant that had been seen near the tent early in the morning.

Wallace, with the Rhatamahatmeya and the trackers, had arrived, and we resolved to start for Cowdellé at daybreak on the following morning.

Nov. 21. — Having made our preparations overnight for an early start, we were off at daybreak, carrying with us the cook with his utensils, and the canteen containing everything that could be required for breakfast. We were thus prepared for a long day's work, should it be necessary.

After a ride of about eight miles along a sandy path, bordered by dense jungle, we arrived at the open but marshy ground upon which we had seen the tracks of the herd a few days previous. Fresh elephant tracks had accompanied us the whole way along our path, and a herd was evidently somewhere in the vicinity, as the path was obstructed in many places by the branches of trees upon which they had been feeding during the night. The sandy ground was likewise printed with innumerable tracks of elk, deer, hogs, and leopards. We halted under some wide-spreading trees, beneath which a clear stream of water rippled over a bed of white pebbles, with banks of fine green sward. In this spot were unmistakeable tracks of elephants where they had been recently drinking. The country was park-like, but surrounded upon its borders with thick jungles; clumps of thorny bushes were scattered here and there, and an abundance of good grass and water ensured a large quantity of game. The elephants were evidently not far off, and of course were well secured in the thorny jungles.

Wortley had never yet seen a wild elephant, and a dense jungle is by no means a desirable place for an introduction to this kind of game. It is a rule of mine never to follow elephants in such ground, where they generally have it all their own way; but as there are exceptions to all rules, we determined to find them, after having taken so much trouble in making our arrangements.

We unsaddled, and ordered breakfast to be ready for our return beneath one of the most shady trees, and having loaded, we started off upon the tracks. As I had expected, they led to a thick thorny jungle, and slowly and cautiously we followed the leading tracker. The jungle became worse and worse as we advanced, and had it not been for the path which the elephants had formed, we could not have moved an inch. The leaves of the bushes were wet with dew, and we were obliged to cover up all the gun-locks to prevent any of them missing fire. We crept for about a quarter of a mile upon this track, when the sudden snapping of a branch, a hundred paces in advance, plainly showed that we were up with the game.

This is the exciting moment in elephant-shooting, and every breath is held for a second intimation of the exact position of the herd. A deep, guttural sound, like the rolling of very distant thunder, is heard, accompanied by the rustling and cracking of the branches, as they rub their tough sides against the trees. Our advance had been so stealthy that they were perfectly undisturbed. Silently and carefully we crept up, and in a few minutes I distinguished two immense heads exactly facing us at about ten paces distant. Three more indistinct forms loomed in the thick bushes just behind the leaders.

A quiet whisper to Wortley to take a cool shot at the left-hand elephant, in the exact centre of the forehead, and down went the two leaders, Wortley's and mine; quickly we ran into the herd, before they knew what had happened, and down went another to V. Baker's shot. The smoke hung in such thick volumes that we could hardly see two yards before us, when straight into the cloud of smoke an elephant rushed towards us. V. Baker fired, but missed; and my left-hand barrel extinguished him. Running through the smoke with a spare rifle I killed the last elephant. They were all bagged — five elephants within thirty seconds from the first shot fired. Wortley had commenced well, having killed his first elephant with one shot.

We found breakfast ready on our return to the horses, and having disturbed this part of the country by the heavy volley at the herd, we returned to Minneria.

I was convinced that we could expect no sport in this neighbourhood; we therefore held a consultation as to our line of country.

Some years ago I had entered the north of the Veddah country from this point, and I now proposed that we should start upon a trip of discovery, and endeavour to penetrate from the north to the south of the Veddah country into the "Park." No person had ever shot over this route, and the wildness of the idea only increased the pleasure of the trip. We had not the least idea of the distance, but we knew the direction by a pocket compass.

There was but one objection to the plan, and this hinged upon the shortness of V. Baker's leave. We had only ten days unexpired, and it seemed rash, with so short a term, to plunge into an unknown country; however, he was determined to push on, as he trusted in the powers of an extraordinary poney that would do any distance on a push. This determination however destroyed a portion of the trip, as we were obliged to push quickly through a lovely sporting country, to arrive at a civilized, or rather an acknowledged line of road by which he could return to Kandy. Had we, on the contrary, travelled easily through this country, we should have killed an extraordinary amount of game.

We agreed that our route should be this. We were to enter the Veddah country at the north, and strike down to the south. I knew a bridle-path from Badulla to Batticaloa, which cut through the Veddah country from west to east; therefore we should meet it at right angles. From this point V. Baker was to bid adieu, and turn to the west and reach Badulla, from thence to Newera Ellia, and to his regiment in Kandy. We were to continue our direction southward, which I knew wou ld eventually bring us to the Park.

Nov. 22.—We moved our encampment, accompanied by the headman and his followers, and after a ride of fourteen miles we arrived at the country of Hengiriwatdowané, a park-like spot of about twelve square miles, at which place we were led to expect great sport. The appearance of the ground was all that we could wish; numerous patches of jungle and single trees were dotted upon the surface of fine turf.

In the afternoon, after a cooling shower, we all separated, and started with our respective gun-bearers in different directions, with the understanding that no one was to fire a shot at any game but elephants. We were to meet in the evening and describe the different parts of the country so that we should know how to proceed on the following day.

I came upon herds of deer in several places, but I of course did not fire, although they were within certain shot. I saw no elephants.

Everyone saw plenty of deer, but V. Baker was the only lucky individual in meeting with elephants. He came upon a fine herd, but they winded him and escaped. There was evidently plenty of game, but V. B. having fired at the elephants, we knew that this part of the country was disturbed;

we therefore had no hesitation in discharging all the guns and having them well cleaned for the next morning, when we proposed to move the tent a couple of miles further off.

Nov. 23. — A most unfortunate day, proving the disadvantage of being ignorant of the ground. Although I knew the whole country by one route, from Minneria to the north of the Veddah country, we had now diverged from that route to visit this particular spot, which I had never before shot over. We passed on through beautiful open country interspersed with clumps of jungle, but without one large tree that would shade the tent.

A single roofed tent exposed to the sun is perfectly unbearable, and we continued to push on in the hope of finding a tree of sufficient size to afford shelter.

Some miles were passed; fresh tracks of elephants and all kinds of game were very numerous, and the country was perfection for shooting.

At length the open plains became more contracted, and the patches of jungle larger and more frequent. By degrees the open ground ceased altogether, and we found ourselves in a narrow path of deep mud passing through impenetrable thorny jungle. Nevertheless our guide insisted upon pushing on to a place which he compared to that which we had unfortunately left behind us. Instead of going two miles, as we had originally intended, we had already ridden sixteen at the least, and still the headman persisted in pushing on. No coolies were up; the tents and baggage were far behind; we had nothing to eat; we had left the fine open country, which was full of game, miles behind us, and we were in a close jungle country where a rifle was not worth a bodkin. It was too annoying. I voted for turning back to the lovely hunting-ground that we had deserted; but after a long consultation we came to the conclusion that every day was of such importance to V. Baker, that we could not afford to retrace a single step.

Thus all this beautiful country, abounding with every kind of game, was actually passed over without firing a single shot.

I killed a few couple of snipe in a neighbouring swamp to pass the time until the coolies arrived with the baggage; they were not up until four o'clock P. M., therefore the whole day was wasted, and we were obliged to sleep here.

Nov. 24. — This being Sunday, the guns were at rest. The whole of this country was dense chenar jungle; we therefore pushed on, and after a ride of fourteen miles, we arrived at the Rhatamahatmeya's residence at Doolana. He insisted upon our taking breakfast with him, and he accordingly commenced his preparations. Borrowing one of our hunting-knives, two of his men gave chase to a kid, and cut his head off. Half an hour afterwards we were eating it in various forms, all of which were excellent.

We had thus travelled over forty-four miles of country from Minneria, without killing a single head of game. Had we remained a week in the country through which we had passed so rapidly, we must have had most excellent sport. All this was the effect of being hurried for time.

In the neighbourhood of Doolana I had killed many elephants some years ago, and I have no doubt we could have had good sport at this time; but V. Baker's leave was so fast expiring, and the natives' accounts of the distance through the Veddah country were so vague, that we had no choice except to push straight through as fast as we could travel, until we should arrive on the Batticaloa path.

We took leave of our friend the Rhatamahatmeya; he had provided us with good trackers, who were to accompany us through the Veddah country to the Park; but I now began to have my doubts as to the knowledge of the ground. However we started, and after skirting the Doolana tank for some distance, we rode five miles through fine forest, and then arrived on the banks of the Mahawellé river. The stream was at this time very rapid, and was a quarter of a mile in width, rolling along between its steep banks through a forest of magnificent trees. Some hours were consumed in transporting the coolies and baggage across the river, as the canoe belonging to the village of Monampitya, on the opposite bank, would only hold four coolies and their loads at one voyage.

We swam the horses across, and, attending carefully to the safety of the cook before any other individual, we breakfasted on the opposite bank, while the coolies were crossing the river.

After breakfast, a grave question arose, viz., Which way were we to go? The trackers that the headman had given us now confessed that they did not know an inch of the Veddah country into which we had arrived by crossing the river, and they refused to go a step further. Here was a "regular fix!" as the Americans would express it.

The village of Monampitya consists of about six small huts; and we now found out that there was no other village within forty miles in the direction that we wished to steer. Not a soul could we obtain as a guide—no offer of reward would induce a man to start — as they declared that no one knew the country, and that the distance was so great that the people would be starved, as they could get nothing to eat. We looked hopelessly at the country before us. We had a compass, certainly, which might be useful enough on a desert or a prairie, but in a jungle country it was of little value.

Just as we were in the greatest despair, and we were gazing wistfully in the direction which the needle pointed out as the position of the "Park," now separated from us by an untravelled district of an unknown distance, we saw two figures with bows and arrows coming from the jungle. One of these creatures bolted back again into the bushes the moment he perceived us; the other one had a fish in his hand, of about four pounds weight, which he had shot with his bow and arrow, and, while he was hesitating whether he should run or stand still, we caught him.

Of all the ugly little devils I ever saw, he was superlative. He squinted terribly; his hair was greyish and matted with filth; he was certainly not more than four feet and a half high, and he carried a bow two feet longer than himself. He could speak no language but his own, which throughout the Veddah country is much the same, intermixed with so many words resembling Cingalese that a native can generally understand their meaning. By proper management, and some little presents of rice and tobacco, we got the animal into a good humour, and we gathered the following information:—

He knew nothing of any place except the northern portion of the Veddah country. This was his world; but his knowledge of it was extremely limited, as he could not undertake to guide us further than Oomanoo, a Veddah village, which he described as three days' journey from where we then stood. We made him point out the direction in which it lay. This he did, after looking for some moments at the sun; and, upon comparing the position with the compass, we were glad to see it at South-South-East, being pretty close to the course that we wished to steer. From Oomanoo, he said, we could procure another Veddah to guide us still further; but he himself knew nothing more.

Now this was all satisfactory enough so far; but I had been completely wrong in my idea of the distance from Doolana to the "Park." We now heard of *three days'* journey to Oomanoo, which was certainly somewhere in the very centre of the Veddah country; and our quaint little guide had never even heard of the Batticaloa road. There was no doubt, therefore, that it was a long way from Oomanoo, which village might be any distance from us, as a Veddah's description of a day's journey might vary from ten to thirty miles.

I certainly looked forward to a short allowance of food both for ourselves and coolies. We had been hurrying through the country at such a rate that we had killed no deer; we had, therefore, been living upon our tins of preserved provisions, of which we had now only four remaining.

At the village of Monampitya there was no rice procurable, as the natives lived entirely upon korrakan *, at which our coolies turned up their noses, when I advised them to lay in a stock before starting.

There was no time to be lost, and we determined to push on as fast as the coolies could follow, as they had only two days' provisions; we had precisely the same, and those could not be days of

* A small seed, which they make into hard uneatable cakes.

feasting. We were, in fact, like sailors going to sea with a ship only half victualled; and, as we followed our little guide, and lost sight of the village behind us, I foresaw that our stomachs would suffer unless game was plentiful on the path.

We passed through beautiful open country for about eight miles, during which we saw several nerds of deer; but we could not get a shot. At length we pitched the tent, at four o'clock P. M., at the foot of "Gunner's Coin," a solitary rocky mountain of about two thousand feet in height, which rises precipitously from the level country. We then divided into two parties — W. and P., and V. B. and I. We strolled off with our guns in different directions.

The country was perfectly level, being a succession of glades of fine low grass divided into a thousand natural paddocks by belts of jungle.

We were afraid to stroll more than a mile from the tent, lest we should lose our way; and we took a good survey of the most prominent points of the mountain, that we might know our direction by their position.

After an hour's walk, and just as the sun was setting, a sudden crash in a jungle a few yards from us brought the rifles upon full cock. The next moment, out came an elephant's head, and I knocked him over by a front shot. He had held his head in such a peculiar position, that a ball could not reach the brain, and he immediately recovered himself, and, wheeling suddenly round, he retreated into the jungle, through which we could not follow.

We continued to stroll on from glade to glade, expecting to find him; and, in about a quarter of an hour, we heard the trumpet of an elephant. Fully convinced that this was the wounded animal, we pushed on towards the spot; but, on turning a corner of the jungle, we came suddenly upon a herd of seven of the largest elephants that I ever saw together; they must have been all bulls. Unfortunately, they had our wind, and, being close to the edge of a thick thorny jungle, they disappeared like magic. We gave chase for a short distance, but were soon stopped by the thorns. We had no chance with them.

It was now dusk, and we therefore hastened towards the tent, seeing three herds of deer and one of hogs on our way; but it was too dark to get a shot. The deer were basking in every direction, and the country was evidently alive with game.

On arrival at the tent, we found that W. and P. had met with no better luck than ourselves. Two of our tins of provisions were consumed at dinner, leaving us only two remaining. Not a moment was to be lost in pushing forward; and we determined upon a long march on the following day.

Nov. 25. — Sunrise saw us in the saddles. The coolies, with the tents and baggage, kept close up with the horses, being afraid to lag behind, as there was not a semblance of a path, and we depended entirely upon our small guide, who appeared to have an intimate knowledge of the whole country. The little Veddah trotted along through the winding glades; and we travelled for about five miles without a word being spoken by one of the party, as we were in hopes of coming upon deer. Unfortunately, we were travelling down wind; we accordingly did not see a single head of game, as they of course winded us long before we came in view.

We had ridden about eight miles, when we suddenly came upon the fresh tracks of elephants, and, immediately dismounting, we began to track up. The ground being very dry, and the grass short and parched, the tracks were very indistinct, and it was tedious work. We had followed for about half a mile through alternate glades and belts of jungle, when we suddenly spied a Veddah hiding behind a tree about sixty yards from us. The moment that he saw he was discovered, he set off at full speed; but two of our coolies who acted as gunbearers, started after him. These fellows were splendid runners, and, after a fine course, they ran him down; but when caught, instead of expressing any fear, he seemed to think it a good joke. He was a rather short but stout built fellow, and he was immediately recognized by our little guide as one of the best hunters among the northern Veddahs. He soon understood our object; and, putting down his bow and arrows and a little pipkin of sour curd (his sole provision on his hunting trip), he started at once upon the track.

Without any exception, he was the best tracker I have ever seen: although the ground was as hard as a stone, and the footprints constantly invisible, he went like a hound upon a scent at a pace that kept us in an occasional jog-trot. After half an hour's tracking, and doubling backwards and forward in thick jungle, we came up with three elephants. V. B. killed one, and I killed another at the same moment. V. B. also fired at the third; but, instead of falling, he rushed towards us, and I killed him with my remaining barrel, Palliser joining in the shot. They were all killed in about three seconds. The remaining portion of the herd were at a distance, and we heard them crashing through the thick jungle. We followed them for about a mile, but they had evidently gone off to some other country. The jungle was very thick, and we had a long journey to accomplish; we therefore returned to the horses, and rode on, our party being now increased by the Veddah tracker.

After having ridden about twenty miles, the last eight of which had been through alternate forest and jungle, we arrived at a small plain of rich grass of about a hundred acres: this was surrounded by forest. Unfortunately, the nights were not moonlight, or we could have killed a deer, as they came out in immense herds just at dusk. We luckily bagged a good supply of snipe, upon which we dined, and we reserved our tins of meat for some more urgent occasion.

Nov. 26. — All vestiges of open country had long ceased. We now rode for seventeen miles through magnificent forest, containing the most stupendous Banian trees that I have ever beheld. The ebony trees were also very numerous, and grew to an immense size. This forest was perfectly open. There was not a sign of either underwood or grass beneath the trees, and no track was discernible, beyond the notches in the trees made at some former time by the Veddah's axe. In one part of this forest a rocky mountain appeared at some period to have burst into fragments; and, for the distance of about a mile, it formed the apparent ruins of a city of giants. Rocks as large as churches lay piled one upon the other, forming long dark alleys and caves that would have housed some hundred men.

The effect was perfectly fairylike, as the faint silver light of the sun, mellowed by the screen of tree tops, half lighted up these silent caves. The giant stems of the trees sprung like tall columns from the foundations of the rocks, and shadowed them with their dense foliage. Two or three families of "Cyclops" would not have been out of place in this spot; they were just the class of people that one would expect to meet in such a place.

Late in the afternoon, we arrived at the long talked of village of Oomanoo, about eighteen miles from our last encampment. It was a squalid miserable place of course, and nothing was obtainable. Our coolies had not tasted food since the preceding evening; but, by good luck, we met a travelling Moorman, who had just arrived at the village with a little rice to exchange with the Veddahs for dried venison. As the villagers did not happen to have any meat to barter, we purchased all the rice at an exorbitant price; but it was only sufficient for half a meal for each servant and cooley, when equally divided.

Fortunately, we killed four snipe and two doves: these were added to our last two tins of provisions, which were "hotch potch," and stewed all together. This made a good dinner. We had now nothing left but our biscuits and groceries. All our hams and preserved meats were gone, and we only had one meal on that day.

Nov. 27. — Our horses had eaten nothing but grass for many days; this, however, was excellent, and old Jack looked fat, and was as hardy as ever. We now discharged our Veddah guides, and took on others from Oomanoo. These men told us that we were only four miles from the Batticaloa road, and, with great glee, we started at break of day, determined to breakfast on arrival at the road.

The old adage of "Many a slip 'twixt the cup and the lip" was here fully exemplified. Four miles! We rode twenty-five miles! without drawing the rein once, and at length we then did reach the road; that is to say, a narrow track of grass, which is the track to Batticaloa, for which we had been steering during our journey. A native hut in this wilderness rendered the place worthy of a name; it is therefore known upon the government maps as "Pyeley."

From this place we were directed on to "Curhellulai," a village represented to us as a small London, abounding with every luxury. We obtained a guide and started, as they assured us it was only two miles distant.

After riding three miles through a country of open glades and thick jungle, the same guide who had at first told us it was two miles from "Pyeley," now said it was only "*three miles further on.*" We knew these fellows' ideas of distance too well to proceed any further. We had quitted the Batticaloa track, and we immediately dismounted, unsaddled, and turned the horses loose upon the grass.

Having had only one meal the day before, and no breakfast this morning, we looked forward with impatience to the arrival of the coolies, although I confess I did not expect them, as they were too weak from want of food to travel far. They had only half a meal the day before, and nothing at all the day before that.

We had halted in a grassy glade surrounded by thick jungle. There were numerous fresh tracks of deer and elk, but the animals themselves would not show.

As evening approached we collected a quantity of dead timber and lighted a good fire, before which we piled the rifles, three and three, about ten feet apart. Across these we laid a pole, and then piled branches from the ground to the pole in a horizontal position. This made a shed to protect us from the dew, and, with our saddles for pillows, we all lay down together and slept soundly till morning.

Nov. 28.—We woke hungry, and accordingly tightened our belts by two or three holes. V. Baker had to be in Kandy by the evening of the 30th, and he was now determined to push on. His pony had thrown all his shoes, and had eaten nothing but grass for many days.

I knew our position well, as I had been lost near this spot about two years ago. We were fifty-three miles from Badulla. Nevertheless, V. B. started off, and arrived in Badulla that evening. On the same pony he pushed on to Newera Ellia, thirty-six miles, the next day, and then taking a fresh horse, he rode into Kandy, forty-seven miles, arriving in good time on the evening of the 30th November.

Having parted with V. B., we saddled and mounted, and, following our guide through a forest-path, we arrived at Curhellulai after a ride of four miles. Nothing could exceed the wretchedness of this place, from which we had been led to expect so much. We could not even procure a grain of rice from the few small huts which composed the village. The headman, who himself looked half-starved, made some cakes of korrakan; but as they appeared to be composed of two parts of sand, one of dirt, and one of grain, I preferred a prolonged abstinence to such filth. The abject poverty of the whole of this country is beyond description.

Our coolies arrived at eight A.M., faint and tired; they no longer turned up their noses at korrakan, as they did at Monampitya, but they filled themselves almost to bursting.

I started off V. B.'s coolies after him, also eight men whose loads had been consumed, and, with a diminished party, we started for Bibillé, which the natives assured us was only nineteen miles from this spot. For once they were about correct in their ideas of distance. The beautiful park country commenced about four miles from Curhellulai, and, after a lovely ride through this scenery for sixteen miles, we arrived at the luxurious and pretty village of Bibillé, which had so often been my quarters.

We had thus ridden about 140 miles from Minneria, through a country abounding with game of all kinds, sixty miles of which had never been shot over, and yet the whole bag in this lovely country consisted of only three elephants. So much for hurrying through our ground. If we had remained for a week at the foot of the Gunner's Coin, we could have obtained supplies of all kinds from Doolana, and we should have enjoyed excellent sport through the whole country. Our total bag was now wretchedly small, considering the quantity of ground that we had passed over. We had killed nine elephants and two deer. V. Baker had a miserable time of it, having only killed two elephants when he was obliged to return. The trip might, in fact, be said to commence from Bibillé.

This is a very pretty, civilised village, in the midst of a wild country. It is the residence of a Rhatamahatmeya, and he and his family were well known to me. They were perfectly astonished when they heard by which route we had arrived, and upon hearing of our forty-eight hours of fasting, they lost no time in preparing dinner. We were now in a land of plenty, and we shortly fell to at a glorious dinner of fowls in various shapes, curries, good coffee, rice cakes, plantains, and sweet potatoes. After our recent abstinence and poor fare, it seemed a perfect banquet.

Nov. 29.—The coolies did not arrive till early this morning; they were soon hard at work at curry and rice, and, after a few hours of rest, we packed up and started for a spot in the park (upon which I had often encamped) about ten miles from Bibillé.

The horses had enjoyed their paddy as much as we had relished our change of diet, and the coolies were perfectly refreshed. I sent orders to Kotoboya (about twenty miles from Bibillé) for several bullock loads of paddy and rice to meet us at an appointed spot, and with a good supply of fowls and rice, &c. for the present, we arrived at our place of encampment at three P. M., after a delightful ride.

The grass was beautifully green; a few large trees shaded the tents which were pitched near a stream, and the undulations of the ground, interspersed with clumps of trees, and ornamented by rocky mountains, formed a most lovely scene. We sent a messenger to Nielgala for Banda, and another to Dimbooldîné for old Medima, and the trackers, with orders to meet us at our present encampment. We then took our rifles and strolled out to get a deer. We shortly found a herd, and Wortley got a shot at about sixty yards, and killed a doe. We could have killed other deer shortly afterwards, but we did not wish to disturb the country by firing unnecessary shots, as we had observed fresh tracks of elephants.

We carried the deer to the tent, and rejoiced our coolies with the sight of venison: the doe was soon divided among them, one haunch only being reserved for our own use.

Nov. 30. — This being Sunday, was a day of rest for man and beast after our recent wanderings, and we patiently awaited the arrival of Banda and the trackers. The guns were all in beautiful order, and stood arranged against a temporary rack in readiness for the anticipated sport on the following day.

Banda and the trackers arrived in the afternoon. His accounts were very favourable as to the number of elephants, and we soon laid down a plan for beating the Park in a systematic manner.

Upon this arrangement the duration of sport in this country materially depends. If the shooting is conducted thoughtlessly here and there, without reference to the localities, the whole Park becomes alarmed at once, and the elephants quit the open country and retire to the dense chenar jungles.

I proposed that we should commence shooting at our present encampment, then beat towards the Cave, shoot over that country towards Pattapalaar, from thence to cross the river and make a circuit of the whole of that portion of the Park, and finish off in the environs of Nielgala.

Banda approved of this plan, as we should then be driving the borders of the Park, instead of commencing in the centre.

Dec. 1. — The scouts were sent out at daybreak. At two o'clock P.M. they returned: they had found elephants, but they were four miles from the tent, and two men had been left to watch them.

Upon questioning them as to their position, we discovered that they were in total ignorance of the number in the herd, as they had merely heard them roaring in the distance. They could not approach nearer, as a notoriously vicious rogue elephant was consorting with the herd. This elephant was well known to the natives from a peculiarity in having only one tush, which was about eighteen inches long.

In November and December elephant-shooting requires more than ordinary caution at the Park, as the rogue elephants, who are always bulls, are in the habit of attending upon the herds. The danger lies in their cunning. They are seldom seen in the herd itself, but they are generally within a few hundred paces, and just as the guns may have been discharged at the herd, the rogue will, perhaps, appear in full charge from his ambush. This is exquisitely dangerous, and is the manner in which I was caught near this spot in 1850.

Banda was very anxious that this rogue should be killed before we attacked the herd, and he begged me to give him a shoulder shot with the four-ounce rifle, while Wortley and Palliser were to fire at his head. A shot through the shoulder with the heavy rifle would be certain death, although he might not drop immediately; but the object of the natives was simply to get him killed on account of his mischievous habits.

We therefore agreed to make our first attack upon the rogue: if we should kill him on the spot, so much the better; if not, we knew that a four-ounce ball through his lungs would kill him eventually, and, at all events, he would not be in a humour to interrupt our pursuit of the herd, which we were to push for, the moment we had put the rogue out of the way.

These arrangements being made, we started. After a ride of about four miles through beautiful country, we saw a man in the distance, who was beckoning to us. This was one of the watchers, who pointed to a jungle into which the elephant had that moment entered. From the extreme caution of the trackers, I could see that this rogue was worthy of his name.

The jungle into which he had entered was a long but narrow belt, about a hundred yards in width; it was tolerably good, but still it was so close that we could not see more than six paces in advance. I fully expected that he was lying in wait for us, and would charge when least expected. We therefore cautiously entered the jungle, and, sending Banda on in advance, with instructions to retreat upon the guns if charged, we followed him at about twenty paces distance.

Banda immediately untied his long hair, which fell to his hips, and divesting himself of all clothing except a cloth round his loins, he crept on in advance as stealthily as a cat. So noiselessly did he move, that we presently saw him gliding back to us without a sound. He whispered that he had found the elephant, who was standing on the patina, a few yards beyond the jungle. We immediately advanced, and, upon emerging from the jungle, we saw him within thirty paces on our right, standing with his broadside exposed. Crack went the four-ounce through his shoulder, and the three-ounce and No. 8, with a similar good intention, into his head. Nevertheless, he did not fall, but started off at a great pace, though stumbling nearly on his knees, his head and tail both hanging down, his trunk hanging listlessly upon the ground, and his ears, instead of being cocked, were pressed tightly back against his neck. He did not look much like a rogue at that moment, with upwards of half a pound of lead in his carcase. Still we could not get another shot at him before he reached a jungle about seventy paces distant; and here we stopped to load before we followed him, thinking that he was in dense chenar. This was a great mistake, for, on following him a minute later, we found the jungle was perfectly open, being merely a fringe of forest on the banks of a broad river;

in crossing this we must have killed him had we not stopped to load.

On the sandy bed of this river we found the fresh tracks of several elephants, who had evidently only just retreated, being disturbed by the shots fired; these were a portion of the herd, and the old rogue having got his quietus, we pushed on as fast as we could upon the tracks through fine open forest.

For about an hour we pressed on through forests, plains, rivers, and thick jungles alternately, till at length, upon arriving on some rising ground, we heard the trumpet of an elephant.

It was fine country, but overgrown with lemon grass ten feet high. Clumps of trees were scattered here and there among numerous small dells. Exactly opposite lay several large masses of rock, shaded by a few trees, and on our left lay a small hollow of high lemon grass, bordered by jungle.

In this hollow we counted seven elephants, their heads and backs were just discernible above the grass, as we looked over them from some rising ground at about seventy yards distance. Three more elephants were among the rocks, browsing upon the long grass.

We now heard unmistakeable sounds of a large

number of elephants in the jungle below us, from which the seven elephants in the hollow had only just emerged, and we quietly waited for the appearance of the whole herd, this being their usual feeding time.

One by one they majestically stalked from the jungle. We were speculating on the probable number of this large herd, when one of them suddenly winded us, and, with magical quickness, they all wheeled round and rushed back into the jungle.

Calling upon my little troop of gun-bearers to keep close up, away we dashed after them at full speed; down the steep hollow and through the high lemon grass, now trampled into lanes by the retreating elephants.

In one instant the jungle seemed alive; there were upwards of *fifty* elephants in the herd. The trumpets rang through the forest, the young trees and underwood crashed in all directions with an overpowering noise, as this mighty herd, bearing everything before it, crashed in one united troop through the jungle.

At the extreme end of the grassy hollow there was a snug corner formed by an angle in the jungle. A glade of fine short turf stretched for a short distance into the forest, and, as the herd seemed to be bearing down in this direction, Wortley and I posted off as hard as we could go, hoping to intercept them if they crossed the glade. We arrived there in a few moments, and, taking our position on this fine level sward, about ten paces from the forest, we awaited the apparently irresistible storm that was bursting exactly upon us.

No pen, no tongue can describe the magnificence of the scene; the tremendous roaring of the herd, mingled with the shrill screams of other elephants; the bursting stems of the broken trees; the rushing sound of the leafy branches as though a tempest were howling through them, all this concentrating with great rapidity upon the very spot upon which we were standing. This was an exciting moment, especially to nerves unaccustomed to the sport.

The whole edge of the forest was faced with a dense network of creepers; from the highest tree tops to the ground they formed a leafy screen like a green curtain which clothed the forest as ivy covers the walls of a house. Behind this opaque mass the great actors in the scene were at work, and the whole body would evidently in a few seconds burst through this leafy veil and be right upon us.

On they came, the forest trembling with the onset; the leafy curtain burst into tatters, the jungle ropes and snaky stems tearing the branches from the tree tops were in a few moments heaped in a tangled and confused ruin. One dense mass of elephant's heads, in full career, presented themselves through the shattered barrier of creepers.

Running towards them with a loud holloa, they were suddenly checked by our unexpected apparition, but the confused mass of elephants made the shooting very difficult. Two elephants rushed out to cross the little nook within four yards of me, and I killed both by a right and left shot. Wallace immediately pushed a spare rifle into my hand, just as a large elephant, meaning mischief, came straight towards me, with ears cocked, from the now staggered body of the herd. I killed her with the front shot, both barrels having gone off at once, the heavy charge of powder in the right hand barrel having started the trigger of the left barrel by the concussion. Round wheeled the herd, leaving their three leaders dead; and now the race begun.

It was splendid forest, and the elephants rushed off at about ten miles an hour, in such a compact troop that their sterns formed a living barrier, and not a head could be seen. At length, after a burst of about two hundred yards, the deep and dry bed of a torrent formed a trench about ten feet in width.

Not hesitating at this obstacle, down went the herd without missing a step; the banks crumbled and half filled the trench as the leaders scrambled across, and the main body rushed after them at an extraordinary pace.

I killed a large elephant in the act of crossing; he rolled into the trench, but struggling to rise, I gave him the other barrel in the nape of the neck, which, breaking his spine, extinguished him. He made a noble bridge, and jumping upon his carcase, we cleared the ravine, and again the chase continued, although the herd had now gained about thirty paces.

Upon a fine meadow of grass, about four feet high, the herd now rushed along in a compact mass extending in a broad line of massive hind-quarters over a surface of half an acre. This space formed a complete street in their wake as they levelled everything before them; and the high grass stood up on either side of this road like a wall.

Along this level road we ran at full speed, and by great exertions, managed to keep within twenty yards of the game. Full a quarter of a mile was passed at this pace without a shot being fired. At length one elephant turned and faced about exactly in front of me. My three double-barrelled rifles were now all empty, and I was carrying the little No. 16 gun. I killed him with the right hand barrel, but I lost ground by stopping to fire.

A jungle lay about two hundred yards in front of the herd, and they increased their speed to arrive at this place of refuge.

Giving the little gun, with one barrel still loaded, to Wallace, I took the four-ounce rifle in exchange, as I knew I could not close up with the herd before they reached the jungle, and a long shot would be my last chance. With this heavy gun (21 lbs.), I had hard work to keep my distance, which was about forty yards from the herd.

Palliser and Wortley were before me, and within twenty yards of the elephants. They neared the jungle; I therefore ran off to my left as fast as I could go, so as to ensure a side shot. I was just in time to command their flank as the herd reached the jungle. A narrow river, with steep banks of twenty feet in height, bordered the edge, and I got a shot at a large elephant just as he arrived upon the brink of the chasm. He was fifty paces off, but I hit him in the temple with the four-ounce, and rolled him down the precipitous bank into the river. Here he lay groaning, so taking the little gun, with one barrel still loaded, I extinguished him from the top of the bank.

Oh, for half a dozen loaded guns! I was now unloaded, and the fun began in real earnest. The herd pushed for a particular passage down the steep bank. It was like a rush at the door of the Opera; they jostled each other in a confused *mêlée*, and crossed the river with the greatest difficulty. By some bad luck, Palliser and Wortley only killed one as the herd was crossing the river, but they immediately disappeared in pursuit, as the elephants, having effected their passage, retreated in thick jungle on the other side.

I was obliged to halt to load, which I did as quickly as possible. While I was ramming the balls down, I heard several shots fired in quick succession, and, when loaded, I ran on with my gun-bearers towards the spot.

It was bad thorny jungle, interspersed with numerous small glades of fine turf.

Upon arriving in one of these glades, about a quarter of a mile beyond the river, I saw a crowd of gun-bearers standing around some person lying upon the ground; neither Palliser nor Wortley were to be seen, and for an instant a chill ran through me as I felt convinced that some accident had happened. "Where are masters?" I shouted to the crowd of men, and the next moment I was quite relieved by seeing only a cooley lying on the ground. On examining the man, I found he was more frightened than hurt, although he was cut in several places, and much bruised.

Upon giving a shout, Palliser and Wortley returned to the spot. They now explained the mystery. They were running on the fresh tracks in this glade, no elephants being then in sight, when they suddenly heard a rush in the jungle, and in another instant two elephants charged out upon them. Wortley and he both fired, but without effect — the gun-bearers bolted — an elephant knocked one man over, and tried to butt him against the ground; but two more shots from both Palliser and Wortley turned him, but they were immediately obliged to run in their turn, as the other elephant charged and just grazed Palliser with his trunk behind. Fortunately they doubled short round, instead of continuing a straight course, and the elephants turned into the jungle. They followed them for some little distance, but the jungles were so bad that there was no chance, and they returned when I had shouted.

The man who was hurt was obliged to be supported home. Two of the guns were lost, which the gun-bearers, in their fright, had thrown away. After a long search we found them lying in the high bushes.

We now returned along the line of hunt to cut off the elephants' tails. I had fired at six, all of which were bagged, which we accordingly found in their various positions. One of them was a very large female with her udder full of milk. Being very thirsty, both Wortley and I took a long pull at this, to the evident disgust of the natives. It was very good, being exactly like cow's milk. This was the elephant that I had killed doubly by the left hand barrel exploding by accident, and the two balls were only a few inches apart in the forehead.

There had been very bad luck with this herd; the only dead elephant, in addition to these six, was that which Wortley and Palliser had both fired at in the river, and another which Palliser had knocked down in the high grass when we had just commenced the attack — at which time he had separated from us to cut off the three elephants that we had just seen among the rocks.

On arrival at the spot where the elephants had first burst from the jungle, a heavy shower came down, and the locks of the guns were immediately covered each with a large leaf, and then tied up securely with a handkerchief. A large Banian tree afforded us an imaginary shelter, but we were drenched to the skin in a few seconds. In the meantime, Palliser walked through the high lemon-grass to look for his dead elephant.

On arriving at the spot, instead of finding a *dead* elephant, he found him standing up, and only just recovered from the stunning effect of his wound.

The elephant charged him immediately, and Palliser having the lock of his gun tied up, was perfectly defenceless, and he was obliged to run as hard as his long legs would carry him.

"Look out!! look out!! an elephant's coming!! Look out!!"

This we heard shouted as we were standing beneath the tree, and the next moment we saw Palliser's tall form of six feet four come flying through the high grass. Luckily the elephant lost him, and turned off in some other direction. If he had continued the chase he would have made a fine diversion, as the locks were so tightly tied up that we could not have got a gun ready for some time. In a few minutes the shower cleared off, and on examining the place where the elephant had fallen, we found a large pool of clotted blood.

We now rode homewards, but we had not gone a quarter of a mile before we heard an elephant roaring loudly in a jungle close to us. Thinking that it was the wounded brute who had just hunted Palliser, we immediately dismounted and approached the spot. The roaring continued until we were close to it, and we then saw a young elephant standing in the bed of a river, and he it was who was making all the noise, having been separated from the herd in the late *mêlée*. Wortley shot him, this making eight killed.

When within a mile of the tent, as we were riding along a path through a thick thorny jungle, an immense rogue elephant stalked across our road. I fired the four-ounce through his shoulder, to the great satisfaction of Banda and the natives, although we never had a chance of proving what the effect had been, as he was soon lost in the thick jungle. A short time after this we reached the tent, having had the perfection of sport in elephant-shooting, although luck had been against us in making a large bag.

Dec. 2nd.— The scouts having been sent out at daybreak, returned early, having found another herd of elephants. On our way to the spot Palliser fired at a rogue, but without effect.

On arrival at the jungle in which the elephants were reported to be, we heard from the watchers that a rogue was located in the same jungle in attendance upon the herd. This was now a regular thing to expect, and compelled us to be exceedingly cautious.

Just as we were stalking through the jungle, on the track of the herd, we came upon the rogue himself. Wortley fired at him, but without effect, and unfortunately the shot frightened the herd, which was not a quarter of a mile distant, and the elephants retreated to a large tract of thick jungle country, where pursuit was impracticable. Our party was too large for shooting "rogues" with any degree of success. These brutes, being always on the alert, require the most careful stalking. There is only one way to kill them with any certainty. Two persons, at most, to attack; each person to be accompanied by only one gun-bearer who should carry two spare guns. One good tracker should lead this party of five people in single file. With great caution and silence, being well to leeward of the elephant, he can thus generally be approached till within twelve paces, and he is then killed by one shot before he knows that danger is near. What with our gun-bearers, trackers, watchers, and ourselves, we were a party of sixteen persons; it was therefore impossible to get near a rogue unperceived.

On the way to the tent I got a shot at a deer at full gallop — on old "Jack." It was a doe, who

A SHOT FROM HORSEBACK.

bounded over the plain at a speed that soon distanced my horse, and I took a flying shot from the saddle with one of my No. 10 rifles. I did not get the deer, although she was badly wounded, as we followed the blood-tracks for some distance through thick jungle without success.

This was altogether a blank day; and having thoroughly disturbed this part of the park, we determined to up stick and move our quarters on the following day towards the "cave," according to the plan that we had agreed upon for beating the country.

Dec. 3rd.—With the cook and the canteen in company we started at break of day, leaving the servants to pack up and bring the coolies and tents after us. By this arrangement we were sure of our breakfast wherever we went, and we were free from the noise of our followers, whose scent alone was enough to alarm miles of country down wind. We had our guns all loaded, and carried by our respective gun-bearers close to the horses, and, with Banda, old Medima, and a couple of trackers, we were ready for anything.

We had ridden about six miles when we suddenly came upon fresh elephant tracks, in a grassy hollow surrounded by low rocky hills. We immediately sent the men off upon the tracks, while we waited upon a high plateau of rock for their return. They came back in about a quarter of an hour, having found the elephants within half a mile.

They were in high lemon grass, and upon arrival at the spot, we could distinguish nothing, as the grass rose some feet above our heads. It was like shooting in the dark, and we ascended some rising ground to improve our position. Upon arrival on this spot we looked over an undulating sea of this grass, interspersed with rocky hills and small patches of forest. Across a valley we now distinguished the herd much scattered, going off in all directions. They had winded us, and left us but a poor chance of catching them in such ground. Of course we lost no time in giving chase. The sun was intensely hot, — not a breath of air was stirring, and the heat in the close parched grass was overpowering. With the length of start that the elephants had got, we were obliged to follow at our best pace, which, over such tangled ground, was very fatiguing; fortunately, however, the elephants had not yet seen us, and they had accordingly halted now and then, instead of going straight off.

There were only four elephants together, and, by a great chance, we came up with them just as they were entering a jungle. I got a shot at the last elephant and killed him, but the others put on more steam, and all separated, fairly beating us, as we were almost used up by the heat.

This was very bad luck, and we returned, in despair of finding the scattered herd. We had proceeded some distance through the high grass, having just descended a steep rocky hill, when we suddenly observed two elephants approaching along the side of the very hill that we had just left. Had we remained in the centre of the hill, we should have met them as they advanced. One was a large female, and the other was most probably her calf, being little more than half-grown.

It was a beautiful sight to see the caution with which they advanced, and we lay down to watch them without being seen. They were about 200 yards from us, and, as they slowly advanced along the steep hill-side they occasionally halted, and, with their trunks thrown up in the air, they endeavoured, but in vain, to discover the enemy that had so recently disturbed them. We had the wind all right, and we now crept softly up the hill so as to meet them at right angles. The hill-side was a mass of large rocks overgrown and concealed by the high lemon-grass, and it was difficult to move without making a noise, or falling into the cavities between the rocks.

I happened to be at the head of our line, and, long before I expected the arrival of the elephants, I heard a rustling in the grass, and the next moment I saw the large female passing exactly opposite me, within five or six paces. I was on half-cock at the time, as the ground was dangerous to pass over with a gun on full cock, but I was just quick enough to knock her over before the high grass should conceal her at another step. She fell in a small chasm, nearly upsetting the young elephant, who was close behind her. Wortley killed him while I took the last kick out of the old one by another shot, as she was still moving.

We had thus only killed three elephants out of the herd, and, without seeing more, we returned to the horses.

On finding them we proceeded on our road towards the "Cave," but had not ridden above two miles further when we again came upon fresh tracks of elephants. Sending on our trackers, like hounds upon their path, we sat down and breakfasted under a tree. We had hardly finished the last cup of coffee when the trackers returned, having found another herd. They were not more than half a mile distant, and they were reported to be in open forest, on the banks of a deep and broad river.

Our party was altogether too large for elephant-shooting, as we never could get close up to them without being discovered. As usual they winded us before we got near them, but by quick running we overtook them just as they arrived on the banks of the river and took to water. Wortley knocked over one fellow just as he thought he was safe in running along the bottom of a deep gully; I floored his companion at the same moment, thus choking up the gully, and six elephants closely packed together forded the deep stream. The tops of their backs and heads were alone above water. I fired the four-ounce into the nape of one elephant's neck as the herd crossed, and he immediately turned over and lay foundered in the middle of the river, which was sixty or seventy yards across. In the meantime, Palliser and Wortley kept up a regular volley, but no effects could be observed until the herd reached and begun to ascend the steep bank on the opposite side. I had reloaded the four-ounce, and the heavy battery now begun to open in concert with the general volley as the herd scrambled up the precipitous bank. Several elephants fell, and recovered themselves and disappeared. At length the volley ceased, and two were seen, one dead on the top of the bank, and the other still struggling in the shallow water at the foot of the bank. Once more a general battery opened and he was extinguished. Five were killed, and if noise and smoke add to the fun, there was certainly plenty of it. Wortley and my man Wallace now swam across the river, and cut off the elephants' tails.

We returned to the horses, and moved to the "cave," meeting with no further incidents that day.

Dec. 4th. — We saw nothing but deer the whole of the day, and they were so wild that we could not get a shot. It was therefore a blank.

Dec. 5th. — We started early, and for five miles we tracked a large herd of elephants through fine open country, until we were at length stopped by impenetrable jungle of immense extent, forming the confines of the "park" on this side. We therefore reluctantly left the tracks, and directed our course towards Pattapalaar, about twelve miles distant.

We had passed over a lovely country, and

were within a mile of our proposed resting-place, when Banda, who happened to be a hundred yards in advance, came quickly back, saying that he saw a rogue elephant feeding on the patina not far from us. Wortley had gone in another direction with old Medima a few minutes previous to look for a deer; and Palliser and I resolved to stalk him carefully. We therefore left all the people behind, except two gun-bearers, each of whom carried one of my double-barrelled rifles. I carried my four-ounce, and Palliser took the two-ounce.

It was most difficult ground for stalking, being entirely open, on a spot which had been high lemon-grass, but recently burnt, the long reeds in many places still remaining.

We could not get nearer than fifty yards in such ground, and I accordingly tried a shot at his temple with the four-ounce. The long unburnt stalks of the lemon-grass waving to and fro before the sights of my rifle so bothered me that I missed the fatal spot, and fired about two inches too high. Stumbling only for a moment from the blow, he rushed down hill towards a jungle, but at the same instant Palliser made a capital shot with the long two-ounce, and knocked him over. I never saw an elephant fall with such a crash: they generally sink gently down; but this fellow was going at such speed down hill, that he fairly pitched upon his head.

We arrived at our resting-place, and having pitched the tents, we gave them up to Banda and the servants, while we took possession of a large "amblam," or open building, massively built by the late Major Rodgers, which is about twenty-five feet square. This we arranged in a most comfortable manner, and here we determined to remain for some days while we beat the whole country thoroughly.

Dec. 6th. — We started at our usual early hour with Banda and the trackers, and after a walk of about a mile we found fresh tracks and followed up. Crossing a small river upon the track, we entered a fine open forest, through which the herd had only just passed, and upon following them for about a quarter of a mile, we came to a barrier of dense chénar jungle, into which the elephants had retreated.

There was a rogue with this herd, and we were rather doubtful of his position. We stood in the open forest, within a few feet of the thick jungle, to the edge of which the elephants were so close that we could hear their deep breathing; and by stooping down we could distinguish the tips of their trunks and their feet, although the animals themselves were invisible. We waited about half an hour in the hope that some of the elephants might again enter the open forest; at length two, neither of whom were above five feet high, came out and faced us. My dress of elastic green tights had become so browned by constant washing and exposure, that I matched exactly with the stem of a tree against which I was leaning, and one of the elephants kept advancing towards me until I could nearly touch him with my rifle; still he did not see me, and I did not wish to fire, as I should alarm the herd, which would then be lost for ever. Unfortunately, just at this moment the other elephant saw Palliser, and the alarm was given. There was no help for it, and we were obliged to fire. Mine fell dead, but the other fell, and recovering himself immediately, he escaped in the thick jungle.

This was bad luck, and we returned towards the "amblam" to breakfast. On our way there we found that the "rogue" had concealed himself in a piece of thick jungle, backed by hills of very high lemon grass. From this stronghold we tried to drive him, and posted ourselves in a fine position to receive him, should he break cover; but he was too cunning to come out, and the beaters were too knowing to go in to drive such bad jungle; it was therefore a drawn game, and we were obliged to leave him.

When within a short distance of the "amblam," a fine black partridge got up at about sixty yards. I was lucky enough to knock him over with a rifle, and still more fortunate in not injuring him much with the ball, which took his wing off close to his body. Half an hour afterwards he formed part of our breakfast.

During our breakfast a heavy shower of rain came down and continued for about two hours.

In the afternoon we sallied out, determined to shoot at any large game that we might meet. We had lately confined our sport to elephants, as we did not wish to disturb the country by shooting at other game, but having fired in this neighbourhood in the morning, we were not very particular.

We walked through a lovely country for about five miles, seeing nothing whatever in the shape of game, not even a track, as all the old marks were washed out by the recent shower. At length we heard the barking of deer in the distance, and, upon approaching the direction, we saw a fine herd of about thirty. They were standing in a beautiful meadow of about a hundred acres in extent, perfectly level, and interspersed with trees, giving it the appearance of an immense orchard rather thinly planted. One side of this plain was bounded by a rocky mountain, which rose precipitously from its base, the whole of which was covered with fine open forest.

We were just stalking towards the deer when we came upon a herd of wild buffalos in a small hollow within a close shot.

Palliser wanted a pair of horns, and he was just preparing for a shot when we suddenly heard the trumpet of an elephant in the forest at the foot of the rocky mountain, close to us.

Elephants, buffalos, and deer were all within a hundred yards of each other: we almost expected to see Noah's Ark on the top of the hill.

Of course the elephants claimed our immediate attention. It was Palliser's turn to lead the way; and upon entering the forest at the foot of the mountain, we found that the elephants were close to us. The forest was a perfect place for elephant shooting. Large rocks were scattered here and there among fine trees, free from underwood;

these rocks formed alleys of various widths, and upon such ground an elephant had no chance.

There was a large rock the size of a small house lying within a few yards from the entrance of the forest. This rock was split in two pieces, forming a passage of two feet wide, but of several yards in length. As good luck would have it, an elephant stood exactly on the other side, and Palliser leading the way, we advanced through this secure fort to the attack.

On arrival at the extreme end, Palliser fired two quick shots, and taking a spare gun, he fired a third before we could see what was going on, we being behind him in this narrow passage. Upon passing through we thought the fun was over; he had killed three elephants, and no more were to be seen anywhere.

Hardly had he re-loaded, however, when we heard a tremendous rushing through the forest in the distance; and, upon quickly running to the spot, we came upon a whole herd of elephants, who were coming to meet us in full speed. Upon seeing us, however, they checked their speed for a moment, and Palliser and Wortley both fired, which immediately turned them. This was at rather too long a distance, and no elephants were killed.

A fine chase now commenced through the open forest, the herd rushing off at great speed. This pace soon took us out of it, and we burst upon an open plain of high lemon-grass. Here I got a shot at an elephant, who separated from the main body, and I killed him.

The pace was now so great that the herd fairly distanced us in the tangled lemon-grass, which, though play to them, was very fatiguing to us.

Upon reaching the top of some rising ground, I noticed several elephants, at about a quarter of a mile distant upon my left, in high grass, while the remaining portion of the herd (three elephants) were about two hundred yards ahead, and were stepping out at full speed straight before us.

Wortley had now had plenty of practice, and shot his elephants well. He and Palliser followed the three elephants, while I parted company, and ran towards the other section of the herd, who were standing on some rising ground, and were making a great roaring.

On arriving within a hundred yards of them, I found I had caught a "Tartar." It is a very different thing, creeping up to an unsuspecting

SKETCHED BY S. W. BAKER.

HARD AT IT.

herd and attacking them by surprise, to marching up upon sheer open ground, to a hunted one with wounded elephants among them, who have regularly stood at bay. This was now the case — the ground was perfectly open, and the lemon-grass was above my head: thus I could only see the exact position of the elephants every now and then, by standing upon the numerous little rocks that were scattered here and there. The elephants were standing upon some rising ground, from which they watched every movement as I approached. They continued to growl without a moment's intermission, being enraged, not only from the noise of the firing, but on account of two calves which they had with them, and which I could not see in the high grass. There was a gentle rise in the ground within thirty paces of the spot upon which they stood; and to this place I directed my steps with great care, hiding in the high grass as I crept towards them.

During the whole of this time guns were firing without intermission in the direction taken by Palliser and Wortley, thus keeping my game terribly on the *qui vive.* What they were firing so many shots at I could not conceive.

At length I reached the rising ground. The

moment that I was discovered by them, the two largest elephants came towards me, with their ears cocked and their trunks raised.

I waited for a second or two, till they lowered their trunks, which they presently did; and taking a steady shot with one of my double-barrelled No. 10 rifles, I floored them both by a right and left. One, however, immediately recovered, and, with the blood streaming from his forehead, he turned and retreated with the remainder of the herd at great speed through the high grass.

The chase required great caution; however, they fortunately took to a part of the country where the grass was not higher than my shoulders, and I could thus see well over it. Through this I managed to keep within fifty yards of the herd, and I carried the heavy four-ounce rifle, which I knew would give one of them a benefit if he turned to charge.

I was following the herd at this distance, when they suddenly halted, and the wounded elephant turned quickly round, and charged with a right good intention. He carried his head thrown back in such a position that I could not get a fair shot; but, nevertheless, the four-ounce ball stopped him, and away he went again with the herd at full speed, the blood gushing in streams from the wounds in his head.

My four-ounce is a splendid rifle for loading quickly, it being so thick in the metal that the deep groove catches the belt of the ball immediately. I was loaded in a few seconds, and again set off in pursuit. I saw the herd at about two hundred yards distant; they had halted, and they had again faced about.

I had no sooner approached within sixty paces of them, when the wounded elephant gave a trumpet, and again rushed forward out of the herd. His head was so covered with blood, and was still thrown back in such a peculiar position, that I could not get a shot at the exact mark. Again the four-ounce crashed through his skull, and, staggered with the blow, he once more turned, and retreated with the herd.

Loading quickly, I poured the powder down *ad libitum;* and ran after the herd, who had made a circuit to arrive in the same forest in which we had first found them. A sharp run brought me up to them; but, upon seeing me, they immediately stopped, and, without a moment's pause, round came my old antagonist again straight at me, with his head still raised in the same knowing position.

The charge of powder was so great that it went off like a young fieldpiece, and the elephant fell upon his knees; but, again recovering himself, he turned and went off at such a pace that he left the herd behind, and in a few minutes I was within twenty yards of them; but I would not fire, as I was determined to bag my wounded bird before I fired a single shot at another.

They now reached the forest; but, instead of retreating, the wounded elephant turned short round upon the very edge of the jungle and faced me; the remaining portion of the herd (consisting of two large elephants, and two calves), had passed on into the cover.

This was certainly a plucky elephant; his whole face was a mass of blood, and he stood at the very spot where the herd had passed into the forest as though he was determined to guard the entrance. I was now about twenty-five yards from him, when, gathering himself together for a decisive charge, he once more came on.

I was on the point of pulling the trigger when he reeled and fell without a shot from sheer exhaustion; but recovering himself immediately, he again faced me, but did not move. This was a fatal pause; he forgot the secret of throwing his head far back, and he now held it in the natural position, offering a splendid shot at about twenty yards. Once more the four-ounce buried itself in his skull, and he fell dead.

THE LAST CHARGE.

Palliser and Wortley came up just as I was endeavouring to track up the herd which I had now lost sight of in the forest. Following upon their tracks, we soon came in view of them. Away we went as fast as we could run towards them, but I struck my shin against a fallen tree, which cut me to the bone, and pitched me upon my head. The next moment, however, we were up with the elephants: they were standing upon a slope of rock facing us, but regularly dumbfounded at their unremitting pursuit, and they all rolled over to a volley as we came up, two of them being calves. Palliser killed the two biggest right and left, he being some paces in advance.

This was one of the best hunts that I have ever shared in. The chase had lasted for nearly an hour. There were thirteen elephants originally in the herd, every one of which had been bagged by fair running. Wortley had fired uncommonly well, as he had killed the three elephants which he and Palliser had chased, one of which had given them a splendid run and had proved restive. This elephant took fifteen shots before she fell, and this accounted for the continual firing which I had heard during my chase of the other section. We had killed fourteen elephants during the day, and we returned to the "amblam," having had as fine sport as Ceylon can afford.

Dec. 7th. — This being Sunday, was passed in quiet; but a general cleaning of guns took place, to be ready for the morrow.

Dec. 8th.—We went over many miles of ground without seeing a fresh track. We had evidently disturbed the country on this side of the river, and we returned towards the "amblam," determined to cross the river after breakfast and try the opposite side.

When within a mile of the "amblam" we heard deer barking, and leaving all our gun-bearers and people behind, we carefully stalked to the spot. The ground was very favourable, and having the wind, we reached an excellent position among some trees within sixty yards of the herd of deer who were standing in a little glade. Wortley and I each killed a buck; Palliser wounded a doe, which we tracked for a great distance by the blood, but at length lost altogether.

After breakfast we crossed the large river which flows near the "amblam," and then entered a part of the park that we had not yet beaten.

Keeping to our left we entered a fine forest and skirted the base of a range of rocky mountains. In this forest we saw deer and wild buffalo, but we would not fire a shot, as we had just discovered the fresh track of a rogue elephant. We were following upon this when we heard a bear in some thick jungle. We tried to circumvent him, but in vain; Bruin was too quick for us, and we did not get a sight of him.

We were walking quietly along the dry bed of

a little brook bordered by thick jungle upon either side, when we were suddenly roused by a tremendous crash through the jungle, which was evidently coming straight upon us.

We were in a most unfavourable position, but there was no time for any further arrangement than bringing the rifle on full cock, before six elephants, including the "rogue," whose tracks we were following, burst through the jungle straight at us.

Banda was nearly run over, but with wonderful agility he ran up some tangled creepers hanging from the trees, just as a spider would climb his web. He was just in time, as the back of one of the elephants grazed his feet as it passed below him.

In the meantime the guns were not idle. Wortley fired at the leading elephant which had passed under Banda's feet, just as he was crossing the brook on our left. His shot did not produce any effect, but I killed him by a temple shot just as he was passing on. Palliser, who was on our right, killed two, and knocked down a third, who was about half grown. This fellow got up again, and Wortley and Palliser, both firing at the same moment, extinguished him.

The herd had got themselves into a mess by rushing down upon our scent in this heedless manner, as four of them lay dead within a few paces of each other. The "rogue," who knew how to take care of himself, escaped with only one companion. Upon these tracks we now followed without loss of time.

An hour was thus occupied. We tracked them through many glades and jungles, till we at length discovered in a thick chénar the fresh tracks of another herd, which the "rogue" and his companion had evidently joined, as his immense foot-print was very conspicuous among the numerous marks of the herd. Passing cautiously through a thick jungle, we at length emerged upon an extensive tract of high lemon-grass. There was a small pool of water close to the edge of the jungle which was surrounded with the fresh dung of elephants, and the muddy surface of the water was still agitated by the recent visit of some of these thirsty giants.

Carefully ascending some slightly rising ground, and keeping close to the edge of the jungle, we peered over the high grass.

We were in the very centre of the herd, who were much scattered. It was very late, being nearly dusk; but we counted six elephants here and there in the high grass within sixty paces of us, while the rustling in the jungle to our left warned us that a portion of the herd had not yet quitted this cover. We knew that the "rogue" was somewhere close at hand, and after his recent defeat he would be doubly on the alert. Our plans therefore required the greatest vigilance.

There was no doubt as to the proper course to pursue, which was to wait patiently until the whole herd had left the jungle and concentrated in the high grass; but the waning daylight did not permit of such a steady method of proceeding. I then proposed that we should choose our elephants, which were scattered in the high grass, and advance separately to the attack. Palliser voted that we should creep up to the elephants that were in the jungle close to us, instead of going into the high grass.

I did not much like this plan, as I knew that it would be much darker in the jungle than in the patina, and there was no light to spare. However, Palliser crept into the jungle, towards the spot where we heard the elephants crashing the bushes.

Instead of following behind him, I kept almost in a line, but a few feet on one side, otherwise I knew that should he fire I should see nothing for the smoke of his shot. This precaution was not thrown away. The elephants were about fifty yards from the entrance to the jungle, and we were of course up with them in a few minutes. Palliser took a steady shot at a fine elephant about eight yards from him, and fired.

The only effect produced was a furious charge right into us!

Away went all the gun-bearers except Wallace

PANIC AMONG THE GUN-BEARERS.

as hard as they could run, completely panic-stricken. Palliser and Wortley jumped to one side to get clear of the smoke, which hung like a cloud before them, and having taken my position with the expectation of something of this kind, I had a fine clear forehead shot as the elephant came rushing on, and I dropped him dead.

The gun-bearers were in such a fright that they never stopped till they got out on the patina.

The herd had of course gone off at the alarm of the firing, and we got a glimpse of the old "rogue" as he was taking to the jungle. Palliser fired an ineffectual shot at him at a long range, and the day closed. It was moonlight when we reached the "amblam": the bag for that day being five elephants and two bucks.

Dec. 9th.—We had alarmed this part of the country, and after spending a whole morning in wandering over a large extent of ground without seeing a fresh track of an elephant, we determined to move on to Nielgala, eight miles from the "amblam." We accordingly packed up, and started off our coolies by the direct path, while we made a long circuit by another route in the hope of meeting with heavy game.

After riding about four miles our path lay through a dense forest up the steep side of a hill. Over this was a narrow road, most difficult for a horse to ascend, on account of the large masses of rocks which choked the path from the base to the summit. Leaving the horse-keepers with the horses to scramble up as they best could, we took our guns and went on in advance. We had nearly reached the summit of this pass, when we came suddenly upon some fragments of chewed leaves and branches lying in the middle of the path. The saliva was still warm upon them, and the dung of an elephant lay in the road in a state which proved his close vicinity. There were no tracks, of course, as the path was nothing but a line of piled rocks, from which the forest had been lately cleared, and the elephants had just been disturbed by the clattering of the horses' hoofs in ascending the rugged pass.

Banda had run on in front about fifty yards before us, but we had no sooner arrived on the summit of the hill than we saw him returning at a flying pace towards us with an elephant chasing him in full speed.

It was an exciting scene while it lasted: with the activity of a deer he sprang from rock to rock, while we of course ran to his assistance, and arrived close to the elephant just as Banda had reached a high block of stone, which rendered him an asylum. A shot from Palliser brought the elephant upon his knees, but, immediately recovering himself, he ran round a large rock. I ran round the other side, and killed him dead within four paces.

BANDA'S ESCAPE FROM A "ROGUE."

Upon descending the opposite side of the pass we arrived in flat open country, and on the left of the road we saw another elephant, a "rogue," in high lemon-grass. We tried to get a shot at him, but it was of no use; the grass was so high and thick, that, after trying several experiments, we declined following him in such ground. We arrived at Nielgala in the evening without further sport: here we killed a few couple of snipe in the paddy fields, which added to our dinner.

Dec. 10*th.*—Having beaten several miles of country without seeing any signs of elephants, we came unexpectedly upon a herd of wild buffalos; they were standing in beautiful open ground, interspersed with trees, about a hundred and ten paces from us. I gave Palliser my heavy rifle, as he was very anxious to get a pair of good horns, and with the pleasure of a spectator I watched the sport. He made a good shot with the four-ounce, and dropped the foremost buffalo; the herd gallopped off, but he broke the hind leg of another buffalo with one of the No. 10 rifles, and, after a chase of a couple of hundred yards, he came up with the wounded beast, who could not extricate himself from a deep gully of water, as he could not ascend the steep bank on three legs. A few more shots settled him.

We gave up all ideas of elephants for this day after so much firing, but, curious enough, just as we were mounting our horses we heard the roar of an elephant in a jungle on the hill side, about half a mile distant. There was no mistaking the sound, and we were soon at the spot. This jungle was very extensive, and the rocky bed of a mountain torrent divided it into two portions; on the right hand was fine open forest, and on the left hand thick thorny chénar. The elephants were in the open forest, close to the edge of the torrent.

The herd winded us just as we were approaching up the steep ascent of the rocky stream, and they made a rush across the bed of the torrent to gain the thick jungle on the opposite bank. Banda immediately beckoned to me to come into the thick jungle, with the intention of meeting the elephants as they entered, while Palliser was to command the narrow passage, in which there was only space for one person to shoot without confusion.

In the meantime Palliser knocked over three elephants as they crossed the stream; while we, on reaching the thick jungle, found it was so dense that we could see nothing. Just as we were thinking of returning again to the spot that we had left, we heard a tremendous rush in the thick jungle, coming straight towards us. In another instant I saw a mass of twisted and matted thorns rushing in a heap upon me. I had barely time to jump on one side, as the elephant nearly grazed me, and I fired both barrels into the tangled mass that he bore upon his head. I then bolted, and took up a good position at a few yards' distance. The shots in the head had so completely stunned the elephant that she could not move, and she stood in a piece of jungle so dense that we could not see her, and Palliser creeping up to her, while we stood ready to back him, fired three shots at her without the least effect. She did not even move, being senseless with the wound. One of my men then gave him my four-ounce rifle. A loud report from the old gun sounded the elephant's knell, and closed the sport for that trip.

We returned to Nielgala—the whole of that day's bag belonging to Palliser—four elephants and two buffalos. We packed up our traps, and early the next morning we started direct for Newera Ellia, having in three weeks from the day of our departure from Kandy bagged fifty elephants, five deer, and two buffalos; of which Wortley had killed to his bag ten elephants and two deer; Palliser sixteen elephants and two buffalos; V. Baker, up to the time of his leaving us, two elephants.

CHAP. XIII.

CONCLUSION.

Thus ended a trip, which exhibited the habits and character of elephants in a most perfect manner. From the simple experience of these three weeks' shooting, a novice might claim a knowledge of the elephant; and the journal of this tour must at once explain, even to the most uninitiated, the exact proportion of risk with which this sport is attended, when followed up in a sportsmanlike manner. These days will always be looked back to by me with the greatest pleasure; the moments of sport lose none of their brightness by age, and when the limbs become enfeebled by time, the mind can still cling to scenes long past with the pleasure of youth.

One great addition to the enjoyment of wild sport is, the companionship of thorough sportsmen. A confidence in each other is absolutely necessary; without this, I would not remain a day in the jungle. An even temper, not easily disturbed by the little annoyances inseparable from a trip in a wild country, is also indispensable; without this, a man would be insufferable. Our party was an emblem of contentment. The day's sport concluded, the evenings were most enjoyable, and will never be forgotten. The well-arranged tent, the neatly-spread table, the beds forming a triangle around the walls, and the clean guns piled in a long row against the gun-rack, will often recall a *tableau* in after years, in countries far from this land of independence. The acknowledged sports of England will appear child's play; the exciting thrill will be wanting, when a sudden rush in the jungle brings the rifle on full cock; and the heavy guns will become useless mementos of past days, like the dusty helmets of yore, hanging up in an old hall. The belt and the hunting-knife will alike share the fate of the good rifle, and the blade, now so keen, will blunt from sheer neglect. The slips, which have held the necks of dogs of such staunch natures, will hang neglected from the wall; and all these *souvenirs* of wild sports, contrasted with the puny implements of the English chase, will awaken once more the longing desire for the "Rifle and the Hound in Ceylon."

THE END.

A CATALOGUE

OF

NEW WORKS AND NEW EDITIONS

IN

General and Miscellaneous Literature,

PUBLISHED BY

LONGMAN, BROWN, GREEN, AND LONGMANS,

39, PATERNOSTER ROW, LONDON.

CLASSIFIED INDEX.

Agriculture and Rural Affairs.

Arts, Manufactures, and Architecture.

Biography.

Books of General Utility.

Botany and Gardening.

Chronology.

Commerce and Mercantile Affairs.

Criticism, History, and Memoirs.

Geography and Atlases.

Juvenile Books.

Medicine.

CLASSIFIED INDEX—*continued.*

Miscellaneous and General Literature.

Natural History in General.

One-Volume Encyclopædias and Dictionaries.

Religious and Moral Works.

Poetry and the Drama.

Political Economy and Statistics.

The Sciences in General and Mathematics.

Rural Sports.

Veterinary Medicine, &c.

Voyages and Travels.

Works of Fiction.

An Alphabetical Catalogue

OF

NEW WORKS AND NEW EDITIONS

PUBLISHED BY

MESSRS. LONGMAN, BROWN, GREEN, & LONGMANS,

PATERNOSTER ROW, LONDON.

MISS ACTON'S MODERN COOKERY-BOOK.

Modern Cookery in all its Branches, reduced to a System of Easy Practice. For the use of Private Families. In a Series of Receipts, all of which have been strictly tested, and are given with the most minute exactness. By ELIZA ACTON. New Edition; with Directions for Carving, and other Additions. Fcp. 8vo. with Plates and Woodcuts, 7s. 6d. cloth.

ADAMS.—A SPRING IN THE CANTERBURY SETTLE-

MENT. By C. WARREN ADAMS, Esq. With 5 Illustrations. Post 8vo. price 5s. 6d. cloth.

ADDISON.—HISTORY OF THE KNIGHTS TEMPLARS.

By C. G. ADDISON, of the Inner Temple, Esq., Barrister-at-Law. 3d Edition, corrected and improved; with 4 Lithographic and 3 Woodcut Illustrations. Square crown 8vo. 10s. 6d. cloth.

AIKIN.—SELECT WORKS OF THE BRITISH POETS,

From Ben Jonson to Beattie. With Biographical and Critical Prefaces by Dr. AIKIN. New Edition, with Supplement, by LUCY AIKIN; consisting of additional Selections from more recent Poets. 8vo. 18s. cloth.

ANCELL.—A TREATISE ON TUBERCULOSIS,

The Constitutional Origin of Consumption and Scrofula. By HENRY ANCELL, late Lecturer on Materia Medica and Therapeutics, and on Medical Jurisprudence, at the School of Anatomy and Medicine adjoining St. George's Hospital. 8vo. price 21s. cloth.

ANTHONY.—FOOTSTEPS TO HISTORY:

Being an Epitome of the Histories of England and France; to which are added, slight Sketches of Literature, Arts, and Manufactures. By LOUISA ANTHONY. The Second Edition, thoroughly revised, with considerable Additions. Fcp. 8vo. price 5s. 6d. cloth.

A TREATISE ON THE STEAM ENGINE,

in its Application to Mines, Mills, Steam Navigation, and Railways. By the Artisan Club. Edited by JOHN BOURNE, C.E. New Edition. With 30 Steel Plates and 349 Wood Engravings. 4to. 27s. cloth.

JOANNA BAILLIE'S DRAMATIC & POETICAL WORKS,

Complete in One Volume: Comprising the Plays of the Passions, Miscellaneous Dramas, Metrical Legends, Fugitive Pieces (including several now first published), and Ahalya Baee. Second Edition; including a Life of Joanna Baillie, now first published: With a Portrait engraved by H. Robinson, and a Vignette View of Bothwell Manse. Square crown 8vo. 21s. cloth; or 42s. bound in morocco by Hayday.

BAINES.—THE LIFE OF EDWARD BAINES,

late M.P. for the Borough of Leeds. By his Son, EDWARD BAINES, Author of *The History of the Cotton Manufacture.* With a Portrait engraved in line by Greatbach. 8vo. 9s. cloth.

BALFOUR.—SKETCHES OF ENGLISH LITERATURE

from the Fourteenth to the Present Century. By CLARA LUCAS BALFOUR, Author of *Women of Scripture,* &c. Fcp. 8vo. 7s. cloth.

BANFIELD.—THE STATISTICAL COMPANION:

Exhibiting the most interesting Facts in Moral and Intellectual, Vital, Economical, and Political Statistics, at Home and Abroad. Corrected to the Present Time; and including the Results of the Census of the British Population taken in 1851. Compiled from Official and other Authentic Sources, by T. C. BANFIELD, Esq., Statistical Clerk to the Council of Education. Fcp. 8vo. price 5s. cloth.

BAYLDON'S ART OF VALUING RENTS & TILLAGES,

And Tenant's Right of Entering and Quitting Farms, explained by several Specimens of Valuations; with Remarks on the Cultivation pursued on Soils in different Situations. Adapted to the Use of Landlords, Land-Agents, Appraisers, Farmers, and Tenants. New Edition; corrected and revised by John Donaldson. 8vo. 10s. 6d. cloth.

LORD BELFAST.—LECTURES ON THE ENGLISH POETS

and POETRY of the NINETEENTH CENTURY. By the Right Hon. the EARL of BELFAST. Fcp. 8vo. price 6s. 6d. cloth.

BLACK'S PRACTICAL TREATISE ON BREWING,

Based on Chemical and Economical Principles: with Formulæ for Public Brewers, and Instructions for Private Families. New Edition, with Additions. 8vo. 10s. 6d. cloth.

BLAINE'S ENCYCLOPÆDIA OF RURAL SPORTS;

Or, a complete Account, Historical, Practical, and Descriptive, of Hunting, Shooting, Fishing, Racing, and other Field Sports and Athletic Amusements of the present day. A new and thoroughly revised Edition; with copious Additions and Improvements, and numerous additional Illustrations. The Hunting, Racing, and all relative to Horses and Horsemanship, revised by HARRY HIEOVER; Shooting and Fishing by EPHEMERA; and Coursing by Mr. A. GRAHAM. With upwards of 600 Woodcuts. 8vo. 50s. half-bound.

BLAIR'S CHRONOLOGICAL AND HISTORICAL TABLES,

From the Creation to the present time: with Additions and Corrections from the most authentic Writers; including the Computation of St. Paul, as connecting the Period from the Exode to the Temple. Under the revision of Sir HENRY ELLIS, K.H., Principal Librarian of the British Museum. New Edition, with Corrections. Imperial 8vo. 31s. 6d. half-morocco.

BLOOMFIELD.—THE GREEK TESTAMENT:

With copious English Notes, Critical, Philological, and Explanatory. Especially formed for the use of advanced Students and Candidates for Holy Orders. By Rev. S. T. BLOOMFIELD, D.D. F.S.A. New Edition. 2 vols. 8vo. with a Map of Palestine, £2, cloth.

THE REV. DR. BLOOMFIELD'S ADDITIONAL ANNOTATIONS

On the NEW TESTAMENT: Being a Supplement to his larger Edition of *The Greek Testament with English Notes.* New Edition. 8vo. 15s. cloth.

BLOOMFIELD.—COLLEGE AND SCHOOL GREEK TESTA-

MENT: With shorter English Notes, Critical, Philological, and Explanatory, formed for use in Colleges and the Public Schools. By the Rev. S. T. BLOOMFIELD, D.D. F.S.A. New Edition, greatly enlarged and improved. Fcp. 8vo. 10s. 6d. cloth.

BOURNE.—A TREATISE ON THE SCREW PROPELLER:

With various Suggestions of Improvement. By JOHN BOURNE, C.E., Editor of *The Artisan Club's Treatise on the Steam Engine.* With 20 large Plates and numerous Woodcuts. 4to. price 38s. cloth.

BOURNE.—A CATECHISM OF THE STEAM ENGINE,

Illustrative of the Scientific Principles upon which its Operation depends, and the Practical Details of its Structure, in its applications to Mines, Mills, Steam Navigation, and Railways: with various Suggestions of Improvement. By JOHN BOURNE, C.E. New Edition, corrected. Fcp. 8vo. 6s. cloth.

BRANDE.—A DICTIONARY OF SCIENCE, LITERATURE,

and ART; comprising the History, Description, and Scientific Principles of every Branch of Human Knowledge; with the Derivation and Definition of all the Terms in General Use. Edited by W. T. BRANDE, F.R.S.L. & E.; assisted by Dr. J. CAUVIN. The Second Edition, revised and corrected; including a Supplement, and numerous Wood Engravings. 8vo. price 60s. cloth.—The SUPPLEMENT separately, price 3s. 6d.

BULL.—THE MATERNAL MANAGEMENT OF CHILDREN

in HEALTH and DISEASE. By T. BULL, M.D. Member of the Royal College of Physicians; formerly Physician-Accoucheur to the Finsbury Midwifery Institution. New Edition, revised and enlarged. Fcp. 8vo. 5s. cloth.

BULL.—HINTS TO MOTHERS,

For the Management of their Health during the Period of Pregnancy and in the Lying-in Room: with an Exposure of Popular Errors in connexion with those subjects, &c.; and Hints upon Nursing. By T. BULL, M.D. New Edition, revised and enlarged. Fcp. 8vo. 5s. cloth.

BUNSEN.—HIPPOLYTUS AND HIS AGE;

Or, Doctrine and Practice of the Church of Rome under Commodus and Alexander Severus: And Ancient and Modern Christianity and Divinity compared. By C. C. J. BUNSEN, D.C.L. With the Effigy of Hippolytus. 4 vols. post 8vo. price 42s. cloth.

"The volumes will be acceptable to every right-minded theologian. The candid inquirer will receive them gratefully as suggesting new views, enforcing sound principles, presenting interesting pictures of the past for the instruction of the present and the guidance of the future. The tone of them is healthful and bracing. They must benefit the true spirits of the age who look to the future for a new and better era of Christianity, in which the sickliness of modern piety, with the formalism, superstition, and unsophisticalness of a selfish age shall disappear; and the true Church, the Church of believers, present the spectacle of a loving brotherhood, embodying the life of religion in forms of ever-expanding development pervaded by the intellectual and devotional in due proportions." KITTO'S JOURNAL OF SACRED LITERATURE.

BUNSEN.—EGYPT'S PLACE IN UNIVERSAL HISTORY:

An Historical Investigation, in Five Books. By C. C. J. BUNSEN, D.C.L. Translated from the German, by C. H. COTTRELL, Esq. M.A.—Vol. I. containing the First Book, or Sources and Primeval Facts of Egyptian History: with an Egyptian Grammar and Dictionary, and a complete List of Hieroglyphical Signs; an Appendix of Authorities, embracing the complete Text of Manetho and Eratosthenes, Ægyptiaca from Pliny, Strabo, &c.; and Plates representing the Egyptian Divinities. With many Illustrations. 8vo. 28s. cloth.

*** The Second Volume is preparing for publication.

BURTON.—THE HISTORY OF SCOTLAND,

From the Revolution to the Extinction of the last Jacobite Insurrection (1689—1748). By JOHN HILL BURTON, Author of *The Life of David Hume*, &c. 2 vols. 8vo. [*In the press.*

BISHOP BUTLER'S GENERAL ATLAS OF MODERN AND

ANCIENT GEOGRAPHY; comprising Fifty-one full-coloured Maps; with complete Indices. New Edition, nearly all re-engraved, enlarged, and greatly improved; with Corrections from the most authentic sources in both the Ancient and Modern Maps, many of which are entirely new. Edited by the Author's Son, the Rev. T. BUTLER. Royal 4to. 24s. half-bound.

Separately { The Modern Atlas. 28 full-coloured Maps. Royal 8vo. 12s. half-bound.
The Ancient Atlas. 23 full-coloured Maps. Royal 8vo. 12s. half-bound.

BISHOP BUTLER'S SKETCH OF MODERN & ANCIENT

GEOGRAPHY. New Edition, carefully revised, with such Alterations introduced as continually progressive Discoveries and the latest Information have rendered necessary. Edited by the Author's Son, the Rev. T. BUTLER. 8vo. 9s. cloth.

THE CABINET GAZETTEER:

A Popular Exposition of all the Countries of the World; their Government, Population, Revenues, Commerce and Industries; Agricultural, Manufactured, and Mineral Products; Religion, Laws, Manners, and Social State: With brief Notices of their History and Antiquities. From the latest Authorities. By the Author of *The Cabinet Lawyer*. In One Volume, with a coloured Map. Fcp. 8vo. price 10s. 6d. cloth; or 13s. calf lettered.

THE CABINET LAWYER:

A Popular Digest of the Laws of England, Civil and Criminal; with a Dictionary of Law Terms, Maxims, Statutes, and Judicial Antiquities; Correct Tables of Assessed Taxes, Stamp Duties, Excise Licenses, and Post-Horse Duties; Post-Office Regulations, and Prison Discipline. 15th Edition, with Supplements. Fcp. 8vo. 10s. 6d. cloth.

CAIRD.—ENGLISH AGRICULTURE IN 1850 AND 1851;

Its Condition and Prospects. By JAMES CAIRD, Esq. of Baldoon, Agricultural Commissioner of *The Times*. Second Edition. 8vo. 14s. cloth.

THE CALLING & RESPONSIBILITIES OF A GOVERNESS.

By AMICA. Fcp. 8vo. price 4s. 6d. cloth.

CATLOW.—POPULAR CONCHOLOGY;

Or, the Shell Cabinet arranged: being an Introduction to the Modern System of Conchology: with a sketch of the Natural History of the Animals, an account of the Formation of the Shells, and a complete Descriptive List of the Families and Genera. By AGNES CATLOW. With 312 Woodcuts. Fcp. 8vo. 10s. 6d. cloth.

CAYLEY.—DANTE'S DIVINE COMEDY.

Translated in the Original Ternary Rhyme. By C. B. CAYLEY, B.A. Vol. I. The Vision of Hell. Fcp. 8vo. price 6s. cloth.—Vol. II. The Purgatory. Fcp. 8vo. price price 6s. cloth.

CECIL.—STABLE PRACTICE;

Or, Hints on Training for the Turf, the Chase, and the Road; with Observations on Racing and Hunting, Wasting, Race Riding, and Handicapping: addressed to Owners of Racers, Hunters, and other Horses, and to all who are concerned in Racing, Steeple Chasing, and Fox Hunting. By CECIL. Fcp. 8vo. with Plate, price 5s. half-bound.

CECIL.—THE STUD FARM;

Or, Hints on Breeding Horses for the Turf, the Chase, and the Road. Addressed to Breeders of Race Horses and Hunters, Landed Proprietors, and especially to Tenant Farmers. By CECIL. Fcp. 8vo. with Frontispiece, price 5s. half-bound.

THE CHILDREN'S OWN SUNDAY-BOOK.

By JULIA CORNER, Author of *Questions on the History of Europe*. With Two Illustrations engraved on Steel. Square fcp. 8vo. 5s. cloth.

CONVERSATIONS ON BOTANY.

New Edition, improved. Fcp. 8vo. with 22 Plates, price 7s. 6d. cloth; with the plates coloured, price 12s. cloth.

CONYBEARE AND HOWSON.—THE LIFE & EPISTLES

of SAINT PAUL; Comprising a complete Biography of the Apostle, and a Translation of his Epistles inserted in Chronological Order. By the Rev. W. J. CONYBEARE, M.A. late Fellow of Trinity College, Cambridge; and the Rev. J. S. HOWSON, M.A. Principal of the Collegiate Institution, Liverpool. With 40 Engravings on Steel and 100 Woodcuts: Including Views of the Principal Places visited by the Apostle, from Original Drawings made on the spot by W. H. Bartlett and other Travellers; also Maps, Charts, Plans, Coins, Antiquities, &c. 2 vols. 4to. price £2. 8s. cloth.

COPLAND.—A DICTIONARY OF PRACTICAL MEDICINE;

Comprising General Pathology, the Nature and Treatment of Diseases, Morbid Structures, and the Disorders especially incidental to Climates, to Sex, and to the different Epochs of Life; with numerous approved Formulæ of the Medicines recommended. By JAMES COPLAND, M.D. Consulting Physician to Queen Charlotte's Lying-in Hospital, &c. Vols. I. and II. 8vo. £3, cloth; and Parts X. to XVI. 4s. 6d. each, sewed.

CRESY.—AN ENCYCLOPÆDIA OF CIVIL ENGINEERING,

Historical, Theoretical, and Practical. By EDWARD CRESY, F.S.A. C.E. Illustrated by upwards of 3,000 Woodcuts explanatory of the Principles, Machinery, and Constructions which come under the Direction of the Civil Engineer. 8vo. price £3. 13s. 6d. cloth.

THE CRICKET-FIELD;

Or, the Science and History of the Game. Illustrated with Diagrams, and enlivened with Anecdotes. By the Author of *Principles of Scientific Batting.* Fcp. 8vo. with 2 Plates, price 5s. half-bound.

DALE.—THE DOMESTIC LITURGY & FAMILY CHAPLAIN,

in Two Parts: The First Part being Church Services adapted for domestic use, with Prayers for every day of the week, selected exclusively from the Book of Common Prayer; Part II. comprising an appropriate Sermon for every Sunday in the year. By the Rev. THOMAS DALE, M.A., Canon Residentiary of St. Paul's Cathedral. 2d Edition. Post 4to. 21s. cloth: or, bound by Hayday, 31s. 6d. calf lettered; £2. 10s. morocco.

Separately { THE FAMILY CHAPLAIN, price 12s. cloth.
THE DOMESTIC LITURGY, price 10s. 6d. cloth.

DAVIS.—CHINA DURING THE WAR AND SINCE THE

PEACE. By Sir J. F. DAVIS, Bart., F.R.S., late H.M. Plenipotentiary in China; Governor and Commander-in-Chief of the Colony of Hongkong. 2 vols. post 8vo. with Woodcuts, price 21s. cloth.

DELABECHE.—THE GEOLOGICAL OBSERVER.

By Sir HENRY T. DELABECHE, F.R.S., Director-General of the Geological Survey of the United Kingdom. New Edition; with numerous Woodcuts. 8vo. 18s. cloth.

DELABECHE.—REPORT ON THE GEOLOGY OF CORN-

WALL, DEVON, and WEST SOMERSET. By Sir HENRY T. DELABECHE, F.R.S. Director-General of the Geological Survey. 8vo. with Maps, Woodcuts, and 12 large Plates, price 14s. cloth.

DE LA RIVE.—A TREATISE ON ELECTRICITY,

In Theory and Practice. By AUG. DE LA RIVE, Professor in the Academy of Geneva. In Two Volumes, with numerous Wood Engravings. Vol. I. 8vo. price 18s. cloth.

DENNISTOUN.—MEMOIRS OF THE DUKES OF URBINO;

Illustrating the Arms, Arts, and Literature of Italy, from MCCCCXL. to MDCXXX. By JAMES DENNISTOUN, of Dennistoun. With numerous Portraits, Plates, Fac-similes, and Engravings on Wood. 3 vols. crown 8vo. £2. 8s. cloth.

DISCIPLINE.

By the Author of *Letters to my Unknown Friends*, &c. Second Edition, enlarged. 18mo. price Half-a-Crown, cloth.

DOUBLEDAY, WESTWOOD, AND HEWITSON.—THE

GENERA of BUTTERFLIES, or DIURNAL LEPIDOPTERA: comprising their Generic Characters, a Notice of their Habits and Transformations, and a Catalogue of the Species of each Genus. By EDWARD DOUBLEDAY, F.L.S., F.Z.S., late Assistant in the Zoological Department of the British Museum; and JOHN O. WESTWOOD, Esq., President of the Entomological Society of London. Illustrated with Eighty-six coloured Plates from Drawings by W. C. HEWITSON, Esq., Author of *British Oology*. 2 vols. imperial 4to. price Fifteen Guineas, half-bound in morocco.

EASTLAKE.—MATERIALS FOR A HISTORY OF OIL

PAINTING. By Sir CHARLES LOCK EASTLAKE, F.R.S. F.S.A., President of the Royal Academy. 8vo. 16s. cloth.

THE ECLIPSE OF FAITH;

Or, a Visit to a Religious Sceptic. New Edition. Post 8vo. price 9s. 6d. cloth.

"It is absolutely necessary to meet them" [infidel writers of the modern school] "on their own ground, and fight them with their own weapons. And this is what the little book at the head of this article professes to do; and it does its work well. It is learned and logical, and at the same time lively and entertaining. Its irony is very powerful and cutting, and yet it is not open to the apparent objection of grave and serious subjects being treated flippantly. Whilst, from the nature of the subject, it might fairly be entitled 'Theological Fragments,' from the method in which the subject is treated it is as interesting as a collection of scenes of society." BRITANNIA.

THE ENGLISHMAN'S GREEK CONCORDANCE OF THE

NEW TESTAMENT: being an Attempt at a Verbal Connexion between the Greek and the English Texts; including a Concordance to the Proper Names, with Indexes, Greek-English and English-Greek. New Edition, with a new Index. Royal 8vo. 42s. cloth.

THE ENGLISHMAN'S HEBREW AND CHALDEE CON-

CORDANCE of the OLD TESTAMENT; being an Attempt at a Verbal Connection between the Original and the English Translations: with Indexes, a List of the Proper Names and their occurrences, &c. 2 vols. royal 8vo. £3. 13s. 6d. cloth; large paper, £4. 14s. 6d.

EPHEMERA.—THE BOOK OF THE SALMON:

Comprising the Theory, Principles, and Practice of Fly-Fishing for Salmon: with Lists of good Salmon Flies for every good River in the Empire; with the Natural History of the Salmon, all Its known Habits described, and the best way of artificially Breeding It explained. With numerous coloured Engravings of Salmon Flies and Salmon Fry. By EPHEMERA; assisted by ANDREW YOUNG, of Invershin, Manager of the Duke of Sutherland's Salmon Fisheries. Fcp. 8vo. with coloured Plates, 14s. cloth.

EPHEMERA.—A HAND-BOOK OF ANGLING;

Teaching Fly-fishing, Trolling, Bottom-fishing, Salmon-fishing; with the Natural History of River Fish, and the best modes of Catching them. By EPHEMERA. New Edition, enlarged. Fcp. 8vo. with numerous Woodcuts, 9s. cloth.

THE EXPERIENCE OF LIFE.

By the Author of *Amy Herbert*, *Gertrude*, &c. Fcp. 8vo. price 7s. 6d. cloth.

FELICE'S HISTORY OF THE PROTESTANTS OF FRANCE,

From 1521 to 1851. Translated from the Second revised and corrected Edition, by E. West. 2 vols. post 8vo. [*In the press.*

FORBES.—DAHOMEY AND THE DAHOMANS:

Being the Journals of Two Missions to the King of Dahomey, and Residence at his Capital, in the Years 1849 and 1850. By FREDERICK E. FORBES, Commander, R.N., F.R.G.S., With 10 Plates and 3 Wood Engravings. 2 vols. post 8vo. 21s. cloth.

FORESTER AND BIDDULPH'S NORWAY.

Norway in 1848 and 1849: containing Rambles among the Fjelds and Fjords of the Central and Western Districts; and including Remarks on its Political, Military, Ecclesiastical, and Social Organisation. By THOMAS FORESTER, Esq.; and Lieutenant M. S. BIDDULPH, Royal Artillery. With Map, Woodcuts, and Ten coloured Plates. 8vo. 18s. cloth.

FOSS.—THE JUDGES OF ENGLAND:

With Sketches of their Lives, and Miscellaneous Notices connected with the Courts at Westminster from the time of the Conquest. By EDWARD FOSS, F.S.A. of the Inner Temple Vols. I. II. III. and IV. 8vo. 56s. cloth.

FRANCIS.—THE HISTORY OF THE BANK OF ENGLAND;

Its Times and Traditions. By JOHN FRANCIS. Third Edition. 2 vols. post 8vo. 21s. cloth.

FRANCIS.—A HISTORY OF THE ENGLISH RAILWAY;

Its social Relations and Revelations. By JOHN FRANCIS. 2 vols. 8vo. 24s. cloth.

FRANCIS.—CHRONICLES AND CHARACTERS OF THE

STOCK EXCHANGE. By JOHN FRANCIS. Second Edition. 8vo. 12s. cloth.

FREEMAN.—THE LIFE OF THE REV. WILLIAM KIRBY,

M.A., F.R.S., F.L.S., &c., Rector of Barham; Author of one of the Bridgewater Treatises; and Joint-Author of the *Introduction to Entomology.* By the Rev. JOHN FREEMAN, M.A., Rector of Ashwicken, Norfolk, and Rural Dean. With a Portrait of Mr. Kirby (engraved by Henry Robinson), a Fac-simile of his Handwriting, and a View of Barham Parsonage. 8vo. price 15s. cloth.

GOLDSMITH. — THE POETICAL WORKS OF OLIVER

GOLDSMITH. Illustrated by Wood Engravings, from Designs by Members of the Etching Club. With a Biographical Memoir, and Notes on the Poems. Edited by BOLTON CORNEY, Esq. Square crown 8vo. price One Guinea, cloth; or, bound in morocco by Hayday, price £1. 16s.

GOSSE.—A NATURALIST'S SOJOURN IN JAMAICA.

By P. H. GOSSE, Esq. With coloured Plates. Post 8vo. 14s. cloth.

GRAHAM.—STUDIES FROM THE ENGLISH POETS:

Comprising Selections from Milton, Shakspeare, Pope, Gray, Goldsmith, Cowper, and Collins; with the strikingly beautiful passages printed in italics; Explanatory Notes and Illustrations; and Examination Questions for exercise in English Composition. By G. F. GRAHAM. 12mo. price 7s. cloth.

GRAHAM.—ENGLISH; OR, THE ART OF COMPOSITION Explained in a Series of Instructions and Examples. By G. F. GRAHAM. New Edition, revised and improved. Fcp. 8vo. 6s. cloth.

MR. W. R. GREG'S CONTRIBUTIONS TO THE EDINBURGH REVIEW.—ESSAYS on POLITICAL and SOCIAL SCIENCE. Contributed chiefly to the *Edinburgh Review*. By WILLIAM R. GREG. 2 vols. 8vo. price 24s. cloth.

GURNEY.—HISTORICAL SKETCHES; Illustrating some Memorable Events and Epochs, from A.D. 1,400 to A.D. 1,546. By the Rev. JOHN HAMPDEN GURNEY, M.A., Rector of St. Mary's, Mary-le-bone. Fcp. 8vo. 7s. 6d. cloth.

GWILT.—AN ENCYCLOPÆDIA OF ARCHITECTURE, Historical, Theoretical, and Practical. By JOSEPH GWILT. Illustrated with more than One Thousand Engravings on Wood, from Designs by J. S. GWILT. Second Edition, with a Supplemental View of the Symmetry and Stability of Gothic Architecture; comprising upwards of Eighty additional Woodcuts. 8vo. price 52s. 6d. cloth.—The SUPPLEMENT separately, price 6s. cloth.

SIDNEY HALL'S GENERAL LARGE LIBRARY ATLAS OF FIFTY-THREE MAPS (size 20 in. by 16 in.), with the Divisions and Boundaries carefully coloured; and an Alphabetical Index of all the Names contained in the Maps. New Edition, corrected from the best and most recent Authorities; with the Railways laid down and many entirely new Maps. Colombier 4to. £5. 5s. half-bound in russia.

HAMILTON.—DISCUSSIONS IN PHILOSOPHY AND LITERATURE, EDUCATION and UNIVERSITY REFORM. Chiefly from the *Edinburgh Review;* corrected, vindicated, enlarged, in Notes and Appendices. By SIR WILLIAM HAMILTON, Bart. 8vo. price 18s. cloth.

HARRISON.—THE LIGHT OF THE FORGE; Or, Counsels drawn from the Sick-Bed of E. M. By the Rev. WILLIAM HARRISON, M.A., Rector of Birch, Essex, and Domestic Chaplain to H.R.H. the Duchess of Cambridge. With 2 Wood Engravings. Fcp. 8vo. price 5s. cloth.

HARRISON.—ON THE RISE, PROGRESS, AND PRESENT STRUCTURE of the ENGLISH LANGUAGE. By the Rev. M. HARRISON, M.A. late Fellow of Queen's College, Oxford. Post 8vo. 8s. 6d. cloth.

HARRY HIEOVER.—THE HUNTING-FIELD. By HARRY HIEOVER. With Two Plates—One representing *The Right Sort;* the other, *The Wrong Sort*. Fcp. 8vo. 5s. half-bound.

HARRY HIEOVER.—PRACTICAL HORSEMANSHIP. By HARRY HIEOVER. With 2 Plates—One representing *Going like Workmen;* the other, *Going like Muffs*. Fcp. 8vo. price 5s. half-bound.

HARRY HIEOVER.—THE STUD, For Practical Purposes and Practical Men: Being a Guide to the Choice of a Horse for use more than for show. By HARRY HIEOVER. With Two Plates—One representing *A pretty good sort for most purposes;* the other, *'Rayther' a bad sort for any purpose*. Fcp. 8vo. 5s. half-bound.

HARRY HIEOVER.—THE POCKET AND THE STUD;

Or, Practical Hints on the Management of the Stable. By HARRY HIEOVER. Second Edition; with Portrait of the Author on his favourite Horse *Harlequin*. Fcp. 8vo. 5s. half-bound.

HARRY HIEOVER.—STABLE TALK AND TABLE TALK;

Or, SPECTACLES for YOUNG SPORTSMEN. By HARRY HIEOVER. New Edition. 2 vols. 8vo. with Portrait, 24s. cloth.

HAWKER.—INSTRUCTIONS TO YOUNG SPORTSMEN

In all that relates to Guns and Shooting. By Lieut.-Col. P. HAWKER. New Edition, corrected, enlarged, and improved; with Eighty-five Plates and Woodcuts by Adlard and Branston, from Drawings by C. Varley, Dickes, &c. 8vo. 21s. cloth.

HAYDN'S BOOK OF DIGNITIES:

Containing ROLLS OF THE OFFICIAL PERSONAGES of the BRITISH EMPIRE, Civil, Ecclesiastical, Judicial, Military, Naval, and Municipal, from the EARLIEST PERIODS to the PRESENT TIME; Compiled chiefly from the Records of the Public Offices. Together with the Soverigns of Europe, from the foundation of their respective States; the Peerage and Nobility of Great Britain, and numerous other Lists. Being a New Edition, improved and continued, of BEATSON'S POLITICAL INDEX. By JOSEPH HAYDN, Compiler of *The Dictionary of Dates*, and other Works. 8vo. 25s. half-bound.

SIR JOHN HERSCHEL.—OUTLINES OF ASTRONOMY.

By Sir JOHN F. W. HERSCHEL, Bart. &c. New Edition; with Plates and Wood Engravings. 8vo. 18s. cloth.

HINTS ON ETIQUETTE AND THE USAGES OF SOCIETY:

With a Glance at Bad Habits. By Αγωγός. "Manners make the man." New Edition, revised (with additions) by a Lady of Rank. Fcp. 8vo. 2s. 6d. cloth.

LORD HOLLAND'S MEMOIRS.

Memoirs of the Whig Party during my Time. By HENRY RICHARD LORD HOLLAND. Edited by his Son, HENRY EDWARD LORD HOLLAND. Vol. I. Post 8vo. 9s. 6d. cloth.

LORD HOLLAND'S FOREIGN REMINISCENCES.

FOREIGN REMINISCENCES. By HENRY RICHARD LORD HOLLAND. Comprising Anecdotes, and an Account of such Persons and Political Intrigues in Foreign Countries as have fallen within his Lordship's observation. Edited by his Son, HENRY EDWARD LORD HOLLAND; with Fac-simile. Second Edition. Post 8vo. 10s. 6d.

HOLLAND.—CHAPTERS ON MENTAL PHYSIOLOGY.

By HENRY HOLLAND, M.D., F.R.S., Physician Extraordinary to the Queen; and Physician in Ordinary to His Royal Highness Prince Albert. Founded chiefly on Chapters contained in *Medical Notes and Reflections* by the same Author. 8vo. price 10s. 6d. cloth.

HOOK.—THE LAST DAYS OF OUR LORD'S MINISTRY:

A Course of Lectures on the principal Events of Passion Week. By WALTER FARQUHAR HOOK, D.D., Chaplain in Ordinary to the Queen. New Edition. Fcp. 8vo. 6s. cloth.

HOOKER.—KEW GARDENS;

Or, a Popular Guide to the Royal Botanic Gardens of Kew. By Sir WILLIAM JACKSON HOOKER, K.H. D.C.L. F.R.A. & L.S. &c. &c. Director. New Edition. 16mo. with numerous Wood Engravings, price Sixpence.

HOOKER AND ARNOTT.—THE BRITISH FLORA;

Comprising the Phænogamous or Flowering Plants, and the Ferns. The Sixth Edition, with Additions and Corrections; and numerous Figures illustrative of the Umbelliferous Plants, the Composite Plants, the Grasses, and the Ferns. By Sir W. J. Hooker, F.R.A. and L.S. &c., and G. A. Walker-Arnott, LL.D. F.L.S. 12mo. with 12 Plates, 14s. cloth; with the Plates coloured, price 21s.

HORNE.—AN INTRODUCTION TO THE CRITICAL STUDY

and KNOWLEDGE of the HOLY SCRIPTURES. By Thomas Hartwell Horne, B.D. of St. John's College, Cambridge; Prebendary of St. Paul's. New Edition, revised and corrected; with numerous Maps and Facsimiles of Biblical Manuscripts. 5 vols. 8vo. 63s. cloth; or £5, bound in calf.

HORNE.—A COMPENDIOUS INTRODUCTION TO THE

STUDY of the BIBLE. By Thomas Hartwell Horne, B.D. of St. John's College, Cambridge. Being an Analysis of his *Introduction to the Critical Study and Knowledge of the Holy Scriptures.* New Edition, corrected and enlarged. 12mo. with Maps and other Engravings, 9s. boards.

HOWITT.—THE CHILDREN'S YEAR.

By Mary Howitt. With Four Illustrations, engraved by John Absolon, from Original Designs by Anna Mary Howitt. Square 16mo. 5s. cloth.

WILLIAM HOWITT'S BOY'S COUNTRY BOOK:

Being the real Life of a Country Boy, written by himself; exhibiting all the Amusements, Pleasures, and Pursuits of Children in the Country. New Edition; with 40 Woodcuts. Fcp. 8vo. 6s. cloth.

HOWITT.—THE RURAL LIFE OF ENGLAND.

By William Howitt. New Edition, corrected and revised; with Engravings on wood, by Bewick and Williams: uniform with *Visits to Remarkable Places.* Medium 8vo. 21s. cloth.

HOWITT.—VISITS TO REMARKABLE PLACES;

Old Halls, Battle-Fields, and Scenes illustrative of Striking Passages in English History and Poetry. By William Howitt. New Edition; with 40 Engravings on Wood. Medium 8vo. 21s. cloth.

SECOND SERIES, chiefly in the Counties of NORTHUMBERLAND and DURHAM, with a Stroll along the BORDER. With upwards of 40 Engravings on Wood. Medium 8vo. 21s. cloth.

HUDSON.—THE EXECUTOR'S GUIDE.

By J. C. Hudson, Esq. late of the Legacy Duty Office, London; Author of *Plain Directions for Making Wills.* New Edition. Fcp. 8vo. 5s. cloth.

HUDSON.—PLAIN DIRECTIONS FOR MAKING WILLS

In Conformity with the Law: with a clear Exposition of the Law relating to the distribution of Personal Estate in the case of Intestacy, two Forms of Wills, and much useful information. By J. C. Hudson, Esq. New Edition, corrected. Fcp. 8vo. 2s. 6d. cloth.

*** These Two works may be had in One Volume, 7s. cloth.

HUGHES (E.)—A NEW SCHOOL ATLAS OF PHYSICAL,

POLITICAL, and COMMERCIAL GEOGRAPHY. By Edward Hughes, F.R.G.S., Head Master of the Royal Naval Lower School, Greenwich Hospital. Containing Seventeen coloured Maps, with Descriptive Letterpress. The Maps engraved on Steel by E. Weller, F.R.G.S. Royal 8vo. price 10s. 6d. half-bound.

HUGHES (W.)—A MANUAL OF MATHEMATICAL GEOGRAPHY: comprehending an Inquiry into the Construction of Maps: with Rules for the Formation of Map Projections. By WILLIAM HUGHES, F.R.G.S., late Professor of Geography in the College for Civil Engineers. Second Edition; with 5 Plates. Fcp. 8vo. price 4s. 6d. cloth.

HUMBOLDT.—ASPECTS OF NATURE

In Different Lands and Different Climates; with Scientific Elucidations. By ALEXANDER VON HUMBOLDT. Translated, with the Author's authority, by Mrs. SABINE. New Edition. 16mo. 6s. cloth: or in 2 vols. 3s. 6d. each, cloth; Half-a-Crown each, sewed.

HUMBOLDT'S COSMOS;

Or, a Sketch of a Physical Description of the Universe. Translated, with the Author's authority by Mrs. SABINE. Vols. I. and II. 16mo. Half-a-Crown each, sewed; 3s. 6d. each, cloth: or in post 8vo. 12s. each, cloth.—Vol. III. post 8vo. 12s. 6d. cloth: or in 16mo. Part I. 2s. 6d. sewed, 3s. 6d. cloth; and Part II. 3s. sewed, 4s. cloth.

HUMPHREYS.—SENTIMENTS AND SIMILES OF SHAKSPEARE: a Classified Selection of Similes, Definitions, Descriptions, and other remarkable Passages in Shakspeare's Plays and Poems. With an elaborately illuminated border in the characteristic style of the Elizabethan Period, and other Embellishments. Bound in very massive carved and pierced covers containing in deep relief a medallion Head and Cypher. The Illuminations and Ornaments designed and executed by HENRY NOEL HUMPHREYS. Square post 8vo. One Guinea.

MRS. JAMESON'S LEGENDS OF THE MONASTIC ORDERS, as represented in the Fine Arts. Containing St. Benedict and the Early Benedictines in Italy, France, Spain, and Flanders; the Benedictines in England and in Germany; the Reformed Benedictines; early Royal Saints connected with the Benedictine Order; the Augustines; Orders derived from the Augustine Rule; the Mendicant Orders; the Jesuits; and the Order of the Visitation of St. Mary. Forming the SECOND SERIES of *Sacred and Legendary Art*. Second Edition, corrected and enlarged; with 11 Etchings by the Author, and 88 Woodcuts. Square crown 8vo. 28s. cloth.

MRS. JAMESON'S SACRED AND LEGENDARY ART;

Or, Legends of the Saints and Martyrs. FIRST SERIES. Containing Legends of the Angels and Archangels; the Evangelists and Apostles; the Greek and Latin Fathers; the Magdalene; the Patron Saints; the Virgin Patronesses; the Martyrs; the Bishops; the Hermits; and the Warrior-Saints of Christendom. Second Edition; with numerous Woodcuts, and 16 Etchings by the Author. Square crown 8vo. 28s. cloth.

MRS. JAMESON'S LEGENDS OF THE MADONNA,

As represented in the Fine Arts. Forming the THIRD SERIES of *Sacred and Legendary Art*. With 55 Drawings by the Author, and 152 Wood Engravings. Square crown 8vo. 28s. cloth.

"Of all our writers upon sacred art, there is none in whose hands the subject acquires so deep an interest, or is treated with such profound knowledge, such genial yet acute criticism, such deep sympathy for the poetic, and such high reverence for the sacred, as we find in the works of Mrs Jameson. A noble style, dignified yet natural, simple yet impressive, at once captivates the reader; while the utter absence of pedantry, even in the fulness of the authoress's knowledge of obscure subjects, adds not its least graceful characteristic to this book.....Mrs. Jameson's very scholarly and artist like volume is one which every art library must possess; and of the high qualities and merits of which, even the faint and meagre sketch which we have drawn can hardly, we hope, fail to afford some indication." MORNING CHRONICLE.

LORD JEFFREY'S CONTRIBUTIONS TO THE EDINBURGH REVIEW. A New Edition, complete in One Volume, uniform with Mr. Macaulay's Essays and Sir James Mackintosh's and the Rev. Sydney Smith's Works; with a Portrait engraved by Henry Robinson, and a Vignette View of Craigcrook engraved by J. Cousen. Square crown 8vo. [*Nearly ready.*

*** Also, the Second Edition, in 3 vols. 8vo. price 42s. cloth.

BISHOP JEREMY TAYLOR'S ENTIRE WORKS: With the Life by Bishop HEBER. Revised and corrected by the Rev. CHARLES PAGE EDEN, Fellow of Oriel College, Oxford. In Ten Volumes. Vols. II. to X. 8vo. price Half-a-Guinea each.

*** The First Volume, comprising Bishop Heber's Life of Jeremy Taylor, extended by the Editor, is nearly ready for publication.

BISHOP JEREMY TAYLOR.—READINGS FOR EVERY DAY in LENT: compiled from the Writings of BISHOP JEREMY TAYLOR. By the Author of *Amy Herbert*, *The Child's First History of Rome*, &c. Fcp. 8vo. price 5s. cloth.

JOHNSTON.—A NEW DICTIONARY OF GEOGRAPHY, Descriptive, Physical, Statistical, and Historical: forming a complete General Gazetteer of the World. By ALEXANDER KEITH JOHNSTON, F.R.S.E. F.R.G.S. F.G.S.; Geographer at Edinburgh in Ordinary to Her Majesty. In One Volume of 1,440 pages; comprising nearly 50,000 Names of Places. 8vo. price 36s. cloth; or strongly half-bound in russia, with flexible back, 41s.

KEMBLE.—THE SAXONS IN ENGLAND: a History of the English Commonwealth till the period of the Norman Conquest. By JOHN MITCHELL KEMBLE, M.A., F.C.P.S., &c. 2 vols. 8vo. 28s. cloth.

KIPPIS.—A COLLECTION OF HYMNS AND PSALMS FOR PUBLIC and PRIVATE WORSHIP. Selected and prepared by ANDREW KIPPIS, D.D., ABRAHAM REES, D.D., the Rev. THOMAS JERVIS, and the Rev. THOMAS MORGAN, LL.D. New Edition; including a New Supplement by the Rev. EDMUND KELL, M.A. 18mo. 4s. cloth; or 4s. 6d. bound in roan.—The SUPPLEMENT separately, price Eightpence.

KIRBY AND SPENCE.—AN INTRODUCTION TO ENTO-MOLOGY; or, Elements of the Natural History of Insects: comprising an account of noxious and useful Insects, of their Metamorphoses, Food, Stratagems, Habitations, Societies, Motions, Noises, Hybernation, Instinct, &c. By W. KIRBY, M.A. F.R.S. & L.S. Rector of Barham; and W. SPENCE, Esq. F.R.S. & L.S. New Edition. 2 vols. 8vo. with Plates, 31s. 6d. cloth.

LAING.—OBSERVATIONS ON THE SOCIAL AND POLI-TICAL STATE of DENMARK and the DUCHIES of SLESWICK and HOLSTEIN in 1851: Being the Third Series of *Notes of a Traveller*. By SAMUEL LAING, Esq. With a Plan of the Battle of Idstedt. 8vo. price 12s. cloth.

LAING.—OBSERVATIONS ON THE SOCIAL AND POLI-TICAL STATE of the EUROPEAN PEOPLE in 1848 and 1849: Being the Second Series of *Notes of a Traveller*. By SAMUEL LAING, Esq. 8vo. 14s. cloth.

LANG. — FREEDOM AND INDEPENDENCE FOR THE GOLDEN LANDS of AUSTRALIA; the Right of the Colonies, and the Interest of Britain and of the World. By JOHN DUNMORE LANG, M.A., D.D. With a coloured Map. Post 8vo. price 7s. 6d. cloth.

LANG.—AN HISTORICAL AND STATISTICAL ACCOUNT of NEW SOUTH WALES; including a Visit to the Gold Regions, and a Description of the Mines, with an Estimate of the probable Results of the Great Discovery. By JOHN DUNMORE LANG, M.A., D.D. Third Edition (three-fourths entirely new), bringing down the History of the Colony to July 1, 1852; with a large coloured Map. 2 vols. post 8vo. price 21s. cloth.

LARDNER'S CABINET CYCLOPÆDIA

OF HISTORY, BIOGRAPHY, LITERATURE, THE ARTS AND SCIENCES, NATURAL HISTORY, AND MANUFACTURES: A Series of Original Works by

SIR JOHN HERSCHEL,
SIR JAMES MACKINTOSH,
ROBERT SOUTHEY,
SIR DAVID BREWSTER,
THOMAS KEIGHTLEY,
JOHN FORSTER,
SIR WALTER SCOTT,
THOMAS MOORE,
Bishop THIRLWALL,
The Rev. G. R. GLEIG,
J. C. L. DE SISMONDI,
JOHN PHILLIPS, F.R.S. G.S.

And other eminent Writers.

Complete in 132 vols. fcp. 8vo. with Vignette Titles, price Nineteen Guineas, cloth.
The works separately, in Sets or Series, price Three Shillings and Sixpence each Volume.

A List of the Works composing the Cabinet Cyclopædia:—

1. Bell's History of Russia......3 vols. 10s. 6d.
2. Bell's Lives of British Poets..2 vols. 7s.
3. Brewster's Optics............1 vol. 3s. 6d.
4. Cooley's Maritime and Inland Discovery ....3 vols. 10s. 6d.
5. Crowe's History of France ..3 vols. 10s. 6d.
6. De Morgan on Probabilities..1 vol. 3s. 6d.
7. De Sismondi's History of the Italian Republics..........1 vol. 3s. 6d.
8. De Sismondi's Fall of the Roman Empire.....................2 vols. 7s.
9. Donovan's Chemistry........1 vol. 3s. 6d.
10. Donovan's Domestic Economy 2 vols. 7s.
11. Dunham's Spain & Portugal 5 vols. 17s. 6d.
12. Dunham's History of Denmark, Sweden, and Norway ......3 vols. 10s. 6d.
13. Dunham's History of Poland..1 vol. 3s. 6d.
14. Dunham's Germanic Empire 3 vols. 10s. 6d.
15. Dunham's Europe during the Middle Ages ....4 vols. 14s.
16. Dunham's British Dramatists 2 vols. 7s.
17. Dunham's Lives of Early Writers of Great Britain ......1 vol. 6d.
18. Fergus's History of the United States ....2 vols. 7s.
19. Fosbroke's Greek and Roman Antiquities................2 vols. 7s.
20. Forster's Lives of the Statesmen of the Commonwealth 5 vols. 17s. 6d.
21. Gleig's Lives of British Military Commanders ....3 vols. 10s. 6d.
22. Grattan's History of the Netherlands ....1 vol. 3s. 6d.
23. Henslow's Botany ....1 vol. 3s. 6d.
24. Herschel's Astronomy ......1 vol. 3s. 6d.
25. Herschel's Discourse on Natural Philosophy ....1 vol. 3s. 6d.
26. History of Rome ....2 vols. 7s.
27. History of Switzerland ......1 vol. 3s. 6d.
28. Holland's Manufactures in Metal ....3 vols. 10s. 6d.
29. James's Lives of Foreign Statesmen ....5 vols. 17s. 6d.
30. Kater & Lardner's Mechanics 1 vol. 3s. 6d.
31. Keightley's Outlines of Hist. 1 vol. 3s. 6d.
32. Lardner's Arithmetic........1 vol. 3s. 6d.
33. Lardner's Geometry ....1 vol. 3s. 6d.
34. Lardner on Heat ....1 vol. 3s. 6d.
35. Lardner's Hydrostatics and Pneumatics ....1 vol. 3s. 6d.
36. Lardner & Walker's Electricity and Magnetism............2 vols. 7s.
37. Mackintosh, Forster, and Courtenay's Lives of British Statesmen ....7 vols. 24s. 6d.
38. Mackintosh, Wallace, & Bell's History of England........10 vols. 35s.
39. Montgomery and Shelley's Eminent Italian, Spanish, and Portuguese Authors....3 vols. 10s. 6d.
40. Moore's History of Ireland..4 vols. 14s.
41. Nicolas's Chronology of Hist. 1 vol. 3s. 6d.
42. Phillips's Treatise on Geology, 2 vols. 7s.
43. Powell's History of Natural Philosophy................1 vol. 3s. 6d.
44. Porter's Treatise on the Manufacture of Silk ....1 vol. 3s. 6d.
45. Porter's Manufactures of Porcelain and Glass ......1 vol. 3s. 6d.
46. Roscoe's British Lawyers....1 vol. 3s. 6d.
47. Scott's History of Scotland..2 vols. 7s.
48. Shelley's Lives of Eminent French Authors. ....2 vols. 7s.
49. Shuckard & Swainson's Insects, 1 vol. 3s. 6d.
50. Southey's Lives of British Admirals ....5 vols. 17s. 6d.
51. Stebbing's Church History ..2 vols. 7s.
52. Stebbing's History of the Reformation ....2 vols. 7s.
53. Swainson's Discourse on Natural History..............1 vol. 3s. 6d.
54. Swainson's Natural History & Classification of Animals..1 vol. 3s. 6d.
55. Swainson's Habits & Instincts of Animals ....1 vol. 3s. 6d.
56. Swainson's Birds ....2 vols. 7s.
57. Swainson's Fish, Reptiles, &c. 2 vols. 7s.
58. Swainson's Quadrupeds......1 vol. 3s. 6d.
59. Swainson's Shells & Shell-fish, 1 vol. 3s. 6d.
60. Swainson's Animals in Menageries ....1 vol. 3s. 6d.
61. Swainson's Taxidermy and Bibliography ....1 vol. 3s. 6d.
62. Thirlwall's History of Greece, 8 vols. 28s.

LARDNER.—THE GREAT EXHIBITION AND LONDON

in 1851. Reviewed by Dr. LARDNER, MICHEL CHEVALIER, JOHN LEMOINNE, and HECTOR BERLIOZ. With Wood Engravings. Crown 8vo. price 14s. cloth.

DR. LATHAM ON DISEASES OF THE HEART.

Lectures on Subjects connected with Clinical Medicine: Diseases of the Heart. By P. M. LATHAM, M.D., Physician Extraordinary to the Queen. New Edition. 2 vols. 12mo. 16s. cl.

DR. FALCK LEBAHN.—GOETHE'S FAUST.

With copious English Notes, containing the whole of the Text, in German and English, classified according to the Rules of Grammar, for Students of the German Language. By FALCK LEBAHN, Ph.D. Author of *German in One Volume*, &c. 8vo. price 15s. cloth.

LEE.—ELEMENTS OF NATURAL HISTORY;

Or, First Principles of Zoology: Comprising the Principles of Classification interspersed with amusing and instructive Accounts of the most remarkable Animals. By Mrs. R. LEE. New Edition, enlarged, with numerous additional Woodcuts. Fcp. 8vo. 7s. 6d. cloth.

L. E. L.—THE POETICAL WORKS OF LETITIA ELIZABETH LANDON;

comprising the IMPROVISATRICE, the VENETIAN BRACELET, the GOLDEN VIOLET, the TROUBADOUR, and other Poetical Remains. New Edition; with 2 Vignettes by Richard Doyle. 2 vols. 16mo. 10s. cloth; morocco, 21s.

LETTERS ON HAPPINESS, ADDRESSED TO A FRIEND.

By the Author of *Letters to My Unknown Friends*, &c. Fcp. 8vo. 6s. cloth.

LETTERS TO MY UNKNOWN FRIENDS.

By a LADY, Author of *Letters on Happiness.* 3d Edition. Fcp. 8vo. 6s. cloth.

LINDLEY.—INTRODUCTION TO BOTANY.

By J. LINDLEY, Ph.D. F.R.S. L.S. &c. Professor of Botany in University College, London. New Edition, with Corrections and copious Additions. 2 vols. 8vo. with Six Plates and numerous Woodcuts, 24s. cloth.

LINWOOD.—ANTHOLOGIA OXONIENSIS,

Sive Florilegium e lusibus poeticis diversorum Oxoniensium Græcis et Latinis decerptum. Curante GULIELMO LINWOOD, M.A. Ædis Christi Alummo. 8vo. 14s. cloth.

LITTON.—THE CHURCH OF CHRIST,

In its Idea, Attributes, and Ministry: With a particular reference to the Controversy on the Subject between Romanists and Protestants. By the Rev. EDWARD ARTHUR LITTON, M.A., Vice-Principal of St. Edmund Hall, Oxford. 8vo. 16s. cloth.

LORIMER.—LETTERS TO A YOUNG MASTER MARINER

On some Subjects connected with his Calling. By the late CHARLES LORIMER. New Edition. Fcp. 8vo. 5s. 6d. cloth.

LOUDON.—THE AMATEUR GARDENER'S CALENDAR:

Being a Monthly Guide as to what should be avoided, as well as what should be done, in a Garden in each Month: with plain Rules *how to do* what is requisite; Directions for Laying Out and Planting Kitchen and Flower Gardens, Pleasure Grounds, and Shrubberies; and a short Account, in each Month, of the Quadrupeds, Birds, and Insects then most injurious to Gardens. By Mrs. LOUDON. 16mo. with Wood Engravings, 7s. 6d. cloth.

LOUDON.—THE LADY'S COUNTRY COMPANION;

Or, How to Enjoy a Country Life Rationally. By Mrs. LOUDON, Author of *Gardening for Ladies*, &c. Fourth Edition; with Plate and Wood Engravings. Fcp. 8vo. 5s. cloth.

LOUDON'S SELF-INSTRUCTION FOR YOUNG GARDENERS, Foresters, Bailiffs, Land Stewards, and Farmers; in Arithmetic, Book-keeping, Geometry, Mensuration, Practical Trigonometry, Mechanics, Land-Surveying, Levelling, Planning and Mapping, Architectural Drawing, and Isometrical Projection and Perspective; with Examples shewing their applications to Horticulture and Agricultural Purposes. With a Portrait of Mr. Loudon, and a Memoir by Mrs. Loudon. 8vo. with Woodcuts, 7s. 6d. cloth.

LOUDON'S ENCYCLOPÆDIA OF GARDENING;

Comprising the Theory and Practice of Horticulture, Floriculture, Arboriculture, and Landscape Gardening: including all the latest improvements; a General History of Gardening in all Countries; and a Statistical View of its Present State: with Suggestions for its Future Progress in the British Isles. Illustrated with many hundred Engravings on Wood by Branston. New Edition, corrected and improved by Mrs. LOUDON. 8vo. 50s. cloth.

LOUDON'S ENCYCLOPÆDIA OF TREES AND SHRUBS:

Being the *Arboretum et Fruticetum Britannicum* abridged: containing the Hardy Trees and Shrubs of Great Britain, Native and Foreign, Scientifically and Popularly Described; with their Propagation, Culture, and Uses in the Arts; and with Engravings of nearly all the Species. Adapted for the use of Nurserymen, Gardeners, and Foresters. With about 2,000 Engravings on Wood. 8vo. £2. 10s. cloth.

LOUDON'S ENCYCLOPÆDIA OF AGRICULTURE:

Comprising the Theory and Practice of the Valuation, Transfer, Laying-out, Improvement, and Management of Landed Property, and of the Cultivation and Economy of the Animal and Vegetable productions of Agriculture: including all the latest Improvements, a general History of Agriculture in all Countries, a Statistical View of its present State, with Suggestions for its future progress in the British Isles. New Edition. 8vo. with 1,100 Woodcuts, 50s. loth.

LOUDON'S ENCYCLOPÆDIA OF PLANTS;

Including all the Plants which are now found in, or have been introduced into, Great Britain; giving their Natural History, accompanied by such descriptions, engraved figures, and elementary details, as may enable a beginner, who is a mere English reader, to discover the name of every Plant which he may find in flower, and acquire all the information respecting it which is useful and interesting. New Edition, corrected throughout, and brought down to the year 1853, by Mrs. LOUDON. [*In the press.*

LOUDON'S ENCYCLOPÆDIA OF COTTAGE, FARM, AND VILLA ARCHITECTURE and **FURNITURE**; containing numerous Designs, from the Villa to the Cottage and the Farm, including Farm Houses, Farmeries, and other Agricultural Buildings; Country Inns, Public Houses, and Parochial Schools; with the requisite Fittings-up, Fixtures, and Furniture, and appropriate Offices, Gardens, and Garden Scenery: each Design accompanied by Analytical and Critical Remarks. New Edition, edited by Mrs. LOUDON. With more than 2,000 Engravings on Wood. 8vo. £3. 3s. cloth.

LOUDON'S HORTUS BRITANNICUS;

Or, Catalogue of all the Plants indigenous to, cultivated in, or introduced into Britain. An entirely New Edition, corrected throughout: With a Supplement, including all the New Plants, and a New General Index to the whole Work. Edited by Mrs. LOUDON; assisted by W. H. BAXTER, and DAVID WOOSTER. 8vo. 31s. 6d. cloth.—The SUPPLEMENT separately, price 14s. cloth.

LOW.—ELEMENTS OF PRACTICAL AGRICULTURE;
Comprehending the Cultivation of Plants, the Husbandry of the Domestic Animals, and the Economy of the Farm. By D. Low, Esq. F.R S.E. New Edition, with 200 Woodcuts. 8vo. 21s. cloth.

MACAULAY.—THE HISTORY OF ENGLAND FROM THE ACCESSION OF JAMES II. By THOMAS BABINGTON MACAULAY. New Edition. Vols. I. and II. 8vo. 32s. cloth.

MR. MACAULAY'S CRITICAL & HISTORICAL ESSAYS CONTRIBUTED to The EDINBURGH REVIEW. Three Editions, as follows:—

1. LIBRARY EDITION (the *Seventh*), in 3 vols. 8vo. price 36s. cloth.
2. Complete in ONE VOLUME, with Portrait and Vignette. Square crown 8vo. price 21s. cloth; or 30s. handsomely bound in calf by Hayday.
3. A NEW EDITION, in 3 vols. fcp. 8vo. price 21s. cloth.

MACAULAY.—LAYS OF ANCIENT ROME,
With IVRY and the ARMADA. By THOMAS BABINGTON MACAULAY. New Edition. 16mo. 4s. 6d. cloth; or 10s. 6d. bound in morocco by Hayday.

MR. MACAULAY'S LAYS OF ANCIENT ROME.
With numerous Illustrations, Original and from the Antique, drawn on Wood by George Scharf, Jun. and engraved by Samuel Williams. New Edition. Fcp. 4to. 21s. boards; or 42s. bound in morocco by Hayday.

MACDONALD.—VILLA VEROCCHIO;
Or, the YOUTH of LEONARDO DA VINCI: a Tale. By the late DIANA LOUISA MACDONALD. Fcp. 8vo. 6s. cloth.

MACKINTOSH.—SIR JAMES MACKINTOSH'S MISCELLANEOUS WORKS; including his Contributions to The EDINBURGH REVIEW. A New Edition, complete in One Volume; with Portrait and Vignette. Square crown 8vo. 21s. cloth; or 30s. calf extra by Hayday.

M'LEOD AND WELLER'S SACRED ATLAS.
An Atlas of Scripture Geography. Adapted for the use of Training Colleges, Pupil Teachers, and the Upper Classes in Elementary Schools. Comprising Fifteen coloured Maps, and a Section, engraved on Ten Plates: with Illustrative Letterpress, by WALTER M'LEOD, F.R.G.S., Head Master of the Model School, and Master of Method in the Royal Military Asylum, Chelsea. The Maps compiled and engraved by EDWARD WELLER, F.R.G.S. Royal 8vo. price 7s. half-bound.

M'CULLOCH.—A TREATISE ON THE CIRCUMSTANCES which DETERMINE the RATE of WAGES and the CONDITION of the LABOURING CLASSES. By J. R. M'CULLOCH, Esq. Fcp. 8vo. 3s. 6d. cloth.

M'CULLOCH.—A DICTIONARY, PRACTICAL, THEORETICAL, and HISTORICAL, of COMMERCE and COMMERCIAL NAVIGATION. Illustrated with Maps and Plans. By J. R. M'CULLOCH, Esq. New Edition, corrected, enlarged, and improved: Including a New Supplement. 8vo. 50s. cloth; or 55s. half-bound in russia with flexible back.—The SUPPLEMENT separately, price 4s. 6d.

M'CULLOCH.—A DICTIONARY, GEOGRAPHICAL, STATISTICAL, and HISTORICAL, of the various Countries, Places, and Principal Natural Objects in the WORLD. By J. R. M'CULLOCH, Esq. Illustrated with 6 large Maps. New Edition; with a Supplement, comprising the Population of Great Britain from the Census of 1851. 2 vols. 8vo. 63s. cloth.—The SUPPLEMENT separately, price 2s. 6d.

M'CULLOCH.—AN ACCOUNT, DESCRIPTIVE & STATISTICAL, of the BRITISH EMPIRE; exhibiting its Extent, Physical Capacities, Population, Industry, and Civil and Religious Institutions. By J. R. M'CULLOCH, Esq. New Edition, corrected, enlarged, and greatly improved. 2 vols. 8vo. 42s. cloth.

M'CULLOCH.—A TREATISE ON THE PRINCIPLES AND PRACTICAL INFLUENCE of TAXATION and the FUNDING SYSTEM. By J. R. M'CULLOCH, Esq. Second Edition, corrected, enlarged, and improved. 8vo. 16s. cloth.

MAITLAND.—THE CHURCH IN THE CATACOMBS: A Description of the Primitive Church of Rome. Illustrated by its Sepulchral Remains. By CHARLES MAITLAND. New Edition; with numerous Woodcuts. 8vo. 14s. cloth.

MRS. MARCET'S CONVERSATIONS ON CHEMISTRY; In which the Elements of that Science are familiarly Explained and Illustrated by Experiments, New Edition, enlarged and improved. 2 vols. fcp. 8vo. 14s. cloth.

MRS. MARCET'S CONVERSATIONS ON NATURAL PHILOSOPHY, in which the Elements of that Science are familiarly explained. New Edition, enlarged and corrected. Fcp. 8vo. with 23 Plates, 10s. 6d. cloth.

MRS. MARCET'S CONVERSATIONS ON POLITICAL ECONOMY, in which the Elements of that Science are familiarly explained. New Edition. Fcp. 8vo. 7s. 6d. cloth.

MRS. MARCET'S CONVERSATIONS ON VEGETABLE PHYSIOLOGY; comprehending the Elements of Botany, with their application to Agriculture. New Edition. Fcp. 8vo. with 4 Plates, 9s. cloth.

MRS. MARCET'S CONVERSATIONS ON LAND & WATER. New Edition, revised and corrected. With a coloured Map, shewing the comparative altitude of Mountains. Fcp. 8vo. 5s. 6d. cloth.

MARIOTTI.—FRA DOLCINO AND HIS TIMES; Being an Account of a General Struggle for Ecclesiastical Reform, and of an Anti-Heretical Crusade in Italy, in the early part of the Fourteenth Century. By L. MARIOTTI, Author of *Italy, Past and Present,* &c. Post 8vo. price 10s. 6d. cloth.

MARTINEAU.—CHURCH HISTORY IN ENGLAND, From the Earliest Times to the period of the Reformation. By the Rev. ARTHUR MARTINEAU, M.A., late Fellow of Trinity College, Cambridge. 12mo. [*In the press.*

MAUNDER'S BIOGRAPHICAL TREASURY; Consisting of Memoirs, Sketches, and brief Notices of above 12,000 Eminent Persons of all Ages and Nations, from the Earliest Period of History; forming a new and complete Dictionary of Universal Biography. A New and carefully-revised Edition, corrected throughout, and extended by the introduction of numerous additional Lives. Fcp. 8vo. 10s. cloth; bound in roan, 12s.; calf lettered, 12s. 6d.

MAUNDER'S HISTORICAL TREASURY: Comprising a General Introductory Outline of Universal History, Ancient and Modern, and a Series of separate Histories of every principal Nation that exists; their Rise, Progress, and Present Condition, the Moral and Social Character of their respective inhabitants, their Religion, Manners and Customs, &c. An entirely New Edition; revised throughout and brought down to the Present Time. Fcp. 8vo. 10s. cloth; bound in roan, 12s.; calf lettered, [12s. 6d.

MAUNDER'S SCIENTIFIC AND LITERARY TREASURY:
A new and popular Encyclopædia of Science and the Belles-Lettres; including all Branches of Science, and every Subject connected with Literature and Art. New Edition. Fcp. 8vo. 10s. cloth; bound in roan, 12s.; calf lettered, 12s. 6d.

MAUNDER'S TREASURY OF NATURAL HISTORY;
Or, a Popular Dictionary of Animated Nature: In which the Zoological Characteristics that distinguish the different Classes, Genera, and Species are combined with a variety of interesting Information illustrative of the Habits, Instincts, and General Economy of the Animal Kingdom. With 900 accurate Engravings on Wood. New Edition. Fcp. 8vo. 10s. cloth; bound in roan, 12s.; calf lettered, 12s. 6d.

MAUNDER'S TREASURY OF KNOWLEDGE,
And LIBRARY of REFERENCE. Comprising an English Dictionary and Grammar, an Universal Gazetteer, a Classical Dictionary, a Chronology, a Law Dictionary, a Synopsis of the Peerage, numerous useful Tables, &c. The Twentieth Edition (1853), carefully revised and corrected throughout: With some Additions. Fcp. 8vo. 10s. cloth; bound in roan, 12s.; calf lettered, 12s. 6d.

MERIVALE.—A HISTORY OF THE ROMANS UNDER
the EMPIRE. By the Rev. CHARLES MERIVALE, B.D., late Fellow of St. John's College, Cambridge. Vols. I. and II. 8vo. 28s. cloth.—Vol. III. completing the History to the Establishment of the Monarchy by Augustus, 8vo. 14s. cloth.

MERIVALE.—THE FALL OF THE ROMAN REPUBLIC:
A Short History of the Last Century of the Commonwealth. By the Rev. CHAS MERIVALE, B.D., late Fellow of St. John's College, Cambridge. 12mo. [*In the press.*

MILNER.—THE HISTORY OF THE CHURCH OF CHRIST.
By the late Rev. JOSEPH MILNER, A.M. With Additions by the late Rev. ISAAC MILNER, D.D., F.R.S. A New Edition, revised, with additional Notes by the Rev. THOS. GRANTHAM, B.D. 4 vols. 8vo. price 52s. cloth.

JAMES MONTGOMERY'S POETICAL WORKS.
With some additional Poems, and the Author's Autobiographical Prefaces. A New Edition, complete in One Volume; with Portrait and Vignette. Square crown 8vo. 10s. 6d. cloth; morocco, 21s.—Or, in 4 vols. fcp. 8vo. with Portrait, and Seven other Plates, 20s. cloth; morocco, 36s.

MONTGOMERY.—ORIGINAL HYMNS
For Public, Social, and Private Devotion. By JAMES MONTGOMERY. 18mo. 5s. 6d. cloth.

MOORE.—HEALTH, DISEASE, AND REMEDY,
Familiarly and practically considered in a few of their relations to the Blood. By GEORGE MOORE, M.D. Member of the Royal College of Physicians. Post 8vo. 7s. 6d. cloth.

MOORE.—MAN AND HIS MOTIVES.
By GEORGE MOORE, M.D., Member of the Royal College of Physicians. Third and cheaper Edition. Fcp. 8vo. 6s. cloth.

MOORE.—THE POWER OF THE SOUL OVER THE BODY,
Considered in relation to Health and Morals. By GEORGE MOORE, M.D. Member of the Royal College of Physicians. Fifth and cheaper Edition. Fcp. 8vo. 6s. cloth.

MOORE.—THE USE OF THE BODY IN RELATION TO
THE MIND. By GEORGE MOORE, M.D. Member of the Royal College of Physicians. Third and cheaper Edition. Fcp. 8vo. 6s. cloth.

MOORE.—MEMOIRS, JOURNAL, & CORRESPONDENCE of THOMAS MOORE. Edited by the Right Hon. LORD JOHN RUSSELL, M.P. With Portraits and Vignette Illustrations. Vols. I. and II. post 8vo. price 21s. cloth.

THE THIRD AND FOURTH VOLUMES OF MOORE'S MEMOIRS, JOURNAL, and CORRESPONDENCE, with Portraits of Sir John Stevenson and Samuel Rogers, Esq.; and Vignettes, by T. Creswick, R.A., of the Meeting of the Waters, and Moore's Residence at Mayfield. Vols. III. and IV. post 8vo. price 21s. cloth.

THOMAS MOORE'S POETICAL WORKS.

Containing the Author's recent Introduction and Notes. Complete in One Volume, uniform with Lord Byron's and Southey's Poems. With a Portrait, and a View of Sloperton Cottage, Chippenham. Medium 8vo. 21s. cloth; morocco by Hayday, 42s.

*** Also a New and cheaper Issue of the First collected Edition of the above, in 10 vols. fcp. 8vo. with Portrait, and 19 Plates, price 35s. cloth.

MOORE.—SONGS, BALLADS, AND SACRED SONGS.

By THOMAS MOORE, Author of "Lalla Rookh," &c. First collected Edition, with Vignette by R. Doyle. 16mo. 5s. cloth; 12s. 6d. smooth morocco, by Hayday.

MOORE'S IRISH MELODIES.

New Edition, with the Autobiographical Preface from the Collective Edition of Mr. Moore's Poetical Works, and a Vignette Title by D. Maclise, R.A. 16mo. 5s. cloth; 12s. 6d. smooth morocco, by Hayday.—Or, with Vignette Title by E. Corbould, fcp. 8vo. 10s. cloth; bound in morocco, 13s. 6d.

MOORE'S IRISH MELODIES.

Illustrated by D. MACLISE, R.A. New and Cheaper Edition; with 161 Designs, and the whole of the Letterpress engraved on Steel, by F. P. Becker. Super-royal 8vo. 31s. 6d.; bound in morocco by Hayday, £2. 12s. 6d.—The Original Edition, in imperial 8vo., price 63s. boards; morocco, by Hayday, £4. 14s. 6d.; proofs, £6. 6s. boards,—may still be had.

MOORE'S LALLA ROOKH: AN ORIENTAL ROMANCE.

New Edition, with the Autobiographical Preface from the Collective Edition of Mr. Moore's Poetical Works, and a Vignette Title by D. Maclise, R.A. 16mo. 5s. cloth; 12s. 6d. smooth morocco, by Hayday.—Or, in fcp. 8vo. with Four Engravings from Paintings by Westall. 10s. 6d. cloth; bound in morocco, 14s.

MOORE'S LALLA ROOKH: AN ORIENTAL ROMANCE.

With 13 highly-finished Steel Plates from Designs by Corbould, Meadows, and Stephanoff, engraved under the superintendence of the late Charles Heath. New Edition. Square crown 8vo. 15s. cloth; morocco, 28s.—A few copies of the Original Edition, in royal 8vo. price One Guinea, still remain.

MOSELEY.—THE MECHANICAL PRINCIPLES OF ENGINEERING AND ARCHITECTURE. By the Rev. H. MOSELEY, M.A., F.R.S., Professor of Natural Philosophy and Astronomy in King's College, London. 8vo. 24s. cloth.

MOSELEY.—ILLUSTRATIONS OF PRACTICAL MECHANICS. By the Rev. H. MOSELEY, M.A., Professor of Natural Philosophy and Astronomy in King's College, London. New Edition. Fcp. 8vo. with numerous Woodcuts, 8s. cloth.

MOSHEIM'S ECCLESIASTICAL HISTORY,

Ancient and Modern. Translated, with copious Notes, by JAMES MURDOCK, D.D. New Edition, revised, and continued to the Present Time, by the Rev. HENRY SOAMES, M.A. 4 vols. 8vo. 48s. cloth.

MURE.—A CRITICAL HISTORY OF THE LANGUAGE AND LITERATURE OF ANCIENT GREECE. By WILLIAM MURE, M.P., of Caldwell. 3 vols. 8vo. 36s. cloth.—Vol. IV. comprising Historical Literature from the Rise of Prose Composition to the Death of Herodotus. 8vo. with Map, price 15s. cloth.

MURRAY'S ENCYCLOPÆDIA OF GEOGRAPHY;
Comprising a complete Description of the Earth: exhibiting its Relation to the Heavenly Bodies, its Physical Structure, the Natural History of each Country, and the Industry, Commerce, Political Institutions, and Civil and Social State of all Nations. Second Edition; with 82 Maps, and upwards of 1,000 other Woodcuts. 8vo. £3, cloth.

NEALE.—RISEN FROM THE RANKS;
Or, Conduct *versus* Caste. By the Rev. ERSKINE NEALE, M.A., Rector of Kirton, Suffolk. Fcp. 8vo. [*Nearly ready.*

NEALE.—THE RICHES THAT BRING NO SORROW.
By the Rev. ERSKINE NEALE, M.A., Rector of Kirton, Suffolk. Fcp. 8vo. 6s. cloth.

NEALE.—THE EARTHLY RESTING PLACES OF THE JUST. By the Rev. ERSKINE NEALE, M.A., Rector of Kirton, Suffolk. Fcp. 8vo. with Woodcuts, 7s. cloth.

NEALE.—THE CLOSING SCENE;
Or, Christianity and Infidelity contrasted in the Last Hours of Remarkable Persons. By the Rev. ERSKINE NEALE, M.A., Rector of Kirton, Suffolk. New Editions of the First and Second Series. 2 vols. fcp. 8vo. 12s. cloth; or separately, 6s. each.

NEWMAN.—DISCOURSES ADDRESSED TO MIXED CON- GREGATIONS. By JOHN HENRY NEWMAN, Priest of the Oratory of St. Philip Neri. Second Edition. 8vo. 12s. cloth.

LIEUTENANT OSBORN'S ARCTIC JOURNAL.
Stray Leaves from an Arctic Journal; or, Eighteen Months in the Polar Regions in Search of Sir John Franklin's Expedition. By Lieut. SHERARD OSBORN, R.N., Commanding H.M.S.V. *Pioneer.* With Map and Four coloured Plates. Post 8vo. price 12s. cloth.

OWEN JONES.—WINGED THOUGHTS:
A Series of Poems. By MARY ANNE BACON. With Illustrations of Birds, designed by E. L. Bateman, and executed in Illuminated Printing by Owen Jones. Imperial 8vo. 31s. 6d. elegantly bound in calf.

OWEN JONES. — FLOWERS AND THEIR KINDRED THOUGHTS: A Series of Stanzas. By MARY ANNE BACON With beautiful Illustrations of Flowers, designed and printed in Colours by Owen Jones. Imperial 8vo. 31s. 6d. elegantly bound in calf.

OWEN JONES.—FRUITS FROM THE GARDEN AND THE FIELD: A Series of Stanzas. By MARY ANNE BACON. With beautiful Illustrations of Fruit, designed and printed in Colours by Owen Jones. Imperial 8vo. 31s. 6d. elegantly bound in calf.

OWEN.—LECTURES ON THE COMPARATIVE ANATOMY and PHYSIOLOGY of the INVERTEBRATE ANIMALS, delivered at the Royal College of Surgeons in 1843. By RICHARD OWEN, F.R.S. Hunterian Professor to the College. New Edition, corrected. 8vo. with Wood Engravings. [*Nearly ready.*

OWEN.—LECTURES ON THE COMPARATIVE ANATOMY

and PHYSIOLOGY of the VERTEBRATE ANIMALS, delivered at the Royal College of Surgeons in 1844 and 1846. By RICHARD OWEN, F.R.S. Hunterian Professor to the College. In 2 vols. The First Volume; with numerous Woodcuts, 8vo. 14s. cloth.

THE COMPLETE WORKS OF BLAISE PASCAL:

With M. Villemain's Essay on Pascal considered as a Writer and Moralist prefixed to the *Provincial Letters;* and the *Miscellaneous Writings, Thoughts on Religion,* and *Evidences of Christianity* re-arranged, with large Additions, from the French Edition of Mons. P. Faugère. Translated from the French, with Memoir, Introductions to the various Works, Editorial Notes, and Appendices, by GEORGE PEARCE, Esq. 3 vols. post 8vo. with Portrait, 25s. 6d. cloth.

Vol. I.—PASCAL'S PROVINCIAL LETTERS: with M. Villemain's Essay on Pascal prefixed, and a new Memoir. Post 8vo. Portrait, 8s. 6d.

Vol. II.—PASCAL'S THOUGHTS on RELIGION and EVIDENCES of CHRISTIANITY, with Additions, from Original MSS.: from M. Faugère's Edition. Post 8vo. 8s. 6d.

Vol. III.—PASCAL'S MISCELLANEOUS WRITINGS, Correspondence, Detached Thoughts, &c.: from M. Faugère's Edition. Post 8vo. 8s. 6d.

PASHLEY.—PAUPERISM AND POOR-LAWS.

By ROBERT PASHLEY, M.A., F.C.P.S., One of Her Majesty's Counsel, and late Fellow of Trinity College, Cambridge; Author of *Travels in Crete.* 8vo. price 10s. 6d. cloth.

CAPTAIN PEEL'S TRAVELS IN NUBIA.

A RIDE through the NUBIAN DESERT. By Captain W. PEEL, R.N. Post 8vo. with a Route Map from Cairo to Kordofan, price 5s. cloth.

"A very pleasant little book, written by one who let nothing worthy of notice escape him, and knows how to describe what he saw. ....His little book, put forward without any pretension, is not only highly amusing, but it is full of the most valuable information." UNITED SERVICE MAGAZINE.

PEREIRA.—A TREATISE ON FOOD AND DIET:

With Observations on the Dietetical Regimen suited for Disordered States of the Digestive Organs; and an Account of the Dietaries of some of the principal Metropolitan and other Establishments for Paupers, Lunatics, Criminals, Children, the Sick, &c. By JON. PEREIRA, M.D. F.R.S. & L.S. Author of *Elements of Materia Medica.* 8vo. 16s. cloth.

PESCHEL'S ELEMENTS OF PHYSICS.

Translated from the German, with Notes, by E. WEST. With Diagrams and Woodcuts. 3 vols. fcp. 8vo. 21s. cloth.

PETERBOROUGH.—A MEMOIR OF CHARLES MORDAUNT,

EARL of PETERBOROUGH and MONMOUTH: with Selections from his Correspondence. By the Author of *Hochelaga* and *The Conquest of Canada.* 2 vols. post 8vo. [*In the press.*

PHILLIPS'S ELEMENTARY INTRODUCTION TO MINERALOGY.

A New Edition, with extensive Alterations and Additions, by H. J. BROOKE, F.R.S., F.G.S.; and W. H. MILLER, M.A., F.R.S., F.G.S. Professor of Mineralogy in the University of Cambridge. With numerous Wood Engravings. Post 8vo. price 18s. cloth.

PHILLIPS.—FIGURES AND DESCRIPTIONS OF THE

PALÆOZOIC FOSSILS of CORNWALL, DEVON, and WEST SOMERSET; observed in the course of the Ordnance Geological Survey of that District. By JOHN PHILLIPS, F.R.S. F.G.S. &c. 8vo. with 60 Plates, comprising very numerous figures, 9s. cloth.

PORTLOCK.—REPORT ON THE GEOLOGY OF THE COUNTY of LONDONDERRY, and of Parts of Tyrone and Fermanagh, examined and described under the Authority of the Master-General and Board of Ordnance. By J. E. PORTLOCK, F.R.S. &c. 8vo. with 48 Plates, 24s. cloth.

POWER.—SKETCHES IN NEW ZEALAND, with Pen and Pencil. By W. TYRONE POWER, D.A.C.G. From a Journal kept in that Country, from July 1846 to June 1848. With 8 Plates and 2 Woodcuts. Post 8vo. 12s. cloth.

PULMAN.—THE VADE-MECUM OF FLY-FISHING FOR TROUT: being a complete Practical Treatise on that Branch of the Art of Angling; with plain and copious Instructions for the Manufacture of Artificial Flies. By G. P. R. PULMAN. Third Edition, re-written and enlarged; with several Woodcuts. Fcp. 8vo. 6s. cloth.

PYCROFT.—A COURSE OF ENGLISH READING, Adapted to every Taste and Capacity: with Literary Anecdotes. By the Rev. JAMES PYCROFT, B.A. Author of *The Collegian's Guide*, &c. New Edition. Fcp. 8vo. 5s. cloth.

DR. REECE'S MEDICAL GUIDE; For the Use of the Clergy, Heads of Families, Schools, and Junior Medical Practitioners; comprising a complete Modern Dispensatory, and a Practical Treatise on the distinguishing Symptoms, Causes, Prevention, Cure, and Palliation of the Diseases incident to the Human Frame. With the latest Discoveries in the different departments of the Healing Art, Materia Medica, &c. Seventeenth Edition, with considerable Additions; revised and corrected by the Author's Son, Dr. HENRY REECE, M.R.C.S. &c. 8vo. 12s. cloth.

RICH.—THE ILLUSTRATED COMPANION TO THE LATIN DICTIONARY AND GREEK LEXICON: forming a Glossary of all the Words representing Visible Objects connected with the Arts, Manufactures, and Every-day Life of the Ancients. With Representations of nearly Two Thousand Objects from the Antique. By ANTHONY RICH, Jun. B.A. Post 8vo. with about 2,000 Woodcuts, 21s. cloth.

JOURNAL OF A BOAT VOYAGE THROUGH RUPERT'S LAND and the ARCTIC SEA, in Search of the Discovery Ships under Command of Sir John Franklin. With an Appendix on the Physical Geography of North America. By Sir JOHN RICHARDSON, M.D., F.R.S., &c., Inspector of Hospitals and Fleets. With a coloured Map, several Plates, and Woodcuts. 2 vols. 8vo. 31s. 6d. cloth.

RIDDLE'S COMPLETE LATIN-ENGLISH AND ENGLISH- LATIN DICTIONARY, for the use of Colleges and Schools. New Edition, revised and corrected. 8vo. price 21s. cloth.

Separately { The English-Latin Dictionary, price 7s. cloth.
The Latin-English Dictionary, price 15s. cloth.

RIDDLE.—A COPIOUS AND CRITICAL LATIN-ENGLISH LEXICON, founded on the German-Latin Dictionaries of Dr. William Freund. By the Rev. J. E. RIDDLE, M.A. of St. Edmund's Hall, Oxford. New Edition. Post 4to. 31s. 6d. cloth.

RIDDLE'S DIAMOND LATIN-ENGLISH DICTIONARY: A Guide to the Meaning, Quality, and right Accentuation of Latin Classical Words. New Edition. Royal 32mo. price 4s. bound.

RIVERS.—THE ROSE-AMATEUR'S GUIDE; Containing ample Descriptions of all the fine leading varieties of Roses, regularly classed in their respective Families; their History and mode of Culture. By T. RIVERS, Jun. New Edition, corrected and improved. Fcp. 8vo. 6s. cloth.

ROBINSON'S LEXICON TO THE GREEK TESTAMENT.

A GREEK and ENGLISH LEXICON of the NEW TESTAMENT. By EDWARD ROBINSON, D.D., LL.D., Author of *Biblical Researches in Palestine*, &c. A New Edition, revised and in great part re-written. 8vo. 18s. cloth.

ROGERS.—ESSAYS SELECTED FROM CONTRIBUTIONS

to the EDINBURGH REVIEW. By HENRY ROGERS. 2 vols. 8vo. 24s. cloth.

ROGERS'S VEGETABLE CULTIVATOR;

Containing a plain and accurate Description of every species and variety of Culinary Vegetables: With the most approved Modes of Cultivating and Cooking them. New and Cheaper Edition. Fcp. 8vo. 5s. cloth.

ROGET.—THESAURUS OF ENGLISH WORDS & PHRASES

Classified and arranged so as to facilitate the Expression of Ideas and assist in Literary Composition. By P. M. ROGET, M.D. F.R S. &c.; Author of the *Bridgewater Treatise on Animal and Vegetable Physiology*, &c. New Edition, revised and enlarged. Medium 8vo. 14s. cloth.

ROWTON.—THE DEBATER;

Being a Series of complete Debates, Outlines of Debates, and Questions for Discussion; with ample References to the best Sources of Information on each particular Topic. By FREDERIC ROWTON. New Edition. Fcp. 8vo. price 6s. cloth.

ST. JOHN (H.)—THE INDIAN ARCHIPELAGO;

Its History and Present State. By HORACE ST. JOHN, Author of *History of the British Conquests in India, Life of Christopher Columbus*, &c. 2 vols. post 8vo. price 21s. cloth.

MR. ST. JOHN'S NEW WORK ON EGYPT.

ISIS: an Egyptian Pilgrimage. By JAMES AUGUSTUS ST. JOHN. 2 vols. post 8vo. 21s. cloth.

THE SAINTS OUR EXAMPLE.

By the Author of *Letters to my Unknown Friends, Letters on Happiness*, &c. Fcp. 8vo. price 7s. cloth.

SIR EDWARD SEAWARD'S NARRATIVE OF HIS SHIP-

WRECK, and consequent Discovery of certain Islands in the Caribbean Sea: with a detail of many extraordinary and highly interesting Events in his Life, from 1733 to 1749, as written in his own Diary. Edited by JANE PORTER. Third Edition; with a Nautical and Geographical Introduction. 2 vols. post 8vo. 21s. cloth.—Also an ABRIDGMENT, in 16mo. price 2s. 6d. cloth.

SELF-DENIAL THE PREPARATION FOR EASTER.

By the Author of *Letters to my Unknown Friends*, &c. Fcp. 8vo. price 2s. 6d. cloth.

SEWELL.—AMY HERBERT.

By a LADY. Edited by the Rev. WILLIAM SEWELL, B.D. Fellow and Tutor of Exeter College, Oxford. New Edition; complete in One Volume. Fcp. 8vo. price 6s. cloth.

SEWELL.—THE EARL'S DAUGHTER.

By the Author of *Amy Herbert*. Edited by the Rev. W. SEWELL, B.D.. 2 vols. fcp. 8vo. price 9s. cloth.

SEWELL.—GERTRUDE:

A Tale. By the Author of *Amy Herbert*. Edited by the Rev. W. SEWELL, B.D. New Edition; complete in One Volume. Fcp. 8vo. price 6s. cloth.

SEWELL.—LANETON PARSONAGE:

A Tale for Children, on the Practical Use of a portion of the Church Catechism. By the Author of *Amy Herbert*. Edited by the Rev. W. SEWELL, B.D. New Edition. 3 vols. fcp. 8vo. price 16s. cloth.

SEWELL.—MARGARET PERCIVAL.

By the Author of *Amy Herbert*. Edited by the Rev. W. SEWELL, B.D. New Edition. 2 vols. fcp. 8vo. price 12s. cloth.

THE FAMILY SHAKSPEARE;

In which nothing is *added* to the Original Text; but those words and expressions are *omitted* which cannot with propriety be read aloud. By T. BOWDLER, Esq. F.R.S. New Edition (1853), in Volumes for the Pocket. 6 vols. fcp. 8vo. price 30s. cloth.

*** Also a Library Edition; with 36 Engravings on Wood, from designs by Smirke, Howard, and other Artists. 8vo. 21s. cloth.

SHAKSPEARE'S SONGS ILLUSTRATED BY THE ETCH-

ING CLUB.—SONGS and BALLADS of SHAKSPEARE illustrated in Eighteen Plates by the Etching Club. Imperial 4to. price 42s. boards.

*** The first Nine Plates were originally published in 1843; and the Subscribers to that Part may purchase the last Nine Plates separately, price One Guinea.

SHARP'S NEW BRITISH GAZETTEER,

Or TOPOGRAPHICAL DICTIONARY of the BRITISH ISLANDS and NARROW SEAS: Comprising concise Descriptions of about Sixty Thousand Places, Seats, Natural Features, and Objects of Note, founded on the best Authorities; full Particulars of the Boundaries, Registered Electors, &c. of the Parliamentary Boroughs; with a reference under every Name to the Sheet of the Ordnance Survey, as far as completed; and an Appendix, containing a General View of the Resources of the United Kingdom, a Short Chronology, and an Abstract of certain Results of the Census of 1851. 2 vols. 8vo. £2. 16s. cloth.

SHORT WHIST:

Its Rise, Progress, and Laws; with Observations to make any one a Whist Player; containing also the Laws of Piquet, Cassino, Ecarté, Cribbage, Backgammon. By Major A*****. New Edition. To which are added, Precepts for Tyros. y Mrs. B****. Fcp. 8vo. 3s. cloth.

SINCLAIR.—THE JOURNEY OF LIFE.

By CATHERINE SINCLAIR. New Edition, corrected and enlarged. Fcp. 8vo. 5s. cloth.

SINCLAIR.—POPISH LEGENDS OR BIBLE TRUTHS.

By CATHERINE SINCLAIR, Author of *The Journey of Life*, &c. Dedicated to her Nieces. Fcp. 8vo. 6s. cloth.

SIR ROGER DE COVERLEY.

From *The Spectator*. With Notes and Illustrations, by W. HENRY WILLS; and Twelve fine Wood Engravings, by John Thompson, from Designs by FREDERICK TAYLER. Crown 8vo. 15s. boards; or 27s. bound in morocco by Hayday.—Also a Cheap Edition, without Wood Engravings, in 16mo. price One Shilling.

SKETCHES BY A SAILOR;

Or, Things of Earth and Things of Heaven. By a Commander in the Royal Navy. Fcp. 8vo. price 3s. 6d. cloth.

CONTENTS:—1. The Shipwreck; 2. The Model Prison; 3. TheFoot Race; 4. A Man Overboard; 5 The Assize Court; 6. The Fugitive.

SMEE.—ELEMENTS OF ELECTRO-METALLURGY.

By ALFRED SMEE, F.R.S., Surgeon to the Bank of England. Third Edition, revised, corrected, and considerably enlarged; with Electrotypes and numerous Woodcuts. Post 8vo. 10s. 6d. cloth.

SMITH.—THE WORKS OF THE REV. SYDNEY SMITH:

Including his Contributions to The Edinburgh Review. New Edition, complete in One Volume; with Portrait, and Vignette View of Combe Florey Rectory, Somerset. Square crown 8vo. 21s. cloth; 30s. calf extra, by Hayday.—Or in 3 vols. 8vo. with Portrait, 36s. cloth.

SMITH.—ELEMENTARY SKETCHES OF MORAL PHILO-

SOPHY, delivered at the Royal Institution in the Years 1804, 1805, and 1806. By the late Rev. SYDNEY SMITH, M.A. Second Edition. 8vo. 12s. cloth.

SMITH.—THE VOYAGE & SHIPWRECK OF ST. PAUL:

With Dissertations on the Sources of the Writings of St. Luke, and the Ships and Navigation of the Antients. By JAMES SMITH, Esq. F.R.S. 8vo. with Illustrations, 14s. cloth.

SNOW.—VOYAGE OF THE PRINCE ALBERT IN SEARCH

of SIR JOHN FRANKLIN: A Narrative of Every-day Life in the Arctic Seas. By W. PARKER SNOW. With a Chart, and 4 Illustrations printed in Colours. Post 8vo. 12s. cloth.

THE LIFE AND CORRESPONDENCE OF THE LATE

ROBERT SOUTHEY. Edited by his Son, the Rev. CHARLES CUTHBERT SOUTHEY, M.A., Vicar of Ardleigh. With numerous Portraits, and Six Landscape Illustrations from Designs by William Westall, A.R.A. 6 vols. post 8vo. 63s. cloth.

SOUTHEY'S THE DOCTOR &c.

Complete in One Volume Edited by the Rev. JOHN WOOD WARTER, B.D. With Portrait, Vignette, Bust, and coloured Plate. New Edition. Square crown 8vo. 21s. cloth.

SOUTHEY'S COMMONPLACE BOOKS.

The COMMONPLACE BOOKS of the late ROBERT SOUTHEY. Comprising—1. Choice Passages: with Collections for the History of Manners and Literature in England; 2. Special Collections on various Historical and Theological Subjects; 3. Analytical Readings in various branches of Literature; and 4. Original Memoranda, Literary and Miscellaneous. Edited by the Rev. J. W. WARTER, B.D. 4 vols. square crown 8vo. £3. 18s. cloth.

Each Commonplace Book, complete in itself, may be had separately as follows:—

FIRST SERIES—CHOICE PASSAGES, &c. 2d Edition; with medallion Portrait. Price 18s.

SECOND SERIES—SPECIAL COLLECTIONS. 18s.

THIRD SERIES—ANALYTICAL READINGS. 21s.

FOURTH SERIES—ORIGINAL MEMORANDA, &c. 21s.

ROBERT SOUTHEY'S COMPLETE POETICAL WORKS;

Containing all the Author's last Introductions and Notes. Complete in One Volume, with Portrait and View of the Poet's Residence at Keswick; uniform with Lord Byron's and Moore's Poems. Medium 8vo. 21s. cloth; 42s. bound in morocco.—Or, in 10 vols. fcp. 8vo. with Portrait and 19 Plates, £2. 10s. cloth; morocco, £4. 10s.

SOUTHEY.—SELECT WORKS OF THE BRITISH POETS;

From Chaucer to Lovelace, inclusive. With Biographical Sketches by the late ROBERT SOUTHEY. Medium 8vo. 30s. cloth.

SOUTHEY.—THE LIFE OF WESLEY;

And Rise and Progress of Methodism. By ROBERT SOUTHEY. New Edition, with Notes by the late Samuel Taylor Coleridge, Esq., and Remarks on the Life and Character of John Wesley, by the late Alexander Knox, Esq. Edited by the Rev. C. C. SOUTHEY, M.A., Vicar of Ardleigh. 2 vols. 8vo. with 2 Portraits, 28s. cloth.

STEEL'S SHIPMASTER'S ASSISTANT,

For the use of Merchants, Owners and Masters of Ships, Officers of Customs, and all Persons connected with Shipping or Commerce: Containing the Law and Local Regulations affecting the Ownership, Charge, and Management of Ships and their Cargoes; together with Notices of other Matters, and all necessary Information for Mariners. New Edition, rewritten throughout; and containing the New Passenger's Act, passed during the last Session of Parliament. Edited by GRAHAM WILLMORE, Esq. M.A. Barrister-at-Law; GEORGE CLEMENTS, of the Customs, London; and WILLIAM TATE, Author of *The Modern Cambist* 8vo. 28s. cloth.

STEPHEN.—LECTURES ON THE HISTORY OF FRANCE;

By the Right Hon. Sir JAMES STEPHEN, K.C.B. LL.D., Professor of Modern History in the University of Cambridge. Second Edition. 2 vols. 8vo. 24s. cloth.

"These masterly *Lectures* by Sir James Stephen, successor to the lamented Professor Smythe in the University of Cambridge, although they take rather new ground, will be found to cast a flood of light on the external and internal histories of the French people, discussing as they do fully and with consummate ability, as was to be expected from the author of *Ecclesiastical Biography*, the monarchical, judicial, and economical institutions of the Great Nation.......The present *Lectures* are at once profound [*and*] discriminative. They are written in a style of singular fascination, and even to the general reader they present historical truth in the attractiveness of romance. We indulge the hope that they will attain a large circulation, especially among those classes who are so latetudinarian as to ignore the painful but palpable facts of ecclesiastical history."
ECLECTIC REVIEW.

STEPHEN.—ESSAYS IN ECCLESIASTICAL BIOGRAPHY;

From The Edinburgh Review. By the Right Honourable Sir JAMES STEPHEN, K.C.B. LL.D. Professor of Modern History in the University of Cambridge. Second Edition. 2 vols. 8vo. 24s. cloth.

SUTHERLAND.—JOURNAL OF A VOYAGE IN BAFFIN'S

BAY and BARROW'S STRAITS, n the Years 1850 and 1851, performed by H.M. Ships *Lady Franklin* and *Sophia*, under the command of Mr. William Penny, in search of the missing Crews of H.M. Ships *Erebus* and *Terror*: with a Narrative of Sledge Excursions on the Ice of Wellington Channel; and Observations on the Natural History and Physical Features of the Countries and Frozen Seas visited. By PETER C. SUTHERLAND, M.D., M.R.C.S.E., Surgeon to the Expedition. With Two coloured Charts by A. PETERMANN, Six Plates (four coloured), and numerous Wood Engravings. 2 vols. post 8vo. price 27s. cloth.

STOW.—THE TRAINING SYSTEM, THE MORAL TRAIN-

ING SCHOOL, and the NORMAL SEMINARY. By DAVID STOW, Esq. Honorary Secretary to the Glasgow Normal Free Seminary. 8th Edition, corrected and enlarged; with Plates and Woodcuts. Post 8vo. 6s. cloth.

SWAIN.—ENGLISH MELODIES.

By CHARLES SWAIN. Fcp. 8vo. 6s. cloth; bound in morocco, 12s.

SYMONS.—THE MERCANTILE MARINE LAW.

By EDWARD WILLIAM SYMONS, Chief Clerk of the Thames Police Court. 5th Edition, including the Act passed in 1851 to amend the Mercantile Marine Act of 1850, and the provisions of the New Act relating to the Merchant Seamen's Fund. 12mo. 5s. cloth.

TATE.—EXERCISES ON MECHANICS AND NATURAL

PHILOSOPHY; or, an Easy Introduction to Engineering. Containing various Applications of the Principle of Work: the Theory of the Steam-Engine, with Simple Machines; Theorems and Problems on Accumulated Work, &c. By THOMAS TATE, F.R.A.S., of Kneller Training College, Twickenham. New Edition. 12mo. 2s. cloth.—KEY: Containing full Solutions of all the unworked Examples and Problems. 12mo. 3s. 6d. cloth.

TATE.—THE PRINCIPLES OF MECHANICAL PHILOSOPHY

applied to INDUSTRIAL MECHANICS. Forming a Sequel to the Author's *Exercises on Mechanics and Natural Philosophy*. By THOMAS TATE, F.R.A.S., of Kneller Training College, Twickenham. With about 200 Wood Engravings. 8vo. price 10s. 6d. cloth.

"The object of this work is to remove an evil pointed out by Professor Moseley in his Report on the Hydraulic Machines of the Great Exhibition—the frequent sacrifice of capital and of much mechanical ingenuity, in English machinery as compared with French, from the want of a knowledge of mechanical laws. Mr. Tate enunciates the principles of his subject, and illustrates them by means of exercises conducted for the most part on algebraical and geometrical principles."
SPECTATOR.

TATE.—ON THE STRENGTH OF MATERIALS;

Containing various original and useful Formulæ, specially applied to Tubular Bridges, Wrought Iron and Cast Iron Beams, &c. By THOMAS TATE, F.R.A.S. 8vo. 5s. 6d. cloth.

TAYLER.—MARGARET; OR, THE PEARL.

By the Rev. CHARLES B. TAYLER, M.A. New Edition. Fcp. 8vo. 6s. cloth.

TAYLER.—LADY MARY; OR, NOT OF THE WORLD.

By the Rev. C. B. TAYLER, M.A. New Edition; with Frontispiece. Fcp. 8vo. 6s. 6d. cloth.

TAYLOR.—THE AUTOBIOGRAPHY OF B. R. HAYDON,

Historical Painter. Edited, and continued to the Time of his Death, from his own Journals, by TOM TAYLOR, M.A. of the Inner Temple, Esq.; late Fellow of Trinity College, Cambridge; and late Professor of the English Language and Literature in University College, London. 3 vols. post 8vo. [*In the press.*

TAYLOR.—LOYOLA: AND JESUITISM IN ITS RUDIMENTS.

By ISAAC TAYLOR. Post 8vo. with Medallion, price 10s. 6d. cloth.

TAYLOR.—WESLEY AND METHODISM.

By ISAAC TAYLOR. With a Portrait of Wesley, engraved by W. Greatbach. Post 8vo. 10s. 6d. cloth.

"All the characteristics of early Methodism are analysed in the present volume with a discrimination, and described with a clearness such as we might expect from the philosophical and eloquent author of the *Natural History of Enthusiasm* ......Of the Methodism of the eighteenth century, the corporeal part remains in the Wesleyan Connexion; the *soul* of it, while partly animating that body, was transfused into all Christian Churches. How that great movement became a starting-point in our modern history, and how it was the source of what is the most characteristic of the present time, as contrasted with the corresponding period of last century, not in religion only, but in the general tone of national feeling, and manners, and literature, Mr. Taylor ably shews." LITERARY GAZETTE.

THIRLWALL.—THE HISTORY OF GREECE.

By the Right Rev. the LORD BISHOP of ST. DAVID'S (the Rev. Connop Thirlwall). An improved Library Edition; with Maps. 8 vols. 8vo. £4. 16s. cloth.—Also, an Edition in 8 vols. fcp. 8vo. with Vignette Titles, £1. 8s. cloth.

HISTORY OF GREECE, FROM THE EARLIEST TIMES

to the TAKING of CORINTH by the ROMANS, B.C. 146, mainly based upon Bishop Thirlwall's History of Greece. By Dr. LEONHARD SCHMITZ, F.R.S.E., Rector of the High School of Edinburgh. Second Edition. 12mo. 7s. 6d. cloth.

THOMAS'S MODERN PRACTICE OF PHYSIC:

Exhibiting the Symptoms, Causes, Prognostics, Morbid Appearances, and Treatment of the Diseases of All Climates. Eleventh Edition, thoroughly revised, corrected, and to a considerable extent re-written, by ALGERNON FRAMPTON, M.D.; HERBERT DAVIES, M.D.; N. PARKER, M.D.; G. CRITCHETT, F.R.C.S.; J. WORDSWORTH, F.R.C.S.; HENRY POWELL, M.D.; and H. LETHEBY, M.D. 2 vols. 8vo. 28s. cloth.

THOMSON'S SEASONS.

Edited by BOLTON CORNEY, Esq. Illustrated with Seventy-seven Designs drawn on Wood by Members of the Etching Club. Engraved by Thompson and other eminent Engravers. Square crown 8vo. 21s. cloth; or, bound in morocco by Hayday, 36s.

THOMSON'S TABLES OF INTEREST,

At Three, Four, Four-and-a-Half, and Five per Cent., from One Pound to Ten Thousand, and from 1 to 365 Days, in a regular progression of single Days; with Interest at all the above Rates, from One to Twelve Months, and from One to Ten Years. Also, numerous other Tables of Exchanges, Time, and Discounts. New Edition. 12mo. 8s. bound.

THE THUMB BIBLE;

Or, Verbum Sempiternum. By J. TAYLOR. Being an Epitome of the Old and New Testaments in English Verse. A New Edition, printed from the Edition of 1693, by C. Whittingham, Chiswick. 64mo. 1s. 6d. bound and clasped.

TOMLINE'S INTRODUCTION TO THE STUDY OF THE

BIBLE: containing Proofs of the Authenticity and Inspiration of the Holy Scriptures; a Summary of the History of the Jews; an Account of the Jewish Sects; and a brief Statement of the Contents of the several Books of the Old and New Testaments. New Edition. Fcp. 8vo. 5s. 6d. cloth.

TOWNSEND'S MODERN STATE TRIALS.

Revised and illustrated with Essays and Notes. By WILLIAM CHARLES TOWNSEND, Esq. M.A., Q.C. 2 vols. 8vo. 30s. cloth.

TOWNSEND.—THE LIVES OF TWELVE EMINENT

JUDGES of the LAST and of the PRESENT CENTURY. By W. CHARLES TOWNSEND, Esq. M.A. Q.C. 2 vols. 8vo. 28s. cloth.

TURNER.—THE SACRED HISTORY OF THE WORLD,

Attempted to be Philosophically considered, in a Series of Letters to a Son. By SHARON TURNER, F.S.A. and R.A.S.L. New Edition, edited by the Rev. SYDNEY TURNER. 3 vols. post 8vo. 31s. 6d. cloth.

TURNER.—A NEW EDITION OF SHARON TURNER'S

HISTORY of ENGLAND during the MIDDLE AGES: comprising the Reigns from William the Conqueror to the Accession of Henry VIII. 4 vols. 8vo. [*In the press.*

TURNER.—THE HISTORY OF THE ANGLO-SAXONS,

From the Earliest Period to the Norman Conquest. By SHARON TURNER, F.S.A. and R.A.S.L. The Seventh Edition. 3 vols. 8vo. 36s. cloth.

DR. TURTON'S MANUAL OF THE LAND AND FRESH-

WATER SHELLS of the BRITISH ISLANDS. A New Edition, with considerable Additions. By JOHN EDWARD GRAY. Post 8vo. with Woodcuts, and 12 coloured Plates, 15s. cloth.

URE.—DICTIONARY OF ARTS, MANUFACTURES, AND

MINES. Containing a clear Exposition of their Principles and Practice. By ANDREW URE, M.D. F.R.S. M.G.S. M.A.S. Lond.; M. Acad. N.L. Philad.; S. Ph. Soc. N. Germ. Hanov.; Mulii. &c. &c. New Edition, corrected. 8vo. with 1,241 Engravings on Wood, 50s. cloth.—Also,

SUPPLEMENT of RECENT IMPROVEMENTS. New Edition. 8vo. with Woodcuts, 14s. cloth.

WATERTON.—ESSAYS ON NATURAL HISTORY,

Chiefly Ornithology. By CHARLES WATERTON, Esq., Author of *Wanderings in South America.* With an Autobiography of the Author, and Views of Walton Hall. New and cheaper Edition. 2 vols. fcp. 8vo. price 10s. cloth.—Separately—Vol. I. (First Series), 5s. 6d. Vol. II. (Second Series), 4s. 6d.

THE TRAVELLER'S LIBRARY,

In course of publication in Parts at One Shilling and in Volumes price Half-a-Crown each. Comprising books of valuable information and acknowledged merit, in a form adapted for reading while Travelling, and also of a character that will render them worthy of preservation; but the *price* of which has hitherto confined them within a comparatively narrow circle of readers.

Already published:—

WARREN ASTINGS. By THOMAS BABINGTON MACAULAY. Reprinted from Mr. Macaulay's *Critical and Historical Essays*. Price One Shilling.

LORD CLIVE. By THOMAS BABINGTON MACAULAY. Reprinted from Mr. Macaulay's *Critical and Historical Essays*. Price One Shilling.

*** Mr. Macaulay's Two Essays on Warren Hastings and Lord Clive may be had in One Volume, price Half-a-Crown.

WILLIAM PITT, EARL of CHATHAM. By THOMAS BABINGTON MACAULAY. Reprinted from Mr. Macaulay's *Critical and Historical Essays*. Price One Shilling.

RANKE'S HISTORY of the POPES. And, GLADSTONE on CHURCH and STATE. By THOMAS BABINGTON MACAULAY. Reprinted from Mr. Macaulay's *Critical and Historical Essays*. Price One Shilling.

*** Mr. Macaulay's Essays on William Pitt, Ranke's *History of the Popes*, and Gladstone *On Church and State*, may be had in One Volume, price Half-a-Crown.

THE LIFE and WRITINGS of ADDISON. And, HORACE WALPOLE. By THOMAS BABINGTON MACAULAY. Reprinted from Mr. Macaulay's *Critical and Historical Essays*. Price One Shilling.

LORD BACON. By THOMAS BABINGTON MACAULAY. Reprinted from Mr. Macaulay's *Critical and Historical Essays*. Price One Shilling.

*** Mr. Macaulay's Three Essays on Addison, Horace Walpole, and Lord Bacon, may be had in One Volume, price Half-a-Crown.

LORD BYRON. And, the COMIC DRAMATISTS of the RESTORATION. By THOMAS BABINGTON MACAULAY. Reprinted from Mr. Macaulay's *Critical and Historical Essays*. Price One Shilling.

LORD JEFFREY'S TWO ESSAYS on SWIFT and RICHARDSON. Reprinted from *Contributions to the Edinburgh Review*. Price One Shilling.

THE AUSTRALIAN COLONIES; their Origin and Present Condition. By WILLIAM HUGHES, F.R.G.S. Two Parts, price One Shilling each; or in One Volume, price Half-a-Crown.

LONDON in 1850 and 1851. By J. R. M'CULLOCH, Esq. Reprinted from Mr. M'Culloch's *Geographical Dictionary*. Price One Shilling.

MR. S. LAING'S JOURNAL of a RESIDENCE in NORWAY during the Years 1834, 1835, and 1836. Two Parts, price One Shilling each; or in One Volume, price Half a-Crown.

EŌTHEN; or, Traces of Travel brought Home from the East. Two Parts, price One Shilling each; or in One Volume, price Half-a-Crown.

IDA PFEIFFER'S LADY'S VOYAGE ROUND the WORLD. A condensed Translation, by Mrs. PERCY SINNETT. Two Parts, price One Shilling each; or in One Volume, price Half-a-Crown.

HUC'S TRAVELS in TARTARY, THIBET, and CHINA. A condensed Translation, by Mrs. PERCY SINNETT. Two Parts, price One Shilling each; or in One Volume, price Half-a-Crown.

Mrs. JAMESON'S SKETCHES in CANADA and RAMBLES among the RED MEN. Two Parts, price One Shilling each; or in One Volume, price Half a-Crown.

WERNE'S AFRICAN WANDERINGS. Translated by J. R. JOHNSTON. Two Parts, price One Shilling each; or in One Volume, price Half-a-Crown.

JERRMANN'S PICTURES from ST. PETERSBURG. Translated from the German by FREDERICK HARDMAN. Two Parts, price One Shilling each; or in One Volume, price Half-a-Crown.

MEMOIRS of a MAITRE D'ARMES; or, Eighteen Months at St. Petersburg. By ALEXANDRE DUMAS. Translated by the MARQUIS OF ORMONDE. Two Parts, price One Shilling each; or in One Volume, price Half-a-Crown.

SIR EDWARD SEAWARD'S NARRATIVE of his SHIPWRECK. Abridged from the last Edition of the Original for the *Traveller's Library*. Two Parts, price One Shilling each; or in One Volume, price Half-a-Crown

BRITTANY and the BIBLE; with Remarks on the French People and their Affairs. By I. HOPE. Price One Shilling.

RANKE'S FERDINAND the FIRST and MAXIMILIAN the SECOND of AUSTRIA; or, a View of the Religious and Political State of Germany after the Reformation. Translated by Lady DUFF GORDON. Price One Shilling.

MEMOIR of the DUKE of WELLINGTON. Reprinted by permission from *The Times* newspaper. Price One Shilling.

THE LEIPSIC CAMPAIGN. By the Rev. G. R. GLEIG, M.A. Chaplain-General of the Forces. Two Parts, price One Shilling each; or in One Volume, price Half-a-Crown.

THOMAS HOLCROFT'S MEMOIRS, written by HIMSELF, and continued from his Diary and Papers. Reprinted (1852). Two Parts, price One Shilling each; or in One Volume, price Half-a-Crown.

LORD CARLISLE'S LECTURES and ADDRESSES: Including a Lecture on the Poetry of Pope, and the Lecture on Lord Carlisle's Travels in America. Price One Shilling.

THE NATURAL HISTORY of CREATION. By T. LINDLEY KEMP, M.D. Author of *Agricultural Physiology*. Price One Shilling.

ELECTRICITY and the ELECTRIC TELEGRAPH. To which is added, The CHEMISTRY of the STARS. By Dr. GEORGE WILSON. Price One Shilling.

SIR ROGER DE COVERLEY. From the *Spectator*. With Notes and Illustrations by W. H. WILLS. Price One Shilling.

ALARIC WATTS'S POETRY AND PAINTING.—LYRICS

OF THE HEART, and other Poems. By ALARIC A. WATTS. With Forty-one highly-finished Line-Engravings, executed expressly for this work by the most eminent Painters and Engravers. Square crown 8vo. price 31s. 6d. boards, or 45s. bound in morocco by Hayday; Proof Impressions, 63s. boards.—Plain Proofs, 41 Plates, demy 4to. (only 100 copies printed) £2. 2s. in portfolio; India Proofs before letters, colombier 4to. (only 50 copies printed), £5. 5s. in portfolio.

WHEATLEY.—THE ROD AND LINE;

Or, Practical Hints and Dainty Devices for the Sure Taking of Trout, Grayling, &c. By HEWETT WHEATLEY, Esq. Senior Angler. Fcp. 8vo. with Nine coloured Plates, 10s. 6d. cloth.

WEBSTER AND PARKES'S ENCYCLOPÆDIA OF DO-

MESTIC ECONOMY; Comprising such subjects as are most immediately connected with Housekeeping: as, The Construction of Domestic Edifices, with the modes of Warming, Ventilating, and Lighting them—A description of the various articles of Furniture, with the nature of their Materials—Duties of Servants, &c. New Edition. 8vo. with nearly 1,000 Woodcuts, 50s. cloth.

LADY WILLOUGHBY'S DIARY (1635 to 1663).

Printed, ornamented, and bound in the style of the period to which *The Diary* refers. New Edition; in Two Parts. Square fcp. 8vo. 8s. each, boards; or 18s. each, bound in morocco.

WILMOT'S ABRIDGMENT OF BLACKSTONE'S COMMEN-

TARIES on the LAWS of ENGLAND, intended for the use of Young Persons, and comprised in a series of Letters from a Father to his Daughter. A New Edition, corrected and brought down to the Present Day, by SIR JOHN E. EARDLEY WILMOT, Bart., Barrister-at-Law, Recorder of Warwick. Inscribed, by permission, to H.R.H. the Princess Royal. 12mo. price 6s. 6d. cloth.

WOOD'S ELEMENTS OF ALGEBRA,

Designed for the use of Students in the University. Fourteenth Edition, revised and enlarged, by THOMAS LUND, B.D., late Fellow and Sadlerian Lecturer of St. John's College, Cambridge. 8vo. price 12s. 6d. cloth.

LUND'S COMPANION TO WOOD'S ALGEBRA,

Containing Solutions of various Questions and Problems in Algebra, and forming a KEY to the chief Difficulties found in the Collection of Examples appended to *Wood's Algebra*. Second Edition, enlarged. Post 8vo. price 6s. cloth.

YOUATT.—THE HORSE.

By WILLIAM YOUATT. With a Treatise of Draught. A New Edition; with numerous Wood Engravings, from Designs by William Harvey. 8vo. 10s. cloth.

☞ Messrs. Longman and Co.'s Edition should be ordered.

YOUATT.—THE DOG.

By WILLIAM YOUATT. A New Edition; with numerous Wood Engravings, from Designs by William Harvey. 8vo. 6s. cloth.

ZUMPT'S LARGER GRAMMAR OF THE LATIN LAN-

GUAGE. Translated and adapted for the use of English Students by Dr. L. SCHMITZ, F.R.S.E., Rector of the High School of Edinburgh: With numerous Additions and Corrections by the Author and Translator. The Third Edition, thoroughly revised; to which is added, an Index (by the Rev. J. T. White, M.A.) of all the Passages of Latin Authors referred to and explained in the Grammar 8vo. 14s. cloth.

[*March* 31, 1853.